The Essential
Thomas Jefferson

———★———

LIBRARY OF FREEDOM

The Essential Thomas Jefferson

———— ★ ————

EDITED, WITH AN INTRODUCTION, BY

John Gabriel Hunt

GRAMERCY BOOKS
NEW YORK • AVENEL

A NOTE ON THE TEXT

The selections in *The Essential Thomas Jefferson* have been taken from the 1853 collection of Jefferson's writings prepared from his original manuscripts and published by the Joint Committee of Congress on the Library. The selections are presented in chronological order and are complete and unabridged. The omissions in some letters, indicated by ellipses—and long dashes for single words and names—are due in most cases to Jefferson's own use of code, or cipher, for certain information. The text has been edited to modernize punctuation and spelling, but Jefferson's language remains unaltered.

Introduction copyright © 1994
by Outlet Book Company, Inc.
All rights reserved.

This 1994 edition is published by Gramercy Books,
distributed by Outlet Book Company, Inc.,
a Random House Company,
40 Engelhard Avenue,
Avenel, New Jersey 07001.

Random House
New York • Toronto • London • Sydney • Auckland

Printed and bound in the United States of America

Library of Congress Cataloging-in-Publication Data
The Essential Thomas Jefferson / edited, with an introduction,
by John Gabriel Hunt.
p. cm.—(Library of Freedom)
ISBN 0-517-10168-8
1. United States—Politics and government—1775–1783—Sources.
2. United States—Politics and government—1783–1815—Sources.
3. Jefferson, Thomas, 1743–1826—Correspondence.
I. Hunt, John Gabriel, 1952–   .   II. Series.
E302.J442   1994b   93–44694
973.4'6—dc20   CIP

8 7 6 5 4 3 2 1

CONTENTS

INTRODUCTION

THOMAS JEFFERSON'S political opponents often characterized
him as a "visionary"—a fairly accurate assessment, and one
that is today more complimentary than it was two hundred
years ago. But Jefferson was also a man dedicated to the power
of reason, a man of vast intellectual curiosity and discipline, and
a man with sufficient political expertise to attain the offices of
secretary of state, vice president, and president of the United
States. This combination of qualities made him the greatest of
the Founding Fathers and allowed him to produce the cogently
reasoned, poetically inspiring, and politically momentous Declaration of Independence.

Thomas Jefferson was born in Albemarle County, Virginia,
on April 13, 1743, the son of Peter Jefferson, a mapmaker and
surveyor, and Jane Randolph, a woman whose distinguished
family background was beneficial in Virginia society. At seventeen, Thomas began attending the College of William and Mary
in the colonial capital of Williamsburg, where he added the
sciences to his existing interest in the classics. But Jefferson
chose to pursue a practical career: he studied law under George
Wythe, and became a lawyer in 1767.

Jefferson's lifelong interest in architecture began in 1769
with the design and building of Monticello, a neoclassical-style
house surrounded by gardens and farmland, on a wooded hill
near his Virginia birthplace; its construction and transforma-
tions occupied Jefferson until the end of his second presidential

term. It was there that he and his wife, Martha Wayles Skelton, settled after their marriage in 1772. Although the couple eventually had six children, only two daughters survived infancy. Martha herself died in 1782, and Jefferson never remarried.

It was a short step from a legal to a political career, and in 1769 the freeholders of Albemarle elected Thomas Jefferson to the Virginia House of Burgesses. When the assembly protested against the British Parliament's Coercive Acts, the colonial body was dissolved by the governor. In 1774 Jefferson was elected a representative to Virginia's first revolutionary convention, which was to choose delegates to the First Continental Congress. Jefferson drafted a document—not adopted by the convention—that called for the right of Americans to govern themselves; the pamphlet was soon published in Williamsburg, and reprinted in Philadelphia and London the same year. *A Summary View of the Rights of British America,* addressed to the king of England, laid out the colonists' grievances "with that freedom of language and sentiment which becomes a free people, claiming their rights as derived from the laws of nature, and not as the gift of their chief magistrate."

Jefferson was a Virginia delegate to the Second Continental Congress in Philadelphia. There, in 1775, he and John Dickinson drew up the Declaration of the Causes and Necessity of Taking Up Arms. By the following year Congress was representing state governments that were independent of England. In June, Jefferson, who was well respected for his literary abilities, was charged with the task of drafting a declaration of independence, which Congress adopted, after making a number of revisions, on July 4, 1776.

That same year Jefferson returned to Virginia as a member of the new House of Delegates, where he presented a series of reforms: he proposed a plan of universal public education, a bill to replace the existing criminal code with a more humane justice system, and a plan for the gradual emancipation of slaves. Although the assembly rejected these efforts, Jefferson finally achieved success in 1786 with the passage of his Act for

Establishing Religious Freedom, which had been originally drafted in 1777.

In June 1779 Jefferson was elected governor of Virginia. Virginia was constantly under attack during this time by British forces; the state government was chased from Richmond to Charlottesville, and eventually Jefferson even had to flee from Monticello. In 1781, after the British surrendered at Yorktown, Jefferson happily retired to the life of a gentleman farmer. But this idyllic existence was ended the following year by his most devasting personal tragedy, the death of his wife.

Before returning to Congress in November 1783, Jefferson's time at Monticello was occupied by a project that eventually resulted in his only complete book, *Notes on Virginia*. It is a startlingly comprehensive compilation of facts and observances on every element of his state, from its rivers, mountains, climate, and history to its religion, laws, colleges, and commerce. *Notes on Virginia* is the product of a man whose quest for knowledge was constant and unquenchable and who could interchangeably wear the mantles of philosopher, inventor, scientist, geographer, architect, book collector, lawyer, educator, farmer, legislator, and statesman.

In 1785 Congress appointed Jefferson to succeed Benjamin Franklin as minister to France. Jefferson was an ardent Francophile who reveled in the cultural life of Paris. During his five years in Europe, Jefferson negotiated commercial treaties with the French with the help of the Marquis de Lafayette and was witness to the momentous events leading up to the French Revolution. His numerous letters to friends and associates in America during this period provide fascinating first-hand accounts of the situation in Europe and of revolutionary events, as well as his thoughts about the U.S. Constitution at the moment of its birth. In a letter to James Madison of December 20, 1787—after the Constitution took its final shape but before it had been adopted by the necessary nine states—Jefferson offers this opinion: "I like the organization of the government into legislative, judiciary, and executive. I like the power given the legislature to levy taxes, and for that reason solely I approve of the greater house being chosen by the people directly. . . . I will now tell you what I do not like. First, the omission of a bill of rights, providing clearly . . . for freedom of religion, freedom of the press, protection against standing armies, restriction of monopolies, the eternal and unremitting force of the habeas corpus laws, and trials by jury. . . . The second feature I dislike, and strongly dislike, is the abandonment, in every instance, of the principle of rotation in office, and most particularly in the case of the president."

Back home in America, Jefferson warmly wrote to Lafayette on April 2, 1790, of his new position in President Washington's government: "Behold me, my dear friend, elected secretary of state, instead of returning to the far more agreeable position which placed me in daily participation of your friendship." During his term as secretary of state, Jefferson's opposition to Secretary of the Treasury Alexander Hamilton's pro-British trade policies and establishment of a national bank developed into full-blown political partisanship. The constant differences between Hamilton and Jefferson—so candidly revealed in memoranda Jefferson made as records of cabinet meetings— eventually led to the formation of the Federalist and Democratic-Republican parties and to Jefferson's own resignation from the government at the end of President Washington's first term.

Once again, Jefferson retired to his farm at Monticello. But by 1796 he was back in politics, drafted by the Democratic-Republicans—often referred to at the time simply as Republicans—as a presidential candidate in a race with Federalist John Adams. Adams won, but Jefferson spent the next four years as vice president. In spite of his position in the new government, Jefferson became the acknowledged leader of his party and opposed the Federalist cry for war following the notorious XYZ Affair, in which agents of the French foreign minister attempted to extort money from American envoys. In response to the repressive Alien and Sedition Acts of Adams and the Federalists,

Jefferson secretly drafted the Kentucky Resolutions of 1798—James Madison wrote the similar Virginia Resolutions—which deemed the Acts unconstitutional and declared that when the national government overstepped its constitutional limits, a state had no need to obey the federal laws or action.

When Jefferson ran for president in the election of 1800, the increasingly unpopular Federalists and their candidate John Adams were easily defeated. But Aaron Burr, the Democratic-Republican nominee for vice president, received electoral votes equal in number to Jefferson's, and thus remained in contention for the presidency. It was the responsibility of the House of Representatives to break the deadlock; after thirty-six ballots, the election was decided in favor of Jefferson—ironically, with the support of Alexander Hamilton.

In his first inaugural address Jefferson called for frugality in government, limited federal authority, and the protection of civil liberties, and expressed his faith in the reasoned will of the majority to rule: "We are all republicans—we are all federalists. If there be any among us who would wish to dissolve this Union or to change its republican form let them stand undisturbed as monuments of the safety with which error of opinion may be tolerated where reason is left to combat it."

During his first term Jefferson and the Democratic-Republicans abolished internal taxes, reduced the size of the army and navy, worked toward the elimination of the national debt, and reestablished the press freedoms curtailed by the Federalists. Concerned with the presence of foreign powers at the southern and western boundaries of the United States ever since his days as secretary of state, President Jefferson and his own secretary of state, James Madison, negotiated with France to purchase its territory between the Mississippi River and the Rocky Mountains. The result was the Louisiana Purchase of 1803, a triumph of foreign policy. Earlier that same year, and before the negotiations with France had borne fruit, Jefferson had sent a message to Congress recommending a western exploring expedition; he then commissioned Meriwether Lewis and William Clark to undertake, as stated in his letter to Captain Lewis dated July 4, 1803, a journey "for the discovery of the course and source of the Missouri, and of the most convenient water communication from thence to the Pacific Ocean."

When he ran again in 1804, President Jefferson's popularity, and that of his Democratic-Republican party, were so great that he received 162 electoral votes to only 14 for the Federalist candidate, Charles C. Pinckney.

Halfway into his second term Jefferson was able to report, in his Sixth Annual Message to Congress, on the success of the Lewis and Clark expedition. The opening of the West brought particular urgency to a major problem facing the growing United States, that of relations with Native-American nations. Jefferson felt it was the duty of the U.S. government to encourage and help the tribal peoples to abandon hunting and settle into stable agricultural communities. His numerous messages to Indian leaders—whom he addressed as "brothers" and "my children"—reveal a warmth and respect that would, unfortunately, be missing in future contacts between the American government and the tribes.

For much of his second term Jefferson was faced with difficult military and foreign-policy matters. The Napoleonic war in Europe set the British on a consistent path of blockading American trade and impressing American seamen. War was nearly caused by the attack of England's HMS *Leopard* on the American frigate *Chesapeake,* but Jefferson sought to avoid military action with the Embargo Act of 1807, which prohibited all American exports and foreign trade and kept American ships home. It was an unpopular policy, and only minimally successful, and the act was repealed at the end of Jefferson's presidency. The other military challenge faced by Jefferson in these years was the bizarre conspiracy by his former vice president, Aaron Burr, to carve out a little empire for himself in the western territories. "It appeared that he contemplated two distinct objects," revealed Jefferson in his January 1807 message to Congress on the affair. "One of these was the severance of the Union of these States by the Allegheny mountains; the other, an attack on Mexico." Burr was tried for treason and, to Jefferson's indignation, acquitted.

Jefferson's letters written after his final retirement to Monticello in 1809 reveal the breadth of his knowledge, the depth of his intellectual curiosity, the passion of his commitment to education, and the warmth of his character. The last seventeen years of his life were devoted in great part to establishing the University of Virginia, and many of Jefferson's letters attest to his constant attention to its creation, funding, curriculum, and, of course, architectural design.

It is, however, the correspondence of a more personal nature written during his years as the Sage of Monticello that best reveal Jefferson's admirable character. In a letter written in 1810 to Thaddeus Kosciusko, Jefferson seems to revel in his retirement: "I am retired to Monticello, where, in the bosom of my family, and surrounded by my books, I enjoy a repose to which I have been long a stranger. My mornings are devoted to correspondence. From breakfast to dinner, I am in my shops, my garden, or on horseback among my farms; from dinner to dark, I give to society and recreation with my neighbors and friends; and from candlelight to early bedtime, I read." To Dr. Vine Utley in 1819 he writes of his health and eating habits: "I have lived temperately, eating little animal food, and that not as an aliment so much as a condiment for the vegetables, which constitute my principal diet. . . . Malt liquors and cider are my table drinks, and my breakfast . . . is of tea and coffee."

In correspondence with Dr. Benjamin Rush, Jefferson ruefully discusses his estrangement of many years from his old colleague John Adams. But in a letter to Rush of December 5, 1811, Jefferson joyfully relates an incident about Adams recently reported to him. Two of Jefferson's neighbors had visited Adams in Massachusetts, and, writes Jefferson, "among other topics, he [Adams] adverted to the unprincipled licentiousness of the press against myself, adding, 'I always loved Jefferson, and still love him.'" Jefferson's next supremely poignant and telling sentence is simply: "This is enough for me."

In his letter to Adams of January 21, 1812, Jefferson resumes a relationship and begins a correspondence that would prove intellectually stimulating and sustaining to both men until their final days. When Thomas Jefferson died at Monticello, it was on the same day as his colleague in the American experiment John Adams. The date was July 4, 1826.

JOHN GABRIEL HUNT

New York
1994

A SUMMARY VIEW OF THE RIGHTS OF BRITISH AMERICA

1774

Resolved, That it be an instruction to the said deputies, when assembled in general Congress, with the deputies from the other states of British America, to propose to the said Congress, that a humble and dutiful address be presented to His Majesty, begging leave to lay before him, as chief magistrate of the British Empire, the united complaints of His Majesty's subjects in America; complaints which are excited by many unwarrantable encroachments and usurpations, attempted to be made by the legislature of one part of the empire, upon the rights which God, and the laws, have given equally and independently to all. To represent to His Majesty that these, his states, have often individually made humble application to his imperial Throne to obtain, through its intervention, some redress of their injured rights; to none of which, was ever even an answer condescended. Humbly to hope that this, their joint address, penned in the language of truth, and divested of those expressions of servility, which would persuade His Majesty that we are asking favors, and not rights, shall obtain from His Majesty a more respectful acceptance; and this His Majesty will think we have reason to expect, when he reflects that he is no more than the chief officer of the people, appointed by the laws, and circumscribed with definite powers, to assist in working the great machine of government, erected for their use, and, consequently, subject to their superintendence; and, in order that these, our rights, as well as the invasions of them, may be laid

1

more fully before His Majesty, to take a view of them, from the origin and first settlement of these countries.

To remind him that our ancestors, before their emigration to America, were the free inhabitants of the British dominions in Europe, and possessed a right, which nature has given to all men, of departing from the country in which chance, not choice, has placed them, of going in quest of new habitations, and of there establishing new societies, under such laws and regulations as, to them, shall seem most likely to promote public happiness. That their Saxon ancestors had, under this universal law, in like manner, left their native wilds and woods in the north of Europe, had possessed themselves of the island of Britain, then less charged with inhabitants, and had established there that system of laws which has so long been the glory and protection of that country. Nor was ever any claim of superiority or dependence asserted over them, by that mother country from which they had migrated: and were such a claim made, it is believed His Majesty's subjects in Great Britain have too firm a feeling of the rights derived to them from their ancestors to bow down the sovereignty of their state before such visionary pretensions. And it is thought that no circumstance has occurred to distinguish, materially, the British from the Saxon emigration. America was conquered, and her settlements made and firmly established, at the expense of individuals, and not of the British public. Their own blood was spilt in acquiring lands for their settlement, their own fortunes expended in making that settlement effectual. For themselves they fought, for themselves they conquered, and for themselves alone they have right to hold. No shilling was ever issued from the public treasures of His Majesty, or his ancestors, for their assistance, till of very late times, after the colonies had become established on a firm and permanent footing. That then, indeed, having become valuable to Great Britain for her commercial purposes, his Parliament was pleased to lend them assistance against an enemy who would fain have drawn to herself the benefits of their commerce, to the great aggrandizement of herself, and danger of Great Britain. Such assistance, and in such circumstances, they had often before given to Portugal and other allied states, with whom they carry on a commercial intercourse. Yet these states never supposed that by calling in her aid they thereby submitted themselves to her sovereignty. Had such terms been proposed, they would have rejected them with disdain, and trusted for better, to the moderation of their enemies, or to a vigorous exertion of their own force. We do not, however, mean to underrate those aids, which, to us, were doubtless valuable, on whatever principles granted: but we would show that they cannot give a title to that authority which the British Parliament would arrogate over us; and that may amply be repaid by our giving to the inhabitants of Great Britain such exclusive privileges in trade as may be advantageous to them, and, at the same time, not too restrictive to ourselves. That settlement having been thus effected in the wilds of America, the emigrants thought proper to adopt that system of laws under which they had hitherto lived in the mother country, and to continue their union with her, by submitting themselves to the same common sovereign, who was thereby made the central link, connecting the several parts of the empire thus newly multiplied.

But that not long were they permitted, however far they thought themselves removed from the hand of oppression, to hold undisturbed the rights thus acquired at the hazard of their lives and loss of their fortunes. A family of princes was then on the British throne, whose treasonable crimes against their people brought on them, afterwards, the exertion of those sacred and sovereign rights of punishment, reserved in the hands of the people for cases of extreme necessity, and judged by the constitution unsafe to be delegated to any other judicature. While every day brought forth some new and unjustifiable exertion of power over their subjects on that side of the water, it was not to be expected that those here, much less able at that time to oppose the designs of despotism, should be exempted from injury. Accordingly, this country which had been acquired by the lives, the labors, and fortunes of individual adventurers, was by these princes, several times, parted out and distributed among the favorites and followers of their fortunes; and, by an assumed right of the Crown alone, were erected into distinct and independent governments; a measure, which it is believed, His Majesty's prudence and understanding would prevent him from imitating at this day; as no exercise of such power, of dividing and dismembering a country, has ever occurred in His Majesty's realm of England, though now of very ancient standing; nor could it be justified or acquiesced under there, or in any part of His Majesty's empire.

That the exercise of a free trade with all parts of the world, possessed by the American colonists, as of natural right, and which no law of their own had taken away or abridged, was next the object of unjust encroachment. Some of the colonies having thought proper to continue the administration of their government in the name and under the authority of His Majesty, King Charles I, whom, notwithstanding his late deposition by the commonwealth of England, they continued in the sovereignty of their state, the Parliament, for the commonwealth, took the same in high offense, and assumed upon themselves the power of prohibiting their trade with all other parts of the world, except the island of Great Britain. This arbitrary act, however, they soon recalled, and by solemn treaty entered into on the 12th day of March 1651, between the said commonwealth, by their commissioners, and the colony of Virginia by their House of Burgesses, it was expressly stipulated by the eighth article of the said treaty that they should have "free trade as the people of England do enjoy to all places and with all nations, according to the laws of that commonwealth." But that, upon the restoration of His Majesty, King Charles II, their rights of free commerce fell once more a victim to arbitrary power; and by several acts of his reign, as well as of some of his successors, the trade of the colonies was laid under such restrictions, as show what hopes they might form from the justice of a British Parliament, were its uncontrolled power admitted over these states. History has informed us that bodies of men as well as of individuals are susceptible of the spirit of tyranny. A view of these acts of Parliament for regulation, as it has been affectedly called, of the American trade, if all other evidences were removed out of the case, would undeniably evince the truth of this observation. Besides the duties they impose on our articles of export and import, they prohibit our going to any markets northward of Cape Finisterra, in the kingdom of Spain, for the sale of commodities which Great Britain will not take from us, and for the purchase of others, with which she cannot supply us; and that, for no other than the arbitrary purpose of purchasing for themselves, by a sacrifice of our rights and interests, certain privileges in their commerce with an allied state, who, in confidence, that their exclusive trade with America will be continued, while the principles and power of the British Parliament be the same, have indulged themselves in every exorbitance which their avarice could dictate or our necessity extort: have raised their commodities called for in America, to the double and treble of what they sold for, before such exclusive privileges were given them, and of what better commodities of the same kind would cost us elsewhere; and, at the same time, give us much less for what we carry thither than might be had at more convenient ports. That these acts prohibit us from carrying, in quest of other purchasers, the surplus of our tobaccos, remaining after the consumption of Great Britain is supplied: so that we must leave them with the British merchant, for whatever he will please to allow us, to be by him reshipped to foreign markets, where he will reap the benefits of making sale of them for full value. That, to heighten still the idea of parliamentary justice, and to show with what moderation they are like to exercise power, where themselves are to feel no part of its weight, we take leave to mention to His Majesty, certain other acts of the British Parliament, by which they would prohibit us from manufacturing, for our own use, the articles we raise on our own lands, with our own labor. By an act passed in the fifth year of the reign of his late Majesty, King George II, an American subject is forbidden to make a hat for himself of the fur which he has taken, perhaps, on his own soil; an instance of despotism, to which no parallel can be produced in the most arbitrary ages of British history. By one other act, passed in the twenty-third year of the same reign, the iron which we make we are forbidden to manufacture; and, heavy as that article is, and necessary in every branch of husbandry, besides commission and insurance, we are to pay freight for it to Great Britain, and freight for it back again, for the purpose of supporting not men but machines, in the island of Great Britain. In the same spirit of equal and impartial legislation, is to be viewed the act of Parliament, passed in the fifth year of the same reign, by which American lands are made subject to the demands of British creditors, while their own lands were still continued unanswerable for their debts; from which, one of these conclusions must necessarily follow: either that justice is not the same thing in America as in Britain, or else, that the British Parliament pay less regard to it here than there. But, that we do not point out to His Majesty the injustice of these acts, with intent to rest on that principle the cause of their nullity; but to show that experience confirms the propriety of those political principles, which exempt us from the jurisdiction of the British Parliament. The true ground on which we declare these acts void is that the British Parliament has no right to exercise authority over us.

That these exercises of usurped power have not been confined to instances alone, in which themselves were interested; but they have also intermeddled with the regulation of the internal affairs of the colonies. The act of the 9th of Anne for establishing a post office in America seems to have had little connection with British convenience, except that of accommodating His Majesty's ministers and favorites with the sale of a lucrative and easy office.

That thus have we hastened through the reigns which preceded His Majesty's, during which the violation of our rights were less alarming, because repeated at more distant intervals, than that rapid and bold succession of injuries, which is likely to distinguish the present from all other periods of American story. Scarcely have our minds been able to emerge from the astonishment into which one stroke of parliamentary thunder has involved us, before another more heavy and more alarming is fallen on us. Single acts of tyranny may be ascribed to the accidental opinion of a day; but a series of oppressions, begun at a distinguished period, and pursued unalterably through every change of ministers, too plainly prove a deliberate, systematical plan of reducing us to slavery.

That the act passed in the fourth year of His Majesty's reign, entitled ["An Act for Granting Certain Duties"];

One other act passed in the fifth year of his reign, entitled ["A Stamp Act"];

One other act passed in the sixth year of his reign, entitled ["An Act Declaring the Right of Parliament over the Colonies"];

And one other act passed in the seventh year of his reign, entitled ["An Act for Granting Duties on Paper, Tea, etc."]—form that connected chain of parliamentary usurpation which has already been the subject of frequent applications to His Majesty, and the Houses of Lords and Commons of Great Britain; and, no answers having yet been condescended to any of these, we shall not trouble His Majesty with a repetition of the matters they contained.

But that one other act passed in the same seventh year of his reign, having been a peculiar attempt, must ever require peculiar mention. It is entitled ["An Act Suspending the Legislature of New York"].

One free and independent legislature hereby takes upon itself to suspend the powers of another, free and independent as itself—thus exhibiting a phenomenon unknown in nature, the creator, and creature of its own power. Not only the principles of common sense, but the common feelings of human nature must be surrendered up, before His Majesty's subjects here can be persuaded to believe that they hold their political existence at the will of a British Parliament. Shall these governments be dissolved, their property annihilated, and their people reduced to a state of nature, at the imperious breath of a body of men whom they never saw, in whom they never confided, and over whom they have no powers of punishment or removal, let their crimes against the American public be ever so great? Can any one reason be assigned why 160,000 electors in the island of

Great Britain should give law to four millions in the States of America, every individual of whom is equal to every individual of them in virtue, in understanding, and in bodily strength? Were this to be admitted, instead of being a free people, as we have hitherto supposed, and mean to continue ourselves, we should suddenly be found the slaves, not of one, but of 160,000 tyrants; distinguished, too, from all others, by this singular circumstance, that they are removed from the reach of fear, the only restraining motive which may hold the hand of a tyrant.

That, by "An Act to Discontinue in Such Manner, and for Such Time as Are Therein Mentioned, the Landing and Discharging, Lading or Shipping of Goods, Wares, and Merchandise, at the Town and Within the Harbor of Boston, in the Province of Massachusetts Bay, in North America," which was past at the last session of the British Parliament, a large and populous town, whose trade was their sole subsistence, was deprived of that trade, and involved in utter ruin. Let us for a while suppose the question of right suspended, in order to examine this act on principles of justice. An act of Parliament had been passed, imposing duties on teas, to be paid in America, against which act the Americans had protested, as inauthoritative. The East India Company, who till that time had never sent a pound of tea to America on their own account, step forth on that occasion, the asserters of parliamentary right, and send hither many shiploads of that obnoxious commodity. The masters of their several vessels, however, on their arrival in America, wisely attended to admonition, and returned with their cargoes. In the province of New England alone, the remonstrances of the people were disregarded, and a compliance, after being many days waited for, was flatly refused. Whether in this the master of the vessel was governed by his obstinacy or his instructions, let those who know, say. There are extraordinary situations which require extraordinary interposition. An exasperated people, who feel that they possess power, are not easily restrained within limits strictly regular. A number of them assembled in the town of Boston, threw the tea into the ocean, and dispersed without doing any other act of violence. If in this they did wrong, they were known, and were amenable to the laws of the land; against which, it could not be objected, that they had ever, in any instance, been obstructed or diverted from the regular course, in favor of popular offenders. They should, therefore, not have been distrusted on this occasion. But that ill-fated colony had formerly been bold in their enmities against the House of Stuart, and were now devoted to ruin, by that unseen hand which governs the momentous affairs of this great empire. On the partial representations of a few worthless ministerial dependants, whose constant office it has been to keep that government embroiled, and who, by their treacheries, hope to obtain the dignity of British knighthood, without calling for a party accused, without asking a proof, without attempting a distinction between the guilty and the innocent, the whole of that ancient and wealthy town, is in a moment reduced from opulence to beggary. Men who had spent their lives in extending the British commerce, who had invested, in that place, the wealth their honest endeavors had merited, found themselves and their families thrown at once on the world for subsistence by its charities. Not the hundredth part of the inhabitants of that town had been concerned in the act complained of; many of them were in Great Britain and in other parts beyond sea; yet all were involved in one indiscriminate ruin, by a new executive power, unheard of till then, that of a British Parliament. A property of the value of many millions of money was sacrificed to revenge, not repay, the loss of a few thousands. This is administering justice with a heavy hand indeed! And when is this tempest to be arrested in its course? Two wharves are to be opened again when His Majesty shall think proper: the residue, which lined the extensive shores of the bay of Boston, are forever interdicted the exercise of commerce. This little exception seems to have been thrown in for no other purpose than that of setting a precedent for investing His Majesty with legislative powers. If the pulse of his people shall beat calmly under this experiment, another and another will be tried, till the measure of despotism be filled up. It would be an insult on common sense to pretend that this exception was made in order to restore its commerce to that great town. The trade, which cannot be received at two wharves alone, must of necessity be transferred to some other place, to which it will soon be followed by that of the two wharves. Considered in this light, it would be an insolent and cruel mockery at the annihilation of the town of Boston. By the act for the suppression of riots and tumults in the town of Boston, passed also in the last session of Parliament, a murder committed there is, if the governor pleases, to be tried in the Court of King's Bench, in the island of Great Britain, by a jury of Middlesex. The witnesses, too, on receipt of such a sum as the governor shall think it reasonable for them to expend, are to enter into recognizance to appear at the trial. This is, in other words, taxing them to the amount of their recognizance; and that amount may be whatever a governor pleases. For who does His Majesty think can be prevailed on to cross the Atlantic for the sole purpose of bearing evidence to a fact? His expenses are to be borne, indeed, as they shall be estimated by a governor; but who are to feed the wife and children whom he leaves behind and who have had no other subsistence but his daily labor? Those epidemical disorders, too, so terrible in a foreign climate—is the cure of them to be estimated among the articles of expense, and their danger to be warded off by the almighty power of a Parliament? And the wretched criminal, if he happen to have offended on the American side, stripped of his privilege of trial by peers of his vicinage, removed from the place where alone full evidence could be obtained, without money, without counsel, without friends, without exculpatory proof, is tried before judges predetermined to condemn. The cowards who would suffer a countryman to be torn from the bowels of their society, in order to be thus offered a sacrifice to parliamentary tyranny, would merit that everlasting infamy now fixed on the authors of the act! A clause, for a similar purpose, had been introduced into an act passed in the twelfth year of His Majesty's reign, entitled "An Act for the Better Securing and Preserving His Majesty's Dockyards, Magazines, Ships, Ammunition, and Stores"—against which, as meriting the same censures, the several colonies have already protested.

That these are the acts of power, assumed by a body of men foreign to our constitutions, and unacknowledged by our laws; against which we do, on behalf of the inhabitants of British America, enter this, our solemn and determined protest. And we do earnestly intreat His Majesty, as yet the only mediatory power between the several states of the British Empire, to recommend to his Parliament of Great Britain the total revocation of these acts, which, however nugatory they may be, may yet prove the cause of further discontents and jealousies among us.

That we next proceed to consider the conduct of His Majesty, as holding the executive powers of the laws of these states, and mark out his deviations from the line of duty. By the constitution of Great Britain, as well as of the several American states, His Majesty possesses the power of refusing to pass into a law any bill which has already passed the other two branches of the legislature. His Majesty, however, and his ancestors, conscious of the impropriety of opposing their single opinion to the united wisdom of two houses of Parliament, while their proceedings were unbiased by interested principles, for several ages past, have modestly declined the exercise of this power, in that part of his empire called Great Britain. But, by change of circumstances, other principles than those of justice simply have obtained an influence on their determinations. The addition of new states to the British Empire has produced an addition of new and, sometimes, opposite interests. It is now, therefore, the great office of His Majesty to resume the exercise of his negative power, and to prevent the passage of laws by any one legislature of the empire which might bear injuriously on the rights and interests of another. Yet this will not excuse the wanton exercise of this power, which we have seen His Majesty practice on the laws of the American legislature. For the most trifling reasons, and sometimes for no conceivable reason at all, His Majesty has rejected laws of the most salutary tendency. The abolition of domestic slavery is the great object of desire in those colonies, where it was, unhappily, introduced in their infant state. But previous to the enfranchisement of the slaves we have, it is necessary to exclude all further importations from Africa. Yet our repeated attempts to effect this, by prohibitions, and by imposing duties which might amount to a prohibition, having been hitherto defeated by His Majesty's negative: thus preferring the immediate advantages of a few British corsairs to the lasting interests of the American States, and to the rights of human nature, deeply wounded by this infamous practice. Nay, the single interposition of an interested individual against a law was scarcely ever known to fail of success, though, in the opposite scale, were placed the interests of a whole country. That this is so shameful an abuse of a power, trusted with His Majesty for other purposes, as if, not reformed, would call for some legal restrictions.

With equal inattention to the necessities of his people here, has His Majesty permitted our laws to lie neglected, in England, for years, neither confirming them by his assent, nor annulling them by his negative: so that such of them as have no suspending clause we hold on the most precarious of all tenures, His Majesty's will; and such of them as suspend themselves till His Majesty's assent be obtained, we have feared might be called into existence at some future and distant period, when time and change of circumstances shall have rendered them destructive to his people here. And, to render this grievance still more oppressive, His Majesty, by his instructions, has laid his governors under such restrictions that they can pass no law, of any moment, unless it have such suspending clause: so that, however immediate may be the call for legislative interposition, the law cannot be executed, till it has twice crossed the Atlantic, by which time the evil may have spent its whole force.

But in what terms reconcilable to His Majesty, and at the same time to truth, shall we speak of a late instruction to His Majesty's governor of the colony of Virginia, by which he is forbidden to assent to any law for the division of a county, unless the new county will consent to have no representative in Assembly? That colony has as yet affixed no boundary to the westward. Their western counties, therefore, are of an indefinite extent. Some of them are actually seated many hundred miles from their eastern limits. Is it possible, then, that His Majesty can have bestowed a single thought on the situation of those people, who, in order to obtain justice for injuries, however great or small, must, by the laws of that colony, attend their county court at such a distance, with all their witnesses, monthly, till their litigation be determined? Or does His Majesty seriously wish, and publish it to the world, that his subjects should give up the glorious right of representation, with all the benefits derived from that, and submit themselves the absolute slaves of his sovereign will? Or is it rather meant to confine the legislative body to their present numbers, that they may be the cheaper bargain, whenever they shall become worth a purchase?

One of the articles of impeachment against Tresilian, and the other judges of Westminster Hall, in the reign of Richard II, for which they suffered death as traitors to their country, was that they had advised the king that he might dissolve his Parliament at any time; and succeeding kings have adopted the opinion of these unjust judges. Since the establishment, however, of the British constitution, at the Glorious Revolution, on its free and ancient principles, neither His Majesty nor his ancestors have exercised such a power of dissolution in the island of Great Britain;* and when His Majesty was petitioned, by the united voice of his people there, to dissolve the present Parliament, who had become obnoxious to them, his ministers were heard to declare, in open Parliament, that His Majesty possessed no such power by the constitution. But how different their language, and his practice, here! To declare, as their duty required,

---

*On further inquiry, I find two instances of dissolutions before the Parliament would, of itself, have been at an end: viz., the Parliament called to meet August 24, 1698, was dissolved by King William, December 19, 1700, and a new one called, to meet February 6, 1701, which was also dissolved, November 11, 1701, and a new one met December 30, 1701.

the known rights of their country, to oppose the usurpation of every foreign judicature, to disregard the imperious mandates of a minister or governor, have been the avowed causes of dissolving Houses of Representatives in America. But if such powers be really vested in His Majesty, can he suppose they are there placed to awe the members from such purposes as these? When the representative body have lost the confidence of their constituents, when they have notoriously made sale of their most valuable rights, when they have assumed to themselves powers which the people never put into their hands, then, indeed, their continuing in office becomes dangerous to the state, and calls for an exercise of the power of dissolution. Such being the cause for which the representative body should, and should not, be dissolved, will it not appear strange, to an unbiased observer, that that of Great Britain was not dissolved, while those of the colonies have repeatedly incurred that sentence?

But Your Majesty, or your governors, have carried this power beyond every limit known or provided for by the laws. After dissolving one House of Representatives, they have refused to call another, so that, for a great length of time, the legislature provided by the laws has been out of existence. From the nature of things, every society must, at all times, possess within itself the sovereign powers of legislation. The feelings of human nature revolt against the supposition of a state so situated, as that it may not, in any emergency, provide against dangers which, perhaps, threaten immediate ruin. While those bodies are in existence to whom the people have delegated the powers of legislation, they alone possess, and may exercise, those powers. But when they are dissolved, by the lopping off one or more of their branches, the power reverts to the people, who may use it to unlimited extent, either assembling together in person, sending deputies, or in any other way they may think proper. We forbear to trace consequences further; the dangers are conspicuous with which this practice is replete.

That we shall, at this time also, take notice of an error in the nature of our land holdings, which crept in at a very early period of our settlement. The introduction of the feudal tenures into the kingdom of England, though ancient, is well enough understood to set this matter in a proper light. In the earlier ages of the Saxon settlement, feudal holdings were certainly altogether unknown, and very few, if any, had been introduced at the time of the Norman Conquest. Our Saxon ancestors held their lands, as they did their personal property, in absolute dominion, disincumbered with any superior, answering nearly to the nature of those possessions which the feudalists term Allodial. William the Norman first introduced that system generally. The lands which had belonged to those who fell in the Battle of Hastings, and in the subsequent insurrections of his reign formed a considerable proportion of the lands of the whole kingdom. These he granted out, subject to feudal duties, as did he also those of a great number of his new subjects, who, by persuasions or threats, were induced to surrender them for that purpose. But still, much was left in the hands of his Saxon subjects, held of no superior, and not subject to feudal conditions. These, therefore, by express laws, enacted to render uniform the system of military defense, were made liable to the same military duties as if they had been feuds; and the Norman lawyers soon found means to saddle them, also, with the other feudal burdens. But still they had not been surrendered to the king, they were not derived from his grant, and therefore they were not holden of him. A general principle was introduced, that "all lands in England were held either mediately or immediately of the Crown"; but this was borrowed from those holdings which were truly feudal, and only applied to others for the purposes of illustration. Feudal holdings were, therefore, but exceptions out of the Saxon laws of possession, under which all lands were held in absolute right. These, therefore, still form the basis or groundwork of the common law, to prevail wheresoever the exceptions have not taken place. America was not conquered by William the Norman, nor its lands surrendered to him or any of his successors. Possessions there are, undoubtedly, of the Allodial nature. Our ancestors, however, who migrated hither, were laborers, not lawyers. The fictitious principle, that all lands belong originally to the king, they were early persuaded to believe real, and accordingly took grants of their own lands from the Crown. And while the Crown continued to grant for small sums and on reasonable rents, there was no inducement to arrest the error and lay it open to public view. But His Majesty has lately taken on him to advance the terms of purchase and of holding to the double of what they were; by which means, the acquisition of lands being rendered difficult, the population of our country is likely to be checked. It is time, therefore, for us to lay this matter before His Majesty, and to declare that he has no right to grant lands of himself. From the nature and purpose of civil institutions, all the lands within the limits which any particular party has circumscribed around itself are assumed by that society, and subject to their allotment; this may be done by themselves assembled collectively, or by their legislature, to whom they may have delegated sovereign authority; and, if they are allotted in neither of these ways, each individual of the society may appropriate to himself such lands as he finds vacant, and occupancy will give him title.

That is, in order to enforce the arbitrary measures before complained of, His Majesty has, from time to time, sent among us large bodies of armed forces, not made up of the people here nor raised by the authority of our laws. Did His Majesty possess such a right as this, it might swallow up all our other rights, whenever he should think proper. But His Majesty has no right to land a single armed man on our shores; and those whom he sends here are liable to our laws, for the suppression and punishment of riots, routs, and unlawful assemblies, or are hostile bodies invading us in defiance of law. When, in the course of the late war, it became expedient that a body of Hanoverian troops should be brought over for the defense of Great Britain, His Majesty's grandfather, our late sovereign, did not pretend to introduce them under any authority he possessed. Such a measure would have given just alarm to his subjects of Great Britain, whose liberties would not be safe if armed men of another country, and of another spirit, might be brought into the realm at any time, without the consent of their legislature. He, therefore, applied to Parliament, who passed an act for that purpose, limiting the number to be brought in, and the time they were to continue. In like manner is His Majesty restrained in every part of the empire. He possesses indeed the executive power of the laws in every state; but they are the laws of the particular state, which he is to administer within that state, and not those of any one within the limits of another. Every state must judge for itself the number of armed men which they may safely trust among them, of whom they are to consist, and under what restrictions they are to be laid. To render these proceedings still more criminal against our laws, instead of subjecting the military to the civil power, His Majesty has expressly made the civil subordinate to the military. But can His Majesty thus put down all law under his feet? Can he erect a power superior to that which erected himself? He has done it indeed by force; but let him remember that force cannot give right.

That these are our grievances, which we have thus laid before His Majesty, with that freedom of language and sentiment which becomes a free people, claiming their rights as derived from the laws of nature, and not as the gift of their chief magistrate. Let those flatter who fear: it is not an American art. To give praise where it is not due might be well from the venal, but would ill beseem those who are asserting the rights of human nature. They know, and will, therefore, say, that kings are the servants, not the proprietors, of the people. Open your breast, Sire, to liberal and expanded thought. Let not the name of George III be a blot on the page of history. You are surrounded by British counselors, but remember that they are parties. You have no ministers for American affairs, because you have none taken from among us, nor amenable to the laws on which they are to give your advice. It behooves you, therefore, to think and to act for yourself and your people. The great principles of right and wrong are legible to every reader; to pursue them requires not the aid of many counselors. The whole art of government consists in the art of being honest. Only aim to do your duty, and mankind will give you credit where you fail. No longer persevere in sacrificing the rights of one part of the empire to the inordinate desires of another; but deal out to all equal and impartial right. Let no act be passed by any one legislature which may infringe on the rights and liberties of another. This is the important post in which fortune has placed you, holding the balance of a great, if a well-poised, empire. This, Sire, is the advice of your great American council, on the observance of which may perhaps depend your felicity and future fame, and the preservation of that harmony which alone can continue, both to Great Britain and America, the reciprocal advantages of their connection. It is neither our wish nor our interest to separate from her. We are willing, on our part, to sacrifice everything which reason can ask to the restoration of that tranquillity for which all must wish. On their part, let them be ready to establish union on a generous plan. Let them name their terms, but let them be just. Accept of every commercial preference it is in our power to give, for such things as we can raise for their use, or they make for ours. But let them not think to exclude us from going to other markets to dispose of those commodities which they cannot use, nor to supply those wants which they cannot supply. Still less, let it be proposed that our properties, within our own territories, shall [not] be taxed or regulated by any power on earth but our own. The God who gave us life gave us liberty at the same time: the hand of force may destroy but cannot disjoin them. This, Sire, is our last, our determined resolution. And that you will be pleased to interpose, with that efficacy which your earnest endeavors may insure, to procure redress of these our great grievances, to quiet the minds of your subjects in British America against any apprehensions of future encroachment, to establish fraternal love and harmony through the whole empire, and that that may continue to the latest ages of time, is the fervent prayer of all British America.

LETTER TO
DR. WILLIAM SMALL

May 7, 1775

Dear Sir:

Within this week we have received the unhappy news of an action of considerable magnitude, between the king's troops and our brethren of Boston, in which it is said five hundred of the former, with the earl of Percy, are slain. That such an action has occurred, is undoubted, though perhaps the circumstances may not have reached us with truth. This accident has cut off our last hope of reconciliation, and a frenzy of revenge seems to have seized all ranks of people. It is a lamentable circumstance that the only mediatory power, acknowledged by both parties, instead of leading to a reconciliation [of] his divided people, should pursue the incendiary purpose of still blowing up the flames, as we find him constantly doing, in every speech and public declaration. This may, perhaps, be intended to intimidate into acquiescence, but the effect has been most unfortunately otherwise. A little knowledge of human nature, and attention to its ordinary workings, might have foreseen that the spirits of the people here were in a state in which they were more likely to be provoked than frightened by haughty deportment. And to fill up the measure of irritation, a proscription of individuals has been substituted in the room of just trial. Can it be believed that a grateful people will suffer those to be consigned to execution, whose sole crime has been the developing and asserting their rights? Had the Parliament possessed the power of reflection, they would have avoided a measure as impotent as it was inflammatory. When I saw Lord Chatham's bill, I entertained high hope that a reconciliation could have been brought about. The difference between his terms, and those offered by our Congress, might have been accommodated, if entered on by both parties with a disposition to accommodate. But the dignity of Parliament, it seems, can brook no opposition to its power. Strange, that a set of men, who have made sale of their virtue to the minister, should yet talk of retaining dignity! But I am getting into politics, though I sat down only to ask your acceptance of the wine, and express my constant wishes for your happiness.

LETTER TO
JOHN RANDOLPH

Monticello, August 25, 1775

Dear Sir:

I am sorry the situation of our country should render it not eligible to you to remain longer in it. I hope the returning wisdom of Great Britain will, ere long, put an end to this unnatural contest. There may be people to whose tempers and dispositions contention is pleasing, and who, therefore, wish a continuance of confusion, but to me it is of all states but one, the most horrid. My first wish is a restoration of our just rights; my second, a return of the happy period, when, consistently with duty, I may withdraw myself totally from the public stage, and pass the rest of my days in domestic ease and tranquillity, banishing every desire of ever hearing what passes in the world. Perhaps (for the latter adds considerably to the warmth of the former wish), looking with fondness towards a reconciliation with Great Britain, I cannot help hoping you may be able to contribute towards expediting this good work. I think it must be evident to yourself, that the Ministry have been deceived by their officers on this side of the water, who (for what purpose I cannot tell) have constantly represented the American opposition as that of a small faction, in which the body of the people took little part. This, you can inform them, of your own knowledge, is untrue. They have taken it into their heads, too, that we are cowards, and shall surrender at discretion to an armed force. The past and future operations of the war must confirm or undeceive them on that head. I wish they were thoroughly and minutely acquainted with every circumstance relative to America, as it exists in truth. I am persuaded this would go far towards disposing them to reconciliation. Even those in Parliament who are called friends to America seem to know nothing of our real determinations. I observe, they pronounced in the last Parliament that the Congress of 1774 did not mean to insist rigorously on the terms they held out, but kept something in reserve, to give up; and, in fact, that they would give up everything but the article of taxation. Now, the truth is far from this, as I can affirm, and put my honor to the assertion. Their continuance in this error may, perhaps, produce very ill consequences. The Congress stated the lowest terms they thought possible to be accepted, in order to convince the world they were not unreasonable. They gave up the monopoly and regulation of trade, and all acts of Parliament prior to 1764, leaving to British generosity to render these, at some future time, as easy to America as the interest of Britain would admit. But this was before blood was spilt. I cannot affirm, but have reason to think, these terms would not now be accepted. I wish no false sense of honor, no ignorance of our real intentions, no vain hope that partial concessions of right will be accepted, may induce the Ministry to trifle with accommodation, till it shall be out of their power ever to accommodate. If, indeed, Great Britain, disjoined from her colonies, be a match for the most potent nations of Europe, with the colonies thrown into their scale, they may go on securely. But if they are not assured of this, it would be certainly unwise, by trying the event of another campaign, to risk our accepting a foreign aid, which, perhaps, may not be obtainable, but on condition of everlasting avulsion from Great Britain. This would be thought a hard condition, to those who still wish for re-union with their parent country. I am sincerely one of those, and would rather be in dependence on Great Britain, properly limited, than on any nation on earth, or than on no nation. But I am one of those, too, who, rather than submit to the rights of legislating for us, assumed by the British Parliament, and which late experience has shown they will so cruelly exercise, would lend my hand to sink the whole island in the ocean.

If undeceiving the minister, as to matters of fact, may change his disposition, it will, perhaps, be in your power, by assisting to do this, to render service to the whole empire, at the most critical time, certainly, that it has ever seen. Whether Britain shall continue the head of the greatest empire on earth, or shall return to her original station in the political scale of Europe, depends, perhaps, on the resolutions of the succeeding winter. God send they may be wise and salutary for us all. I shall be glad to hear from you as often as you may be disposed to think of things here. You may be at liberty, I expect, to communicate some things, consistently with your honor, and the duties you will owe to a protecting nation. Such a communication among individuals may be mutually beneficial to the contending parties. On this or any future occasion, if I affirm to you any facts, your knowledge of me will enable you to decide on their credibility; if I hazard opinions on the dispositions of men or other speculative points, you can only know they are my opinions. My best wishes for your felicity, attend you, wherever you go, and believe me to be assuredly, your friend and servant.

THE DECLARATION OF INDEPENDENCE

1776

A DECLARATION BY THE REPRESENTATIVES OF THE
UNITED STATES OF AMERICA, IN [GENERAL]
CONGRESS ASSEMBLED

When, in the course of human events, it becomes necessary for one people to dissolve the political bands which have connected them with another, and to assume among the powers of the earth the separate and equal station to which the laws of nature and of nature's God entitle them, a decent respect to the opinions of mankind requires that they should declare the causes which impel them to the separation.

We hold these truths to be self-evident: that all men are created equal; that they are endowed by their creator with [*inherent and*] CERTAIN inalienable rights; that among these are life, liberty, and the pursuit of happiness; that to secure these rights, governments are instituted among men, deriving their just powers from the consent of the governed; that whenever any form of government becomes destructive of these ends, it is the right of the people to alter or to abolish it, and to institute new government, laying its foundation on such principles, and organizing its powers in such form, as to them shall seem most likely to effect their safety and happiness. Prudence, indeed, will dictate that governments long established should not be changed for light and transient causes; and accordingly all experience hath shown that mankind are more disposed to suffer

Editor's note. The parts of Jefferson's original draft that were deleted by Congress are printed in italics and enclosed in brackets. Wording added by Congress and appearing in the final Declaration are indicated by small capitals.

while evils are sufferable than to right themselves by abolishing the forms to which they are accustomed. But when a long train of abuses and usurpations, [*begun at a distinguished period and*] pursuing invariably the same object, evinces a design to reduce them under absolute despotism, it is their right, it is their duty to throw off such government, and to provide new guards for their future security. Such has been the patient sufferance of these colonies; and such is now the necessity which constrains them to [*expunge*] ALTER their former systems of government. The history of the present king of Great Britain is a history of [*unremitting*] REPEATED injuries and usurpations, [*among which appears no solitary fact to contradict the uniform tenor of the rest, but all have*] ALL HAVING in direct object the establishment of an absolute tyranny over these states. To prove this, let facts be submitted to a candid world [*for the truth of which we pledge a faith yet unsullied by falsehood*].

He has refused his assent to laws the most wholesome and necessary for the public good.

He has forbidden his governors to pass laws of immediate and pressing importance, unless suspended in their operation till his assent should be obtained; and, when so suspended, he has utterly neglected to attend to them.

He has refused to pass other laws for the accommodation of large districts of people, unless those people would relinquish the right of representation in the legislature, a right inestimable to them, and formidable to tyrants only.

He has called together legislative bodies at places unusual, uncomfortable, and distant from the depository of their public records, for the sole purpose of fatiguing them into compliance with his measures.

He has dissolved representative houses repeatedly [*and continually*] for opposing with manly firmness his invasions on the rights of the people.

He has refused for a long time after such dissolutions to cause others to be elected, whereby the legislative powers, incapable of annihilation, have returned to the people at large for their exercise, the state remaining, in the meantime, exposed to all the dangers of invasion from without and convulsions within.

He has endeavored to prevent the population of these states; for that purpose obstructing the laws for naturalization of foreigners, refusing to pass others to encourage their migrations hither, and raising the conditions of new appropriations of lands.

He has [*suffered*] OBSTRUCTED the administration of justice [*totally to cease in some of these states*] BY refusing his assent to laws for establishing judiciary powers.

He has made [*our*] judges dependent on his will alone for the tenure of their offices, and the amount and payment of their salaries.

He has erected a multitude of new offices, [*by a self-assumed power*] and sent hither swarms of new officers to harass our people and eat out their substance.

He has kept among us in times of peace standing armies [*and ships of war*] without the consent of our legislatures.

He has affected to render the military independent of, and superior to, the civil power.

He has combined with others to subject us to a jurisdiction foreign to our constitutions and unacknowledged by our laws, giving his assent to their acts of pretended legislation for quartering large bodies of armed troops among us; for protecting them by a mock trial from punishment for any murders which they should commit on the inhabitants of these states; for cutting off our trade with all parts of the world; for imposing taxes on us without our consent; for depriving us IN MANY CASES of the benefits of trial by jury; for transporting us beyond seas to be tried for pretended offenses; for abolishing the free system of English laws in a neighboring province, establishing therein an arbitrary government, and enlarging its boundaries, so as to render it at once an example and fit instrument for introducing the same absolute rule into these [*states*] COLONIES; for taking away our charters, abolishing our most valuable laws, and altering fundamentally the forms of our governments; for suspending our own legislatures, and declaring themselves invested with power to legislate for us in all cases whatsoever.

He has abdicated government here [*withdrawing his governors, and declaring us out of his allegiance and protection*] BY DECLARING US OUT OF HIS PROTECTION, AND WAGING WAR AGAINST US.

He has plundered our seas, ravaged our coasts, burnt our towns, and destroyed the lives of our people.

He is at this time transporting large armies of foreign mercenaries to complete the works of death, desolation, and tyranny already begun with circumstances of cruelty and perfidy SCARCELY PARALLELED IN THE MOST BARBAROUS AGES, AND TOTALLY unworthy the head of a civilized nation.

He has constrained our fellow citizens taken captive on the high seas, to bear arms against their country, to become the executioners of their friends and brethren, or to fall themselves by their hands.

He has EXCITED DOMESTIC INSURRECTION AMONG US, AND HAS endeavored to bring on the inhabitants of our frontiers, the merciless Indian savages, whose known rule of warfare is an undistinguished destruction of all ages, sexes, and conditions [*of existence*].

[*He has incited treasonable insurrections of our fellow citizens, with the allurements of forfeiture and confiscation of our property.*

He has waged cruel war against human nature itself, violating its most sacred rights of life and liberty in the persons of a distant people who never offended him, captivating and carrying them into slavery in another hemisphere, or to incur miserable death in their transportation thither. This piratical warfare, the opprobium of infidel powers, is the warfare of the Christian king of Great Britain. Determined to keep open a market where men should be bought and sold, he has prostituted his negative for suppressing every legislative attempt to prohibit or to restrain this execrable commerce. And that this assemblage of horrors might want no fact of distinguished die, he is now exciting those very people to rise in arms among us, and to purchase that liberty of which he has deprived them, by murdering the people on whom he also obtruded them: thus paying off former crimes committed against the liberties of one people, with crimes which he urges them to commit against the lives of another.]

In every stage of these oppressions we have petitioned for redress in the most humble terms: our repeated petitions have been answered only by repeated injuries.

A prince whose character is thus marked by every act which may define a tyrant is unfit to be the ruler of a FREE people *[who means to be free. Future ages will scarcely believe that the hardiness of one man adventured, within the short compass of twelve years only, to lay a foundation so broad and so undisguised for tyranny over a people fostered and fixed in principles of freedom.]*

Nor have we been wanting in attentions to our British brethren. We have warned them from time to time of attempts by their legislature to extend *[a]* AN UNWARRANTABLE jurisdiction over *[these our states]* US. We have reminded them of the circumstances of our emigration and settlement here, *[no one of which could warrant so strange a pretension: that these were effected at the expense of our own blood and treasure, unassisted by the wealth or the strength of Great Britain: that in constituting indeed our several forms of government, we had adopted one common king, thereby laying a foundation for perpetual league and amity with them: but that submission to their parliament was no part of our constitution, nor ever in idea, if history may be credited: and,]* we HAVE appealed to their native justice and magnanimity *[as well as to]* AND WE HAVE CONJURED THEM BY the ties of our common kindred to disavow these usurpations which *[were likely to]* WOULD INEVITABLY interrupt our connection and correspondence. They too have been deaf to the voice of justice and of consanguinity, *[and when occasions have been given them, by the regular course of their laws, of removing from their councils the disturbers of our harmony, they have, by their free election, reestablished them in power. At this very time too, they are permitting their chief magistrate to send over not only soldiers of our common blood, but Scotch and foreign mercenaries to invade and destroy us. These facts have given the last stab to agonizing affection, and manly spirit bids us to renounce forever these unfeeling brethren. We must endeavor to forget our former love for them, and hold them as we hold the rest of mankind, enemies in war, in peace friends. We might have been a free and a great people together; but a communication of grandeur and of freedom, it seems, is below their dignity. Be it so, since they will have it. The road to happiness and to glory is open to us too. We will tread it apart from them, and]* WE MUST THEREFORE acquiesce in the necessity which denounces our [*eternal*] separation [ ] AND HOLD THEM AS WE HOLD THE REST OF MANKIND, ENEMIES IN WAR, IN PEACE FRIENDS!

We, therefore, the representatives of the United States of America in General Congress assembled, [*do in the name, and by the authority of the good people of these states reject and renounce all allegiance and subjection to the kings of Great Britain and all others who may hereafter claim by, through or under them; we utterly dissolve all political connection which may heretofore have subsisted between us and the people or parliament of Great Britain: and finally we do assert and declare these colonies to be free and independent states,*] APPEALING TO THE SUPREME JUDGE OF THE WORLD FOR THE RECTITUDE OF OUR INTENTIONS, DO IN THE NAME, AND BY THE AUTHORITY OF THE GOOD PEOPLE OF THESE COLONIES, SOLEMNLY PUBLISH AND DE-CLARE, THAT THESE UNITED COLONIES ARE, AND OF RIGHT OUGHT TO BE FREE AND INDEPENDENT STATES; THAT THEY ARE ABSOLVED FROM ALL ALLEGIANCE TO THE BRITISH CROWN, AND THAT ALL POLITICAL CONNECTION BETWEEN THEM AND THE STATE OF GREAT BRITAIN IS, AND OUGHT TO BE, TOTALLY DISSOLVED; and that as free and independent states, they have full power to levy war, conclude peace, contract alliances, establish commerce, and to do all other acts and things which independent states may of right do.

And for the support of this declaration, WITH A FIRM RELI-ANCE ON THE PROTECTION OF DIVINE PROVIDENCE, we mutually pledge to each other our lives, our fortunes, and our sacred honor.

LETTER TO GENERAL GEORGE WASHINGTON

Richmond, October 22, 1780

Sir:

I have this morning received certain information of the arrival of a hostile fleet in our bay, of about sixty sail. The debarkation of some light horse, in the neighborhood of Portsmouth, seems to indicate that as the first scene of action. We are endeavoring to collect as large a body to oppose them as we can arm; this will be lamentably inadequate, if the enemy be in any force. It is mortifying to suppose that a people, able and zealous to contend with their enemy, should be reduced to fold their arms for want of the means of defense. Yet no resources, that we know of, insure us against this event. It has become necessary to divert to this new object a considerable part of the aids we had destined for General Gates. We are still, however, sensible of the necessity of supporting him, and have left that part of the country nearest him uncalled on, at present, that they may reinforce him as soon as arms can be received. We have called to the command of our forces Generals Weeden and Muhlenburg, of the line, and Nelson and Stevens of the militia. You will be pleased to make to these such additions as you may think proper. As to the aids of men, I ask for none, knowing that if the late detachment of the enemy shall have left it safe for you to spare aids of that kind, you will not await my application. Of the troops we shall raise, there is not a single man who ever saw the face of an enemy. Whether the Convention troops will be removed or not is yet undetermined. This must depend on the force of the enemy, and the aspect of their movements.

I have the honor to be Your Excellency's most obedient humble servant.

31

LETTER TO COLONEL
JAMES MONROE

Monticello, May 20, 1782

Dear Sir:

I have been gratified with your two favors of the 6th and 11th instant. It gives me pleasure that your county has been wise enough to enlist your talent into their service. I am much obliged by the kind wishes you express of seeing me also in Richmond, and am always mortified when anything is expected from me which I cannot fulfill, and more especially if it relate to the public service. Before I ventured to declare to my countrymen my determination to retire from public employment, I examined well my heart to know whether it were thoroughly cured of every principle of political ambition, whether no lurking particle remained which might leave me uneasy, when reduced within the limits of mere private life. I became satisfied that every fiber of that passion was thoroughly eradicated. I examined also, in other views, my right to withdraw. I considered that I had been thirteen years engaged in public service—that, during that time, I had so totally abandoned all attention to my private affairs as to permit them to run into great disorder and ruin—that I had now a family advanced to years which require my attention and instruction—that to these was added the hopeful offspring of a deceased friend, whose memory must be forever dear to me, and who have no other reliance for being rendered useful to themselves or their country—that by a constant sacrifice of time, labor, parental and friendly duties, I had, so far from gaining the affection of my countrymen, which was the only reward I ever asked or could have felt, even lost the small estimation I had before possessed.

That, however I might have comforted myself under the

disapprobation of the well-meaning but uninformed people, yet, that of their representatives was a shock on which I had not calculated. That this, indeed, had been followed by an exculpatory declaration. But, in the meantime, I had been suspected in the eyes of the world, without the least hint then or afterwards being made public, which might restrain them from supposing that I stood arraigned for treason of the heart, and not merely weakness of the mind; and I felt that these injuries, for such they have been since acknowledged, had inflicted a wound on my spirit which will only be cured by the all-healing grave. If reason and inclination unite in justifying my retirement, the laws of my country are equally in favor of it. Whether the state may command the political services of all its members to an indefinite extent, or, if these be among the rights never wholly ceded to the public power, is a question which I do not find expressly decided in England. Obiter dictums on the subject I have indeed met with, but the complexion of the times in which these have dropped would generally answer them. Besides that, this species of authority is not acknowledged in our possession.

In this country, however, since the present government has been established, the point has been settled by uniform, pointed, and multiplied precedents. Offices of every kind, and given by every power, have been daily and hourly declined and resigned from the Declaration of Independence to this moment. The General Assembly has accepted these without discrimination of office, and without ever questioning them in point of right. If the difference between the office of a delegate and any other could ever have been supposed, yet in the case of Mr. Thompson Mason, who declined the office of delegate, and was permitted so to do by the House, that supposition has been proved to be groundless. But, indeed, no such distinction of offices can be admitted. Reason, and the opinions of the lawyers, putting all on a footing as to this question, and so giving to the delegate the aid of all the precedents of the refusal of other offices. The law then does not warrant the assumption of such a power by the state over its members. For if it does, where is that law? Nor yet does reason. For though I will admit that this does subject every individual, if called on, to an equal tour of political duty, yet it can never go so far as to submit to it his whole existence. If we are made in some degree for others, yet, in a greater, are we made for ourselves. It were contrary to feeling, and indeed ridiculous to suppose that a man had less rights in himself than one of his neighbors, or indeed all of them put together. This would be slavery, and not that liberty which the bill of rights has made inviolable, and for the preservation of which our government has been charged. Nothing could so completely divest us of that liberty as the establishment of the opinion, that the state has a perpetual right to the services of all its members. This, to men of certain ways of thinking, would be to annihilate the blessings of existence, and to contradict the Giver of Life, who gave it for happiness and not for wretchedness. And certainly, to such it were better that they had never been born. However, with these, I may think public service and private misery inseparably linked together, I have not the vanity to count myself among those whom the state would think worth oppressing with perpetual service. I have received a sufficient memento to the contrary. I am persuaded that, having hitherto dedicated to them the whole of the active and useful part of my life, I shall be permitted to pass the rest in mental quiet. I hope, too, that I did not mistake modes any more than the matter of right when I preferred a simple act of renunciation to the taking sanctuary under those disqualifications (provided by the law for other purposes indeed but) affording asylum also for rest to the wearied. I daresay you did not expect by the few words you dropped on the right of renunciation to expose yourself to the fatigue of so long a letter, but I wished you to see that, if I had done wrong, I had been betrayed by a semblance of right at least. I take the liberty of enclosing to you a letter for General Chattellux, for which you will readily find means of conveyance. But I mean to give you more trouble with the one to Pelham, who lives in the neighborhood of Manchester, and to ask the favor of you to send it by your servant—express—which I am in hopes may be done without absenting him from your person, but during those hours in which you will be engaged in the house. I am anxious that it should be received immediately. . . . It will give me great pleasure to see you here whenever you can favor us with your company. You will find me still busy, but in lighter occupations. But in these and all others you will find me to retain a due sense of your friendship, and to be, with sincere esteem, dear sir, your most obedient and most humble servant.

LETTER TO GENERAL
GEORGE WASHINGTON

Annapolis, April 16, 1784

Dear Sir:

I received your favor of April 8, by Colonel Harrison. The subject of it is interesting, and, so far as you have stood connected with it, has been [a] matter of anxiety to me; because, whatever may be the ultimate fate of the institution of the Cincinnati, in its course, it draws to it some degree of disapprobation, [and] I have wished to see you standing on ground separated from it, and that the character which will be handed to future ages at the head of our Revolution may, in no instance, be compromitted [sic] in subordinate altercations. The subject has been at the point of my pen in every letter I have written to you, but has been still restrained by the reflection that you had among your friends more able counselors, and, in yourself, one abler than them all. Your letter has now rendered a duty what was before a desire, and I cannot better merit your confidence than by a full and free communication of facts and sentiments, as far as they have come within my observation. When the army was about to be disbanded, and the officers to take final leave, perhaps never again to meet, it was natural for men who had accompanied each other through so many scenes of hardship, of difficulty, and danger—who, in a variety of instances, must have been rendered mutually dear by those aids and good offices to which their situations had given occasion—it was natural, I say, for these to seize with fondness any proposition which promised to bring them together again, at certain and regular periods. And this, I take for granted, was the origin and object of this institution; and I have no suspicion that they foresaw, much less intended, those mischiefs which exist, perhaps in the forebodings of politicians only. I doubt, however, whether, in its execution, it would be found to answer the wishes of those who framed it, and to foster those friendships it was intended to preserve. The members would be brought together at their annual assemblies, no longer to encounter a common enemy, but to encounter one another in debate and sentiment. For something, I suppose, is to be done at these meetings, and, however unimportant, it will suffice to produce difference of opinion, contradiction, and irritation. The way to make friends quarrel is to put them in disputation under the public eye. An experience of near twenty years has taught me that few friendships stand this test, and that public assemblies, where everyone is free to act and speak, are the most powerful looseners of the bands of private friendship. I think, therefore, that this institution would fail in its principal object, the perpetuation of the personal friendships contracted through the war.

The objections of those who are opposed to the institution shall be briefly sketched. You will readily fill them up. They urge that it is against the Confederation—against the letter of some of our constitutions—against the spirit of all of them; that the foundation on which all these are built is the natural equality of man, the denial of every preeminence but that annexed to legal office, and, particularly, the denial of a preeminence by birth; that, however, in their present dispositions, citizens might decline accepting honorary installments into the order, a time may come when a change of dispositions would render these flattering, when a well-directed distribution of them might draw into the order all the men of talents, of office and wealth, and in this case, would probably procure an ingraftment into the government; that in this, they will be supported by their foreign members, and the wishes and influence of foreign courts; that experience has shown that the hereditary branches of modern governments are the patrons of privilege and prerogative, and not of the natural rights of the people, whose oppressors they generally are; that, besides these evils, which are remote, others may take place more immediately; that a distinction is kept up between the civil and military, which it is for the happiness of both to obliterate; that when the members assemble they will be proposing to do something, and what that something may be will depend on actual circumstances; that being an organized body, under habits of subordination, the first obstruction to enterprise will be already surmounted; that the moderation and virtue of a single character have probably prevented this Revolution from being closed, as most others have been, by a subversion of that liberty it was intended to establish; that he is not immortal, and his successor, or some of his successors, may be led by false calculation into a less certain road to glory.

What are the sentiments of Congress on this subject, and what line they will pursue, can only be stated conjecturally. Congress, as a body, if left to themselves, will, in my opinion, say nothing on the subject. They may, however, be forced into a declaration by instructions from some of the states, or by other incidents. Their sentiments, if forced from them, will be unfriendly to the institution. If permitted to pursue their own path, they will check it by side-blows whenever it comes in their way, and in competitions for office, on equal or nearly equal ground, will give silent preferences to those who are not of the fraternity. My reasons for thinking this are: (1) the grounds on which they lately declined the foreign order proposed to be conferred on some of our citizens; (2) the fourth of the fundamental articles of constitution for the new states; I enclose you the report; it has been considered by Congress, recommitted and reformed by a committee, according to sentiments expressed on other parts of it, but the principle referred to, having not been controverted at all, stands in this as in the original report; it is not yet confirmed by Congress; (3) private conversations on this subject with the members. Since the receipt of your letter, I have taken occasion to extend these; not, indeed, to the military members, because, being of the order, delicacy forbade it, but to the others pretty generally; and among these, I have as yet found but one who is not opposed to the institution, and that with an anguish of mind, though covered under a guarded silence, which

I have not seen produced by any circumstance before. I arrived at Philadelphia before the separation of the last Congress, and saw there and at Princeton some of its members, not now in delegation. Burke's piece happened to come out at that time, which occasioned this institution to be the subject of conversation. I found the same impressions made on them which their successors have received. I hear from other quarters that it is disagreeable, generally, to such citizens as have attended to it, and, therefore, will probably be so to all, when any circumstance shall present it to the notice of all.

This, sir, is as faithful an account of sentiments and facts as I am able to give you. You know the extent of the circle within which my observations are at present circumscribed, and can estimate how far, as forming a part of the general opinion, it may merit notice, or ought to influence your particular conduct.

It remains now to pay obedience to that part of your letter, which requests sentiments on the most eligible measures to be pursued by the society, at their next meeting. I must be far from pretending to be a judge of what would, in fact, be the most eligible measures for the society. I can only give you the opinions of those with whom I have conversed, and who, as I have before observed, are unfriendly to it. They lead to these conclusions: 1) if the society proceed according to its institution, it will be better to make no applications to Congress on that subject, or any other, in their associated character; (2) if they should propose to modify it, so as to render it unobjectionable, I think this would not be effected without such a modification as would amount almost to annihilation; for such would it be to part with its inheritability, its organization, and its assemblies; (3) if they shall be disposed to discontinue the whole, it would remain with them to determine whether they would choose it to be done by their own act only, or by a reference of the matter to Congress, which would infallibly produce a recommendation of total discontinuance.

You will be sensible, sir, that these communications are without reserve. I supposed such to be your wish, and mean them but as materials, with such others as you may collect, for your better judgment to work on. I consider the whole matter as between ourselves alone, having determined to take no active part in this or anything else, which may lead to altercation, or disturb that quiet and tranquillity of mind to which I consign the remaining portion of my life. I have been thrown back by events on a stage where I had never more thought to appear. It is but for a time, however, and as a day laborer, free to withdraw or be withdrawn at will. While I remain, I shall pursue in silence the path of right, but in every situation, public or private, I shall be gratified by all occasions of rendering you service, and of convincing you there is no one to whom your reputation and happiness are dearer than to, sir, your most obedient and most humble servant.

LETTER TO
CHARLES BELLINI

Paris, September 30, 1785

Dear Sir:

Your estimable favor, covering a letter to Mr. Mazzei, came to hand on the 26th instant. The letter to Mr. Mazzei was put into his hands in the same moment, as he happened to be present. I leave to him to convey to you all his complaints, as it will be more agreeable to me to express to you the satisfaction I received on being informed of your perfect health. Though I could not receive the same pleasing news of Mrs. Bellini, yet the philosophy with which I am told she bears the loss of health is a testimony the more how much she deserved the esteem I bear her. Behold me at length on the vaunted scene of Europe! It is not necessary for your information that I should enter into details concerning it. But you are, perhaps, curious to know how this new scene has struck a savage of the mountains of America. Not advantageously, I assure you. I find the general fate of humanity here most deplorable. The truth of Voltaire's observation offers itself perpetually, that every man here must be either the hammer or the anvil. It is a true picture of that country to which they say we shall pass hereafter, and where we are to see God and his angels in splendor, and crowds of the damned trampled under their feet. While the great mass of the people are thus suffering under physical and moral oppression, I have endeavored to examine more nearly the condition of the great, to appreciate the true value of the circumstances in their situation, which dazzle the bulk of spectators, and, especially, to compare it with that degree of happiness which is enjoyed in America by every class of people. Intrigues of love occupy the younger, and those of ambition the elder part of the great. Conjugal love having no existence among them, domestic happiness, of which that is the basis, is utterly unknown. In lieu of this are substituted pursuits which nourish and invigorate all our bad passions, and which offer only moments of ecstasy, amidst days and months of restlessness and torment. Much, very much inferior, this, to the tranquil, permanent felicity with which domestic society in America blesses most of its inhabitants; leaving them to follow steadily those pursuits which health and reason approve, and rendering truly delicious the intervals of those pursuits.

In science, the mass of the people are two centuries behind ours; their literati, half a dozen years before us. Books, really good, acquire just reputation in that time, and so become known to us, and communicate to us all their advances in knowledge. Is not this delay compensated by our being placed out of the reach of that swarm of nonsensical publications which issues daily from a thousand presses, and perishes almost in issuing? With respect to what are termed polite manners, without sacrificing too much the sincerity of language, I would wish my countrymen to adopt just so much of European politeness as to be ready to make all those little sacrifices of self which really render European manners amiable and relieve society from the disagreeable scenes to which rudeness often subjects it. Here, it seems that a man might pass a life without encountering a single rudeness. In the pleasures of the table, they are far before us, because, with good taste they unite temperance. They do not terminate the most sociable meals by transforming themselves into brutes. I have never yet seen a man drunk in France, even among the lowest of the people. Were I to proceed to tell you how much I enjoy their architecture, sculpture, painting, music, I should want words. It is in these arts they shine. The last of them, particularly, is an enjoyment, the deprivation of which with us cannot be calculated. I am almost ready to say it is the only thing which from my heart I envy them, and which, in spite of all the authority of the Decalogue, I do covet. But I am running on in an estimate of things infinitely better known to you than to me, and which will only serve to convince you that I have brought with me all the prejudices of country, habit, and age. But whatever I may allow to be charged to me as prejudice, in every other instance, I have one sentiment at least, founded on reality: it is that of the perfect esteem which your merit and that of Mrs. Bellini have produced, and which will forever enable me to assure you of the sincere regard with which I am, dear sir, your friend and servant.

AN ACT FOR
ESTABLISHING
RELIGIOUS FREEDOM

1786

Well aware that Almighty God hath created the mind free; that all attempts to influence it by temporal punishments or burdens, or by civil incapacitations, tend only to beget habits of hypocrisy and meanness, and are a departure from the plan of the Holy Author of our religion, who being Lord both of body and mind, yet chose not to propagate it by coercions on either, as was in his Almighty power to do; that the impious presumption of legislators and rulers, civil as well as ecclesiastical, who, being themselves but fallible and uninspired men have assumed dominion over the faith of others, setting up their own opinions and modes of thinking as the only true and infallible, and as such endeavoring to impose them on others, hath established and maintained false religions over the greatest part of the world, and through all time; that to compel a man to furnish contributions of money for the propagation of opinions which he disbelieves is sinful and tyrannical; that even the forcing him to support this or that teacher of his own religious persuasion is depriving him of the comfortable liberty of giving his contributions to the particular pastor whose morals he would make his pattern, and whose powers he feels most persuasive to righteousness, and is withdrawing from the ministry those temporal rewards, which proceeding from an approbation of their personal conduct, are an additional incitement to earnest and unremitting labors for the instruction of mankind; that our civil rights have no dependence on our religious opinions, more than our opinions in physics or geometry; that, therefore, the proscribing any citizen as unworthy the public confidence by laying upon him an incapacity of being called to the offices of trust and emolument unless he profess or renounce this or that religious opinion is depriving him injuriously of those privileges and advantages to which in common with his fellow citizens he has a natural right; that it tends also to corrupt the principles of that very religion it is meant to encourage, by bribing, with a monopoly of worldly honors and emoluments, those who will externally profess and conform to it; that though indeed these are criminal who do not withstand such temptation, yet neither are those innocent who lay the bait in their way; that to suffer the civil magistrate to intrude his powers into the field of opinion and to restrain the profession or propagation of principles, on the supposition of their ill tendency is a dangerous fallacy, which at once destroys all religious liberty, because he being of course judge of that tendency, will make his opinions the rule of judgment, and approve or condemn the sentiments of others only as they shall square with or differ from his own; that it is time enough for the rightful purposes of civil government for its officers to interfere when principles break out into overt acts against peace and good order; and finally, that truth is great and will prevail if left to herself, that she is the proper and sufficient antagonist to error, and has nothing to fear from the conflict, unless by human interposition disarmed of her natural weapons, free argument and debate, errors ceasing to be dangerous when it is permitted freely to contradict them.

Be it therefore enacted by the General Assembly, That no man shall be compelled to frequent or support any religious worship, place or ministry whatsoever, nor shall be enforced, restrained, molested, or burdened in his body or goods, nor shall otherwise suffer on account of his religious opinions or belief; but that all men shall be free to profess, and by argument to maintain, their opinions in matters of religion, and that the same shall in no wise diminish, enlarge, or affect their civil capacities.

And though we well know this Assembly, elected by the

people for the ordinary purposes of legislation only, have no power to restrain the acts of succeeding Assemblies, constituted with the powers equal to our own, and that therefore to declare this act irrevocable would be of no effect in law, yet we are free to declare, and do declare, that the rights hereby asserted are of the natural rights of mankind, and that if any act shall be hereafter passed to repeal the present or to narrow its operation, such act will be an infringement of natural right.

LETTER TO
JOHN ADAMS

Paris, July 11, 1786

Dear Sir:

Our instructions relative to the Barbary States having required us to proceed by way of negotiation to obtain their peace, it became our duty to do this to the best of our power. Whatever might be our private opinions, they were to be suppressed, and the line, marked out to us, was to be followed. It has been so, honestly and zealously. It was, therefore, never material for us to consult together, on the best plan of conduct towards these states. I acknowledge, I very early thought it would be best to effect a peace through the medium of war. Though it is a question with which we have nothing to do, yet as you propose some discussion of it, I shall trouble you with my reasons. Of the four positions laid down in your letter of the 3d instant, I agree to the three first, which are, in substance, that the good offices of our friends cannot procure us a peace, without paying its price; that they cannot materially lessen that price; and that paying it, we can have the peace in spite of the intrigues of our enemies. As to the fourth, that the longer the negotiation is delayed the larger will be the demand, this will depend on the intermediate captures: if they are many and rich, the price may be raised; if few and poor, it will be lessened. However, if it is decided that we shall buy a peace, I know no reason for delaying the operation, but should rather think it ought to be hastened; but I should prefer the obtaining it by war.

1. Justice is in favor of this opinion.

2. Honor favors it.

3. It will procure us respect in Europe; and respect is a safeguard to interest.

4. It will arm the federal head with the safest of all the

instruments of coercion over its delinquent members, and prevent it from using what would be less safe. I think that so far, you go with me. But in the next steps, we shall differ.

5. I think it least expensive.

6. Equally effectual. I ask a fleet of 150 guns, the one-half of which shall be in constant cruise. This fleet, built, manned, and victualled for six months will cost £450,000 sterling. Its annual expense will be £300 sterling a gun, including everything; this will be £45,000 sterling a year. I take British experience for the basis of my calculation: though we know, from our own experience, that we can do in this way, for pounds lawful, what costs them pounds sterling. Were we to charge all this to the Algerine war, it would amount to little more than we must pay, if we buy peace. But as is it proper and necessary that we should establish a small marine force (even were we to buy a peace from the Algerines), and as that force, laid up in our dock-yards, would cost us half as much annually, as if kept in order for service, we have a right to say that only £22,500 sterling, per annum, should be charged to the Algerine war. It will be as effectual. To all the mismanagements of Spain and Portugal, urged to show that war against these people is ineffectual, I urge a single fact to prove the contrary, where there is any management. About forty years ago, the Algerines having broke their treaty with France, this court sent Monsieur de Massiac, with one large, and two small frigates; he blockaded the harbor of Algiers three months, and they subscribed to the terms he proposed. If it be admitted, however, that war, on the fairest prospects, is still exposed to uncertainties, I weigh against this, the greater uncertainty of the duration of a peace bought with money, from such a people, from a dey eighty years old, and by a nation who, on the hypothesis of buying peace, is to have no power on the sea to enforce an observance of it.

So far, I have gone on the supposition that the whole weight of this war would rest on us. But,

1. Naples will join us. The character of their naval minister (Acton), his known sentiments with respect to the peace Spain

is officiously trying to make for them, and his dispositions against the Algerines give the best grounds to believe it.

2. Every principle of reason assures us that Portugal will join us. I state this as taking for granted what all seem to believe, that they will not be at peace with Algiers. I suppose, then, that a convention might be formed between Portugal, Naples, and the United States, by which the burden of the war might be quotaed on them, according to their respective wealth; and the term of it should be when Algiers should subscribe to a peace with all three on equal terms. This might be left open for other nations to accede to, and many, if not most of the powers of Europe (except France, England, Holland, and Spain, if her peace be made), would sooner or later enter into the confederacy, for the sake of having their peace with the piratical states guaranteed by the whole. I suppose, that, in this case, our proportion of force would not be the half of what I first calculated on.

These are the reasons which have influenced my judgment on this question. I give them to you to show you that I am imposed on by a semblance of reason, at least, and not with an expectation of their changing your opinion. You have viewed the subject, I am sure, in all its bearings. You have weighed both questions, with all their circumstance. You make the result different from what I do. The same facts impress us differently. This is enough to make me suspect an error in my process of reasoning, though I am not able to detect it. It is of no consequence, as I have nothing to say in the decision, and am ready to proceed heartily on any other plan which may be adopted, if my agency should be thought useful. With respect to the dispositions of the state, I am utterly uninformed. I cannot help thinking, however, that on a view of all the circumstances, they might be united in either of the plans.

Having written this on the receipt of your letter, without knowing of any opportunity of sending it, I know not when it will go; I add nothing, therefore, on any other subject, but assurances of the sincere esteem and respect with which I am, dear sir, your friend and servant.

LETTER TO
BENJAMIN FRANKLIN

Paris, August 14, 1786

Dear Sir:

I received your favor of March 20, and much satisfaction from it. I had been alarmed with the general cry that our commerce was in distress, and feared it might be for the want of markets. But the high price of commodities shows that markets are not wanting. Is it not yet possible, however, that these high prices may proceed from the smallness of the quantity made, and that from the want of laborers? It would really seem as if we did not make produce enough for home consumption, and, of course, had none superfluous to exchange for foreign articles. The price of wheat, for instance, shows it is not exported, because it could not, at such a price, enter into competition at a foreign market with the wheat of any other nation.

I send you some packets which have been put into my hands to be forwarded to you. I cannot send your Encyclopedie by the same conveyance, because it is by the way of England. Nothing worth reading has come from the press, I think, since you left us. There are one or two things to be published soon, which being on the subject of America, may be grateful to you, and shall be sent.

Europe enjoys a perfect repose at present. Venice and the two empires seem to be pecking at the Turks, but only in such a degree as may keep alive certain pretensions for commencing war when they shall see the occasion fit. Whether this will be immediately on the death of the king of Prussia remains to be seen. That event must happen soon. By the little attention paid by this country to their land army, it would seem as if they did not apprehend a war on that element. But to the increase and arrangement of their navy, they are very attentive. There is no longer a doubt but that the harbor of Cherbourg will be completed, will be a most excellent one, and capable of containing the whole navy of France. By having two outlets, vessels may enter and sally with every wind, while in the opposite ports of England particular winds are necessary. Our peace with Morocco is probably signed by this time. We are indebted for it to the court of Spain. Algiers, Tunis, and Tripoli will continue hostile according to present appearances.

Your friends here, within the circle of my acquaintance, are well, and often inquire after you. No interesting change that I recollect has taken place among them. Houdon has just received the block of marble for General Washington's statue. He is married since his return. Trumbull, our young American painter, is come here to have his *Death of Montgomery* and *Battle of Bunker's Hill* engraved. I will beg leave to place here my friendly respects to young Mr. Franklin, and assurances of the esteem and regard with which I have the honor to be, dear sir, your most obedient and most humble servant.

SELECTIONS FROM NOTES ON VIRGINIA

1787

THE COLLEGES AND PUBLIC ESTABLISHMENTS, THE ROADS, BUILDINGS, ETC.

The college of William and Mary is the only public seminary of learning in this state. It was founded in the time of King William and Queen Mary, who granted to it twenty thousand acres of land, and a penny a pound duty on certain tobaccos exported from Virginia and Maryland, which had been levied by the statute of 25 Car. II. The assembly also gave it, by temporary laws, a duty on liquors imported, and skins and furs exported. From these resources it received upwards of three thousand pounds *communibus annis*. The buildings are of brick, sufficient for an indifferent accommodation of perhaps a hundred students. By its charter it was to be under the government of twenty visitors, who were to be its legislators, and to have a president and six professors, who were incorporated. It was allowed a representative in the General Assembly. Under this charter, a professorship of the Greek and Latin languages, a professorship of mathematics, one of moral philosophy, and two of divinity were established. To these were annexed, for a sixth professorship, a considerable donation by Mr. Boyle, of England, for the instruction of the Indians, and their conversion to Christianity. This was called the professorship of Brafferton, from an estate of that name in England, purchased with the monies given. The admission of the learners of Latin and Greek filled the college with children. This rendering it disagreeable and degrading to young gentlemen already prepared for entering on the sciences, they were discouraged from resorting to it, and thus the schools for mathematics and moral philosophy, which might have been of some service, became of very little. The revenues, too, were exhausted in accommodating those who came only to acquire the rudiments of science. After the present Revolution, the visitors, having no power to change those circumstances in the constitution of the college which were fixed by the charter, and being therefore confined in the number of the professorships, undertook to change the objects of the professorships. They excluded the two schools for divinity, and that for the Greek and Latin languages, and substituted others; so that at present they stand thus:

A professorship for law and police;

Anatomy and medicine;

Natural philosophy and mathematics;

Moral philosophy, the law of nature and nations, the fine arts;

Modern languages;

For the Brafferton.

And it is proposed, so soon as the legislature shall have leisure to take up this subject, to desire authority from them to increase the number of professorships, as well for the purpose of subdividing those already instituted as of adding others for other branches of science. To the professorships usually established in the universities of Europe, it would seem proper to add one for the ancient languages and literature of the north, on account of their connection with our own language, laws, customs, and history. The purposes of the Brafferton institution would be better answered by maintaining a perpetual mission among the Indian tribes, the object of which, besides instructing them in the principles of Christianity, as the founder requires, should be to collect their traditions, laws, customs, languages, and other circumstances which might lead to a discovery of their relation with one another, or descent from other nations. When these objects are accomplished with one tribe, the missionary might pass on to another.

The roads are under the government of the county courts,

subject to be controlled by the general court. They order new roads to be opened wherever they think them necessary. The inhabitants of the county are by them laid off into precincts, to each of which they allot a convenient portion of the public roads to be kept in repair. Such bridges as may be built without the assistance of artificers, they are to build. If the stream be such as to require a bridge of regular workmanship, the court employs workmen to build it, at the expense of the whole county. If it be too great for the county, application is made to the General Assembly, who authorize individuals to build it, and to take a fixed toll from all passengers, or give sanction to such other proposition as to them appears reasonable.

Ferries are admitted only at such places as are particularly pointed out by law, and the rates of ferriage are fixed.

Taverns are licensed by the courts, who fix their rates from time to time.

The private buildings are very rarely constructed of stone or brick, much the greatest portion being of scantling and boards, plastered with lime. It is impossible to devise things more ugly, uncomfortable, and happily more perishable. There are two or three plans, on one of which, according to its size, most of the houses in the state are built. The poorest people build huts of logs, laid horizontally in pens, stopping the interstices with mud. These are warmer in winter, and cooler in summer, than the more expensive construction of scantling and plank. The wealthy are attentive to the raising of vegetables, but very little so to fruits. The poorer people attend to neither, living principally on milk and animal diet. This is the more inexcusable, as the climate requires indispensably a free use of vegetable food, for health as well as comfort, and is very friendly to the raising of fruits. The only public buildings worthy mention are the capitol, the palace, the college, and the hospital for lunatics, all of them in Williamsburg, heretofore the seat of our government. The capitol is a light and airy structure, with a portico in front of two orders, the lower of which, being Doric, is tolerably just in its proportions and ornaments, save only that the intercolonations are too large. The upper is Ionic, much too small for that on which it is mounted, its ornaments not proper to the order, nor proportioned within themselves. It is crowned with a pediment, which is too high for its span. Yet, on the whole, it is the most pleasing piece of architecture we have. The palace is not handsome without, but it is spacious and commodious within, is prettily situated, and with the grounds annexed to it, is capable of being made an elegant seat. The college and hospital are rude, misshapen piles, which, but that they have roofs, would be taken for brick-kilns. There are no other public buildings but churches and courthouses, in which no attempts are made at elegance. Indeed, it would not be easy to execute such an attempt, as a workman could scarcely be found capable of drawing an order. The genius of architecture seems to have shed its maledictions over this land. Buildings are often erected, by individuals, of considerable expense. To give these symmetry and taste would not increase their cost. It would only change the arrangement of the materials, the form and combination of the members. This would often cost less than the burden of barbarous ornaments with which these buildings are sometimes charged. But the first principles of the art are unknown, and there exists scarcely a model among us sufficiently chaste to give an idea of them. Architecture being one of the fine arts, and as such within the department of a professor of the college, according to the new arrangement, perhaps a spark may fall on some young subjects of natural taste, kindle up their genius, and produce a reformation in this elegant and useful art. But all we shall do in this way will produce no permanent improvement to our country while the unhappy prejudice prevails that houses of brick or stone are less wholesome than those of wood. A dew is often observed on the walls of the former in rainy weather, and the most obvious solution is that the rain has penetrated through these walls. The following facts, however, are sufficient to prove the error of this solution: (1) this dew upon the walls appears when there is no rain, if the state of the atmosphere be moist; (2) it appears upon the partition as well as the exterior walls; (3) so, also, on pavements of brick or stone; (4) it is more copious in proportion as the walls are thicker; the reverse of which ought to be the case, if this hypothesis were just. If cold water be poured into a vessel of stone, or glass, a dew forms instantly on the outside; but if it be poured into a vessel of wood, there is no such appearance. It is not supposed, in the first case, that the water has exuded through the glass, but that it is precipitated from the circumambient air—as the humid particles of vapor, passing from the boiler of an alembic through its refrigerant, are precipitated from the air, in which they are suspended, on the internal surface of the refrigerant. Walls of brick and stone act as the refrigerant in this instance. They are sufficiently cold to condense and precipitate the moisture suspended in the air of the room, when it is heavily charged therewith. But walls of wood are not so. The question then is whether the air in which this moisture is left floating, or that which is deprived of it, be most wholesome. In both cases the remedy is easy. A little fire kindled in the room, whenever the air is damp, prevents the precipitation on the walls; and this practice, found healthy in the warmest as well as coldest seasons, is as necessary in a wooden as in a stone or brick house. I do not mean to say that the rain never penetrates through walls of brick. On the contrary, I have seen instances of it. But with us it is only through the northern and eastern walls of the house, after a northeasterly storm, this being the only one which continues long enough to force through the walls. This, however, happens too rarely to give a just character of unwholesomeness to such houses. In a house, the walls of which are of well-burnt brick and good mortar, I have seen the rain penetrate through but twice in a dozen or fifteen years. The inhabitants of Europe, who dwell chiefly in houses of stone or brick, are surely as healthy as those of Virginia. These houses have the advantage, too, of being warmer in winter and cooler in summer than those of wood; of being cheaper in their first construction, where lime is convenient, and infinitely more durable. The latter consideration renders it of great importance to eradicate this prejudice from the minds of our countrymen. A country whose buildings are of wood can never increase in its improvements to any considerable degree. Their duration is highly estimated at fifty years. Every half-century, then, our country becomes a tabula rasa, whereon we have to set out anew, as in the first moment of seating it. Whereas when buildings are of durable materials, every new edifice is an actual and permanent acquisition to the state, adding to its value as well as to its ornament.

THE DIFFERENT RELIGIONS RECEIVED INTO THAT STATE

The first settlers in this country were emigrants from England, of the English church, just at a point of time when it was flushed with complete victory over the religious of all other persuasions. Possessed, as they became, of the powers of making, administering, and executing the laws, they showed equal intolerance in this country with their Presbyterian brethren, who had emigrated to the northern government. The poor Quakers were flying from persecution in England. They cast their eyes on these new countries as asylums of civil and religious freedom; but they found them free only for the reigning sect. Several acts of the Virginia Assembly of 1659, 1662, and 1693 had made it penal in parents to refuse to have their children baptized; had prohibited the unlawful assembling of Quakers; had made it penal for any master of a vessel to bring a Quaker into the state; had ordered those already here, and such as should come thereafter, to be imprisoned till they should abjure the country; provided a milder punishment for their first and second return, but death for their third; had inhibited all persons from suffering their meetings in or near their houses, entertaining them individually, or disposing of books which supported their tenets. If no execution took place here, as did in New England, it was not owing to the moderation of the church, or spirit of the legislature, as may be inferred from the law itself, but to historical circumstances which have not been handed down to us. The Anglicans retained full possession of the country about a century. Other opinions began then to creep in, and the great care of the government to support their own church, having begotten an equal degree of indolence in its clergy, two-thirds of the people had become dissenters at the commencement of the present Revolution. The laws, indeed, were still oppressive on them, but the spirit of the one party had subsided into moderation, and of the other had risen to a degree of determination which commanded respect.

The present state of our laws on the subject of religion is this. The Convention of May 1776, in their declaration of rights, declared it to be a truth, and a natural right, that the exercise of religion should be free; but when they proceeded to form on that declaration the ordinance of government, instead of taking up every principle declared in the bill of rights, and guarding it by legislative sanction, they passed over that which asserted our religious rights, leaving them as they found them. The same Convention, however, when they met as a member of the General Assembly in October 1776, repealed all *acts of Parliament* which had rendered criminal the maintaining any opinions in matters of religion, the forbearing to repair to church, and the exercising any mode of worship; and suspended the laws giving salaries to the clergy, which suspension was made perpetual in October 1779. Statutory oppressions in religion being thus wiped away, we remain at present under those only imposed by the common law, or by our own acts of Assembly. At the common law, *heresy* was a capital offense, punishable by burning. Its definition was left to the ecclesiastical judges, before whom the conviction was, till the statute of the I El. c. 1 circumscribed it, by declaring that nothing should be deemed heresy but what had been so determined by authority of the canonical scriptures, or by one of the four first general councils, or by other council, having for the grounds of their declaration the

express and plain words of the scriptures. Heresy, thus circumscribed, being an offense against the common law, our act of
assembly of October 1777, c. 17, gives cognizance of it to the
General Court, by declaring that the jurisdiction of that court
shall be general in all matters at the common law. The execution
is by the writ *De haeretico comburendo*. By our own act of
assembly of 1705, c. 30, if a person brought up in the Christian
religion denies the being of a God, or the Trinity, or asserts
there are more Gods than one, or denies the Christian religion
to be true, or the Scriptures to be of divine authority, he is
punishable on the first offense by incapacity to hold any office
or employment ecclesiastical, civil, or military; on the second by
disability to sue, to take any gift or legacy, to be guardian,
executor, or administrator, and by three years' imprisonment
without bail. A father's right to the custody of his own children
being founded in law on his right of guardianship, this being
taken away, they may of course be severed from him, and put
by the authority of a court into more orthodox hands. This is
a summary view of that religious slavery under which a people
have been willing to remain, who have lavished their lives and
fortunes for the establishment of their civil freedom. The error
seems not sufficiently eradicated that the operations of the mind,
as well as the acts of the body, are subject to the coercion of the
laws. But our rulers can have no authority over such natural
rights, only as we have submitted to them. The rights of conscience we never submitted, we could not submit. We are an-
swerable for them to our God. The legitimate powers of
government extend to such acts only as are injurious to others.
But it does me no injury for my neighbor to say there are twenty
gods, or no God. It neither picks my pocket nor breaks my leg.
If it be said, his testimony in a court of justice cannot be relied
on, reject it then, and be the stigma on him. Constraint may
make him worse by making him a hypocrite, but it will never
make him a truer man. It may fix him obstinately in his errors,
but will not cure them. Reason and free inquiry are the only
effectual agents against error. Give a loose to them, they will

support the true religion by bringing every false one to their tribunal, to the test of their investigation. They are the natural enemies of error, and of error only. Had not the Roman government permitted free inquiry, Christianity could never have been introduced. Had not free inquiry been indulged at the era of the Reformation, the corruptions of Christianity could not have been purged away. If it be restrained now, the present corruptions will be protected, and new ones encouraged. Was the government to prescribe to us our medicine and diet, our bodies would be in such keeping as our souls are now. Thus in France the emetic was once forbidden as a medicine, and the potato as an article of food. Government is just as infallible, too, when it fixes systems in physics. Galileo was sent to the Inquisition for affirming that the earth was a sphere; the government had declared it to be as flat as a trencher, and Galileo was obliged to abjure his error. This error, however, at length prevailed, the earth became a globe, and Descartes declared it was whirled round its axis by a vortex. The government in which he lived was wise enough to see that this was no question of civil jurisdiction, or we should all have been involved by authority in vortices. In fact, the vortices have been exploded, and the Newtonian principle of gravitation is now more firmly established, on the basis of reason, than it would be were the government to step in, and to make it an article of necessary faith. Reason and experiment have been indulged, and error has fled before them. It is error alone which needs the support of government. Truth can stand by itself. Subject opinion to coercion: whom will you make your inquisitors? Fallible men; men governed by bad passions, by private as well as public reasons. And why subject it to coercion? To produce uniformity. But is uniformity of opinion desirable? No more than of face and stature. Introduce the bed of Procrustes then, and as there is danger that the large men may beat the small, make us all of a size, by lopping the former and stretching the latter. Difference of opinion is advantageous in religion. The several sects perform the office of a *censor morum* over such other. Is uniformity attainable? Millions of innocent men, women, and children, since the introduction of Christianity, have been burnt, tortured, fined, imprisoned; yet we have not advanced one inch towards uniformity. What has been the effect of coercion? To make one-half the world fools, and the other half hypocrites; to support roguery and error all over the earth. Let us reflect that it is inhabited by a thousand millions of people. That these profess probably a thousand different systems of religion. That ours is but one of that thousand. That if there be but one right, and ours that one, we should wish to see the nine hundred and ninety-nine wandering sects gathered into the fold of truth. But against such a majority we cannot effect this by force. Reason and persuasion are the only practicable instruments. To make way for these, free inquiry must be indulged; and how can we wish others to indulge it while we refuse it ourselves? But every state, says an inquisitor, has established some religion. No two, say I, have established the same. Is this a proof of the infallibility of establishments? Our sister states of Pennsylvania and New York, however, have long subsisted without any establishment at all. The experiment was new and doubtful when they made it. It has answered beyond conception. They flourish infinitely. Religion is well supported; of various kinds, indeed, but all good enough; all sufficient to preserve peace and order; or if a sect arises, whose tenets would subvert morals, good sense has fair play, and reasons and laughs it out of doors, without suffering the state to be troubled with it. They do not hang more malefactors than we do. They are not more disturbed with religious dissensions. On the contrary, their harmony is unparalleled, and can be ascribed to nothing but their unbounded tolerance, because there is no other circumstance in which they differ from every nation on earth. They have made the happy discovery that the way to silence religious disputes, is to take no notice of them. Let us too give this experiment fair play, and get rid, while we may, of those tyrannical laws. It is true, we are as yet secured against them by the spirit of the times. I doubt whether the people of this country would suffer an execution for heresy, or a three years' imprisonment for not comprehending the mysteries of the Trinity. But is the spirit of the people an infallible, a permanent reliance? Is it government? Is this the kind of protection we receive in return for the rights we give up? Besides, the spirit of the times may alter, will alter. Our rulers will become corrupt, our people careless. A single zealot may commence persecutor, and better men be his victims. It can never be too often repeated that the time for fixing every essential right on a legal basis is while our rulers are honest, and ourselves united. From the conclusion of this war we shall be going downhill. It will not then be necessary to resort every moment to the people for support. They will be forgotten, therefore, and their rights disregarded. They will forget themselves, but in the sole faculty of making money, and will never think of uniting to effect a due respect for their rights. The shackles, therefore, which shall not be knocked off at the conclusion of this war, will remain on us long, will be made heavier and heavier, till our rights shall revive or expire in a convulsion.

THE PARTICULAR CUSTOMS AND MANNERS THAT MAY HAPPEN TO BE RECEIVED IN THAT STATE

It is difficult to determine on the standard by which the manners of a nation may be tried, whether *catholic* or *particular*. It is more difficult for a native to bring to that standard the manners of his own nation, familiarized to him by habit. There must doubtless be an unhappy influence on the manners of our people produced by the existence of slavery among us. The whole commerce between master and slave is a perpetual exercise of the most boisterous passions, the most unremitting despotism on the one part and degrading submissions on the other. Our children see this, and learn to imitate it; for man is an imitative animal. This quality is the germ of all education in him. From his cradle to his grave he is learning to do what he sees others do. If a parent could find no motive either in his philanthropy or his self-love for restraining the intemperance of passion towards his slave, it should always be a sufficient one that his child is present. But generally it is not sufficient. The parent storms, the child looks on, catches the lineaments of wrath, puts on the same airs in the circle of smaller slaves, gives a loose to the worst of passions, and thus nursed, educated, and daily exercised in tyranny, cannot but be stamped by it with odious peculiarities. The man must be a prodigy who can retain his manners and morals undepraved by such circumstances. And with what execration should the statesman be loaded, who, permitting one-half the citizens thus to trample on the rights of the other, transforms those into despots, and these into enemies, destroys the morals of the one part, and the *amor patriae* of the other. For if a slave can have a country in this world, it must be any other in preference to that in which he is born to live and labor for another; in which he must lock up the faculties of his nature, contribute as far as depends on his individual endeavors to the evanishment of the human race, or entail his own miserable condition on the endless generations proceeding from him. With the morals of the people, their industry also is destroyed. For in a warm climate, no man will labor for himself who can make another labor for him. This is so true, that of the proprietors of slaves a very small proportion indeed are ever seen to labor. And can the liberties of a nation be thought secure when we have removed their only firm basis, a conviction in the minds of the people that these liberties are of the gift of God? That they are not to be violated but with his wrath? Indeed I tremble for my country when I reflect that God is just; that his justice cannot sleep forever; that considering numbers, nature, and natural means only, a revolution of the wheel of fortune, an exchange of situation is among possible events; that it may become probable by supernatural interference! The Almighty has no attribute which can take side with us in such a contest. But it is impossible to be temperate and to pursue this subject through the various considerations of policy, of morals, of history natural and civil. We must be contented to hope they will force their way into everyone's mind. I think a change already perceptible, since the origin of the present Revolution. The spirit of the master is abating, that of the slave rising from the dust, his condition mollifying, the way I hope preparing, under the auspices of heaven, for a total emancipation, and that this is disposed, in the order of events, to be with the consent of the masters, rather than by their extirpation.

APPENDIX:
A CONSTITUTION FOR VIRGINIA

In the summer of the year 1783, it was expected that the Assembly of Virginia would call a convention for the establishment of a Constitution. The following draft of a fundamental Constitution for the commonwealth of Virginia was then prepared, with a design of being proposed in such convention had it taken place.

To the citizens of the commonwealth of Virginia, and all others whom it may concern, the delegates for the said commonwealth in convention assembled, send greeting:

It is known to you and to the world that the government of Great Britain, with which the American states were not long since connected, assumed over them an authority unwarrantable and oppressive; that they endeavored to enforce this authority by arms, and that the states of New Hampshire, Massachusetts, Rhode Island, Connecticut, New York, New Jersey, Pennsylvania, Delaware, Maryland, Virginia, North Carolina, South Carolina, and Georgia, considering resistance, with all its train of horrors, as a lesser evil than abject submission, closed in the appeal to arms. It hath pleased the Sovereign

Disposer of all human events to give to this appeal an issue favorable to the rights of the states; to enable them to reject forever all dependence on a government which had shown itself so capable of abusing the trusts reposed in it; and to obtain from that government a solemn and explicit acknowledgment that they are free, sovereign, and independent states. During the progress of that war, through which we had to labor for the establishment of our rights, the legislature of the commonwealth of Virginia found it necessary to make a temporary organization of government for preventing anarchy, and pointing our efforts to the two important objects of war against our invaders, and peace and happiness among ourselves. But this, like all other acts of legislation, being subject to change by subsequent legislatures, possessing equal powers with themselves; it has been thought expedient, that it should receive those amendments which time and trial have suggested, and be rendered permanent by a power superior to that of the ordinary legislature. The General Assembly therefore of this state recommend it to the good people thereof, to choose delegates to meet in general convention, with powers to form a constitution of government for them, and to declare those fundamentals to which all our laws present and future shall be subordinate; and, in compliance with this recommendation, they have thought proper to make choice of us, and to vest us with powers for this purpose.

We, therefore, the delegates, chosen by the said good people of this state for the purpose aforesaid, and now assembled in general convention, do in execution of the authority with which we are invested, establish the following constitution and fundamentals of government for the said state of Virginia:

The said state shall forever hereafter be governed as a commonwealth.

The powers of government shall be divided into three distinct departments, each of them to be confided to a separate body of magistracy; to wit, those which are legislative to one, those which are judiciary to another, and those which are executive to another. No person, or collection of persons, being of one of these departments, shall exercise any power properly belonging to either of the others, except in the instances hereinafter expressly permitted.

The legislature shall consist of two branches, the one to be called the House of Delegates, the other the Senate, and both together the General Assembly. The concurrence of both of these, expressed on three several readings, shall be necessary to the passage of a law.

Delegates for the General Assembly shall be chosen on the last Monday of November in every year. But if an election cannot be concluded on that day, it may be adjourned from day to day till it can be concluded.

The number of delegates which each county may send shall be in proportion to the number of its qualified electors; and the whole number of delegates for the state shall be so proportioned to the whole number of qualified electors in it that they shall never exceed three hundred, nor be fewer than one hundred. Whenever such excess or deficiency shall take place, the House of Delegates so deficient or excessive shall, notwithstanding this, continue in being during its legal term; but they shall, during that term, readjust the proportion, so as to bring their number within the limits before mentioned at the ensuing election. If any county be reduced in its qualified electors below the number authorized to send one delegate, let it be annexed to some adjoining county.

For the election of senators, let the several counties be allotted by the Senate, from time to time, into such and so many districts as they shall find best; and let each county at the time of electing its delegates, choose senatorial electors, qualified as themselves are, and four in number for each delegate their county is entitled to send, who shall convene, and conduct themselves, in such manner as the legislature shall direct, with the senatorial electors from the other counties of their district, and then choose, by ballot, one senator for every six delegates which their district is entitled to choose. Let the senatorial districts be divided into two classes, and let the members elected for one of them be dissolved at the first ensuing general election of delegates, the other at the next, and so on alternately forever.

All free male citizens, of full age, and sane mind, who for one year before shall have been resident in the county, or shall through the whole of that time have possessed therein real property of the value of ———, or shall for the same time have been enrolled in the militia, and no others, shall have a right to vote for delegates for the said county, and for senatorial electors for the district. They shall give their votes personally, and *viva voce*.

The General Assembly shall meet at the place to which the last adjournment was, on the forty-second day after the day of election of delegates, and thenceforward at any other time or place on their own adjournment, till their office expires, which shall be on the day preceding that appointed for the meeting of the next General Assembly. But if they shall at any time adjourn for more than one year, it shall be as if they had adjourned for one year precisely. Neither house, without the concurrence of the other, shall adjourn for more than one week, nor to any other place than the one at which they are sitting. The governor shall also have power, with the advice of the council of state, to call them at any other time to the same place, or to a different one, if that shall have become, since the last adjournment, dangerous from an enemy, or from infection.

A majority of either house shall be a quorum, and shall be requisite for doing business; but any smaller proportion which from time to time shall be thought expedient by the respective houses, shall be sufficient to call for, and to punish, their nonattending members, and to adjourn themselves for any time not exceeding one week.

The members, during their attendance on the General Assembly, and for so long a time before and after as shall be necessary for traveling to and from the same, shall be privileged from all personal restraint and assault, and shall have no other privilege whatsoever. They shall receive during the same time, daily wages in gold or silver, equal to the value of two bushels of wheat. This value shall be deemed one dollar by the bushel till the year 1790, in which, and in every tenth year thereafter, the General Court, at their first sessions in the year, shall cause a special jury, of the most respectable merchants and farmers, to be summoned, to declare what shall have been the averaged value of wheat during the last ten years; which averaged value shall be the measure of wages for the ten subsequent years.

Of this General Assembly, the treasurer, attorney general, register, ministers of the gospel, officers of the regular armies of this state, or of the United States, persons receiving salaries or emoluments from any power foreign to our confederacy, those who are not resident in the county for which they are chosen delegates, or districts for which they are chosen senators, those who are not qualified as electors, persons who shall have committed treason, felony, or such other crime as would subject them to infamous punishment, or who shall have been convicted by due course of law of bribery or corruption, in endeavoring to procure an election to the said Assembly: shall be incapable of being members. All others, not herein elsewhere excluded, who may elect, shall be capable of being elected thereto.

Any member of the said assembly accepting any office of profit under this state, or the United States, or any of them, shall thereby vacate his seat, but shall be capable of being reelected.

Vacancies occasioned by such disqualifications, by death, or otherwise, shall be supplied by the electors, on a writ from the speaker of the respective house.

The General Assembly shall not have power to infringe this constitution; to abridge the civil rights of any person on account of his religious belief; to restrain him from professing and supporting that belief, or to compel him to contributions, other than those he shall have personally stipulated for the support of that or any other; to ordain death for any crime but treason or murder, or military offenses; to pardon, or give a power of pardoning persons duly convicted of treason or felony, but instead thereof they may substitute one or two new trials, and no more; to pass laws for punishing actions done before the existence of such laws; to pass any bill of attainder of treason or felony; to prescribe torture in any case whatever; nor to permit the introduction of any more slaves to reside in this state, or the continuance of slavery beyond the generation which shall be living on the thirty-first day of December, one thousand eight hundred; all persons born after that day being hereby declared free.

The General Assembly shall have power to sever from this state all or any parts of its territory westward of the Ohio, or of the meridian of the mouth of the Great Kanhaway, and to cede to Congress one hundred square miles of territory in any other part of this state, exempted from the jurisdiction and government of this state so long as Congress shall hold their sessions therein, or in any territory adjacent thereto, which may be tendered to them by any other state.

They shall have power to appoint the speakers of their respective houses, treasurer, auditors, attorney general, register, all general officers of the military, their own clerks and serjeants, and no other officers, except where, in other parts of this constitution, such appointment is expressly given them.

The executive powers shall be exercised by a *governor,* who shall be chosen by joint ballot of both houses of Assembly, and when chosen shall remain in office five years, and be ineligible a second time. During his term he shall hold no other office or emolument under this state, or any other state or power whatsoever. By executive powers, we mean no reference to those powers exercised under our former government by the crown as of its prerogative, nor that these shall be the standard of what may or may not be deemed the rightful powers of the governor. We give him those powers only, which are necessary to execute the laws (and administer the government), and which are not in their nature either legislative or judiciary. The application of this idea must be left to reason. We do however expressly deny him the prerogative powers of erecting courts, offices, boroughs, corporations, fairs, markets, ports, beacons, lighthouses, and seamarks; of laying embargoes, of establishing precedence, of retaining within the state, or recalling to it, any citizen thereof, and of making denizens, except so far as he may be authorized from time to time by the legislature to exercise any of those powers. The power of declaring war and concluding peace, of contracting alliances, of issuing letters of marque and reprisal, of raising and introducing armed forces, of building armed vessels, forts, or strongholds, of coining money or regulating its value, of regulating weights and measures, we leave to be exercised under the authority of the confederation; but in all cases respecting them which are out of the said confederation, they shall be exercised by the governor, under the regulation of such laws as the legislature may think it expedient to pass.

The whole military of the state, whether regular, or of militia, shall be subject to his directions; but he shall leave the execution of those directions to the general officers appointed by the legislature.

His salary shall be fixed by the legislature at the session of the Assembly in which he shall be appointed, and before such appointment be made; or if it be not then fixed, it shall be the same which his next predecessor in office was entitled to. In either case he may demand it quarterly out of any money which shall be in the public treasury; and it shall not be in the power of the legislature to give him less or more, either during his continuance in office, or after he shall have gone out of it. The lands, houses, and other things appropriated to the use of the governor shall remain to his use during his continuance in office.

A *Council of State* shall be chosen by joint ballot of both houses of Assembly, who shall hold their offices seven years, and be ineligible a second time, and who, while they shall be of the said council, shall hold no other office or emolument under this state, or any other state or power whatsoever. Their duty shall be to attend and advise the governor when called on by him, and their advice in any case shall be a sanction to him. They shall also have power, and it shall be their duty, to meet at their own will, and to give their advice, though not required by the governor, in cases where they shall think the public good calls for it. Their advice and proceedings shall be entered in books to be kept for that purpose, and shall be signed as approved or disapproved by the members present. These books shall be laid before either house of Assembly when called for by them. The said council shall consist of eight members for the present; but their numbers may be increased or reduced by the legislature, whenever they shall think it necessary; provided such reduction be made only as the appointments become vacant by death, resignation, disqualification, or regular deprivation. A majority of their actual number, and not fewer, shall be a quorum. They shall be allowed for the present ——— each by the year, payable quarterly out of any money which shall be in the public treasury. Their salary, however, may be increased or abated from time to time, at the discretion of the legislature; provided such increase or abatement shall not, by any ways or means, be made to affect either then, or at any future time, anyone of those then actually in office. At the end of each quarter their salary shall be divided into equal portions by the number of days on which, during that quarter, a council has been held, or required by the governor, or by their own adjournment, and one of those portions shall be withheld from each member for every of the said days which, without cause allowed good by the board, he failed to attend, or departed before adjournment without their leave. If no board should have been held during that quarter, there shall be no deduction.

They shall annually choose a *president*, who shall preside in council in the absence of the governor, and who, in case of his office becoming vacant by death or otherwise, shall have authority to exercise all his functions, till a new appointment be made, as he shall also in any interval during which the governor shall declare himself unable to attend to the duties of his office.

The *judiciary* powers shall be exercised by county courts and such other inferior courts as the legislature shall think proper to continue or to erect, by three superior courts, to wit, a Court of Admiralty, a General Court of Common Law, and a High Court of Chancery; and by one Supreme Court, to be called the Court of Appeals.

The judges of the High Court of Chancery, General Court, and Court of Admiralty shall be four in number each, to be appointed by joint ballot of both houses of Assembly, and to hold their offices during good behavior. While they continue judges, they shall hold no other office or emolument, under this state, or any other state or power whatsoever, except that they may be delegated to Congress, receiving no additional allowance.

These judges, assembled together, shall constitute the Court of Appeals, whose business shall be to receive and determine appeals from the three superior courts, but to receive no original causes, except in the cases expressly permitted herein.

A majority of the members of either of these courts, and not fewer, shall be a quorum. But in the Court of Appeals nine members shall be necessary to do business. Any smaller numbers however may be authorized by the legislature to adjourn their respective courts.

They shall be allowed for the present ——— each by the year, payable quarterly out of any money which shall be in the public treasury. Their salaries, however, may be increased or abated, from time to time, at the discretion of the legislature, provided such increase or abatement shall not by any ways or means be made to affect, either then or at any future time, anyone of those then actually in office. At the end of each quarter their salary shall be divided into equal portions by the number of days on which, during that quarter, their respective courts sat, or should have sat, and one of these portions shall be withheld from each member for every of the said days which, without cause allowed good by his court, he failed to attend, or departed before adjournment without their leave. If no court should have been held during the quarter, there shall be no deduction.

There shall, moreover, be a *Court of Impeachments,* to consist of three members of the Council of State, one of each of the superior courts of Chancery, Common Law, and Admiralty, two members of the house of delegates and one of the Senate, to be chosen by the body respectively of which they are. Before this court any member of the three branches of government, that is to say, the governor, any member of the council, of the two houses of legislature, or of the superior courts, may be impeached by the governor, the council, or either of the said houses or courts, and by no other, for such misbehavior in office as would be sufficient to remove him therefrom; and the only sentence they shall have authority to pass shall be that of deprivation and future incapacity of office. Seven members shall be requisite to make a court, and two-thirds of those present must concur in the sentence. The offenses cognizable by this court shall be cognizable by no other, and they shall be triers of the fact as well as judges of the law.

The justices or judges of the inferior courts already erected, or hereafter to be erected, shall be appointed by the governor, on advice of the council of state, and shall hold their offices during good behavior, or the existence of their courts. For breach of the good behavior, they shall be tried according to the laws of the land, before the Court of Appeals, who shall be judges of the fact as well as of the law. The only sentence they shall have authority to pass shall be that of deprivation and future incapacity of office, and two-thirds of the members present must concur in this sentence.

All courts shall appoint their own clerks, who shall hold their offices during good behavior, or the existence of their court; they shall also appoint all other attending officers to continue during their pleasure. Clerks appointed by the supreme or superior courts shall be removable by their respective courts. Those to be appointed by other courts shall have been previously examined, and certified to be duly qualified, by some two members of the General Court, and shall be removable for breach of the good behavior by the Court of Appeals only, who shall be judges of the fact as well as of the law. Two-thirds of the members present must concur in the sentence.

The justices or judges of the inferior courts may be members of the legislature.

The judgment of no inferior court shall be final, in any civil case, of greater value than fifty bushels of wheat, as last rated in the General Court for setting the allowance to the members of the General Assembly, nor in any case of treason, felony, or other crime which should subject the party to infamous punishment.

In all causes depending before any court, other than those of impeachments, of appeals, and military courts, facts put in issue shall be tried by jury, and in all courts whatever witnesses shall give testimony *viva voce* in open court, wherever their attendance can be procured; and all parties shall be allowed counsel and compulsory process for their witnesses.

Fines, amercements, and terms of imprisonment left indefinite by the law, other than for contempts, shall be fixed by the jury, triers of the offense.

The governor, two councilors of state, and a judge from each of the superior courts of Chancery, Common Law, and Admiralty, shall be a council to revise all bills which shall have passed both houses of Assembly, in which council the governor, when present, shall preside. Every bill, before it becomes a law, shall be represented to this council, who shall have a right to advise its rejection, returning the bill, with their advice and reasons in writing, to the house in which it originated, who shall proceed to reconsider the said bill. But if after such reconsideration, two-thirds of the house shall be of opinion that the bill should pass finally, they shall pass and sent it, with the advice and written reasons of the said Council of Revision, to the other house, wherein if two-thirds also shall be of opinion it should pass finally, it shall thereupon become law; otherwise it shall not.

If any bill, presented to the said council, be not, within one week (exclusive of the day of presenting it) returned by them, with their advice of rejection and reasons, to the house wherein it originated, or to the clerk of the said house, in case of its adjournment over the expiration of the week, it shall be law from the expiration of the week, and shall then be demandable by the clerk of the House of Delegates, to be filed of record in his office.

The bills which they approve shall become law from the time of such approbation, and shall then be returned to, or demandable by, the clerk of the House of Delegates, to be filed of record in his office.

A bill rejected on advice of the Council of Revision may again be proposed, during the same session of assembly, with such alterations as will render it comfortable to their advice.

The members of the said Council of Revision shall be appointed from time to time by the board or court of which they respectively are. Two of the executive and two of the judiciary members shall be requisite to do business; and to prevent the evils of nonattendance, the board and courts may at any time name all, or so many as they will, of their members, in the particular order in which they would choose the duty of attendance to devolve from preceding to subsequent members, the preceding failing to attend. They shall have additionally for their services in this council the same allowance as members of assembly have.

The confederation is made a part of this constitution, subject to such future alterations as shall be agreed to by the legislature of this state, and by all the other confederating states.

The delegates to Congress shall be five in number; any three of whom, and no fewer, may be a representation. They shall be appointed by joint ballot of both houses of assembly for any term not exceeding one year, subject to be recalled, within the term, by joint vote of both the said houses. They may at the same time be members of the legislative or judiciary departments, but not of the executive.

The benefits of the writ of habeas corpus shall be extended, by the legislature, to every person within this state, and without fee, and shall be so facilitated that no person may be detained in prison more than ten days after he shall have demanded and been refused such writ by the judge appointed by law, or if none be appointed, then by any judge of a superior court, nor more than ten days after such writ shall have been served on the person detaining him, and no order given, on due examination, for his remandment or discharge.

The military shall be subordinate to the civil power.

Printing presses shall be subject to no other restraint than liableness to legal prosecution for false facts printed and published.

Any two of the three branches of government concurring in opinion, each by the voice of two-thirds of their whole existing number, that a convention is necessary for altering this constitution, or correcting breaches of it, they shall be authorized to issue writs to every county for the election of so many delegates as they are authorized to send to the general assembly, which elections shall be held, and writs returned, as the laws shall have provided in the case of elections of delegates of assembly, *mutatis mutandis,* and the said delegates shall meet at the usual place of holding assemblies, three months after date of such writs, and shall be acknowledged to have equal powers with this present convention. The said writs shall be signed by all the members approving the same.

To introduce this government, the following special and temporary provision is made.

This convention being authorized only to amend those laws which constituted the form of government, no general dissolution of the whole system of laws can be supposed to have taken place; but all laws in force at the meeting of this convention, and not inconsistent with this constitution, remain in full force, subject to alterations by the ordinary legislature.

The present General Assembly shall continue till the forty-second day after the last Monday of November in this present year. On the said last Monday of November in this present year, the several counties shall by their electors qualified as provided by this constitution, elect delegates, which for the present shall be, in number, one for every ———— militia of the said county, according to the latest returns in possession of the governor, and shall also choose senatorial electors in proportion thereto, which senatorial electors shall meet on the fourteenth day after the day of their election, at the courthouse of that county of their present district which would stand first in an alphabetical arrangement of their counties, and shall choose senators in the proportion fixed by this constitution. The elections and returns shall be conducted, in all circumstances not hereby particularly prescribed, by the same persons and under the same forms as prescribed by the present laws in elections of senators and delegates of Assembly. The said senators and delegates shall constitute the first General Assembly of the new government, and shall specially apply themselves to the procuring an exact return from every county of the number of its qualified electors, and to the settlement of the number of delegates to be elected for the ensuing General Assembly.

The present governor shall continue in office to the end of the term for which he was elected.

All other officers of every kind shall continue in office as they would have done had their appointment been under this constitution, and new ones, where new are hereby called for, shall be appointed by the authority to which such appointment is referred. One of the present judges of the General Court, he consenting thereto, shall by joint ballot of both houses of Assembly, at their first meeting, be transferred to the High Court of Chancery.

LETTER TO
ST. JOHN DE CRÈVECOEUR

Paris, January 15, 1787

Dear Sir:

I see by the *Journal* of this morning that they are robbing us of another of our inventions to give it to the English. The writer, indeed, only admits them to have revived what he thinks was known to the Greeks, that is, the making the circumference of a wheel of one single piece. The farmers in New Jersey were the first who practiced it, and they practiced it commonly. Dr. Franklin, in one of his trips to London, mentioned this practice to the man now in London who has the patent for making those wheels. The idea struck him. The doctor promised to go to his shop, and assist him in trying to make the wheel of one piece. The Jersey farmers do it by cutting a young sapling, and bending it, while green and juicy, into a circle; and leaving it so until it becomes perfectly seasoned. But in London there are no saplings. The difficulty was, then, to give to old wood the pliancy of young. The doctor and the workman labored together some weeks, and succeeded; and the man obtained a patent for it, which has made his fortune. I was in his shop in London, he told me the whole story himself, and acknowledged, not only the origin of the idea, but how much the assistance of Dr. Franklin had contributed to perform the operation on dry wood. He spoke of him with love and gratitude. I think I have had a similar account from Dr. Franklin, but cannot be quite certain. I know that, being in Philadelphia when the first set of patent wheels arrived from London, and were spoken of by the gentleman (an Englishman) who brought them as a wonderful discovery, the idea of its being a new discovery was laughed at by the Philadelphians, who, in their Sunday parties across the

Delaware, had seen every farmer's cart mounted on such wheels. The writer in the paper supposes the English workman got his idea from Homer. But it is more likely the Jersey farmer got his idea from thence, because ours are the only farmers who can read Homer; because, too, the Jersey practice is precisely that stated by Homer: the English practice very different. Homer's words are (comparing a young hero killed by Ajax to a poplar felled by a workman) literally thus: "He fell on the ground, like a poplar, which has grown smooth, in the west part of a great meadow; with its branches shooting from its summit. But the chariot maker, with the sharp axe, has felled it, that he may bend a wheel for a beautiful chariot. It lies drying on the banks of the river." Observe the circumstances which coincide with the Jersey practice: (1) it is a tree growing in a moist place, full of juices and easily bent; (2) it is cut while green; (3) it is bent into the circumference of a wheel; (4) it is left to dry in that form. You, who write French well and readily, should write a line for the *Journal,* to reclaim the honor of our farmers. Adieu. Yours affectionately.

LETTER TO THE
MARQUIS DE LAFAYETTE

Nice, April 11, 1787

Your head, my dear friend, is full of notable things; and being better employed, therefore, I do not expect letters from you. I am constantly roving about, to see what I have never seen before, and shall never see again. In the great cities, I go to see what travelers think alone worthy of being seen; but I make a job of it, and generally gulp it all down in a day. On the other hand, I am never satiated with rambling through the fields and farms, examining the culture and cultivators, with a degree of curiosity which makes some take me to be a fool, and others to be much wiser than I am. I have been pleased to find among the people a less degree of physical misery than I had expected. They are generally well clothed, and have a plenty of food, not animal indeed, but vegetable, which is as wholesome. Perhaps they are overworked, the excess of the rent required by the landlord obliging them to too many hours of labor in order to produce that, and wherewith to feed and clothe themselves. The soil of Champagne and Burgundy I have found more universally good than I had expected, and as I could not help making a comparison with England, I found that comparison more unfavorable to the latter than is generally admitted. The soil, the climate, and the productions are superior to those of England, and the husbandry as good, except in one point: that of manure. In England, long leases for twenty-one years, or three lives, to wit, that of the farmer, his wife, and son, renewed by the son as soon as he comes to the possession, for his own life, his wife's, and eldest child's, and so on, render the farms there almost hereditary, make it worth the farmer's while to manure the lands highly, and give the landlord an opportunity of occasionally making his rent keep pace with the improved state of the lands. Here the leases are either during pleasure, or for three, six, or nine years, which does not give the farmer time to repay himself for the expensive operation of well manuring, and, therefore, he manures ill, or not at all. I suppose that could the practice of leasing for three lives be introduced in the whole kingdom, it would, within the term of your life, increase agricultural productions 50 percent; or were any one proprietor to do it with his own lands, it would increase his rents 50 percent, in the course of twenty-five years. But I am told the laws do not permit it. The laws then, in this particular, are unwise and unjust, and ought to give that permission. In the southern provinces, where the soil is poor, the climate hot and dry, and there are few animals, they would learn the art, found so precious in England, of making vegetable manure, and thus improving these provinces in the article in which nature has been least kind to them. Indeed, these provinces afford a singular spectacle. Calculating on the poverty of their soil, and their climate by its latitude only, they should have been the poorest in France. On the contrary, they are the richest, from one fortuitous circumstance. Spurs or ramifications of high mountains, making down from the Alps, and, as it were, reticulating these provinces, give to the valleys the protection of a particular enclosure to each, and the benefit of a general stagnation of the northern winds produced by the whole of them, and thus countervail the advantage of several degrees of latitude. From the first olive fields of Pierrelatte to the orangeries of Hieres has been continued rapture to me. I have often wished for you. I think you have not made this journey. It is a pleasure you have to come, and an improvement to be added to the many you have already made. It will be a great comfort to you, to know, from your own inspection, the condition of all the provinces of your own country, and it will be interesting to them at some future day to be known to you. This is, perhaps, the only moment of your life in which you can acquire that knowledge. And to do it most effectually, you must be absolutely incognito, you must ferret the people out of their hovels as I have done, look into their kettles, eat their bread, loll on their beds under pretense of resting yourself, but in fact, to find if they are soft. You will feel a sublime pleasure in the course of this investigation, and a sublimer one hereafter, when you shall be able to apply your knowledge to the softening of their beds, or the throwing a morsel of meat into their kettle of vegetables.

You will not wonder at the subjects of my letters; they are the only ones which have been presented to my mind for some time past; and the waters must always be what are the fountains from which they flow. According to this, indeed, I should have intermixed, from beginning to end, warm expressions of friendship to you. But according to the ideas of our country, we do not permit ourselves to speak even truths when they may have the air of flattery. I content myself, therefore, with saying once for all, that I love you, your wife, and children. Tell them so, and adieu. Yours affectionately.

LETTER TO
JAMES MADISON

Paris, December 20, 1787

Dear Sir:

My last to you was of October 8, by the Count de Moustier. Yours of July 18, September 6, and October 24 were successively received, yesterday, the day before, and three or four days before that. I have only had time to read the letters; the printed papers communicated with them, however interesting, being obliged to lie over till I finish my dispatches for the packet, which dispatches must go from hence the day after tomorrow. I have much to thank you for; first and most for the ciphered paragraph respecting myself. These little informations are very material towards forming my own decisions. I would be glad even to know when any individual member thinks I have gone wrong in any instance. If I know myself, it would not excite ill blood in me, while it would assist to guide my conduct, perhaps to justify it, and to keep me to my duty, alert. I must thank you, too, for the information in Thomas Burke's case, though you will have found by a subsequent letter that I have asked of you a further investigation of that matter. It is to gratify the lady who is at the head of the convent wherein my daughters are, and who, by her attachment and attention to them, lays me under great obligations. I shall hope, therefore, still to receive from you the result of all the further inquiries my second letter had asked. The parcel of rice which you informed me had miscarried accompanied my letter to the delegates of South Carolina. Mr. Bourgoin was to be the bearer of both, and both were delivered together into the hands of his relation here, who introduced him to me, and who, at a subsequent moment, undertook to convey them to Mr. Bourgoin. This person was an engraver, particularly recommended to Dr. Franklin and Mr. Hopkinson. Perhaps he may have mislaid the little parcel of rice among his baggage. I am much pleased that the sale of western lands is so successful. I hope they will absorb all the certificates of our domestic debt speedily, in the first place, and that then, offered for cash, they will do the same by our foreign ones.

The season admitting only of operations in the cabinet, and these being in a great measure secret, I have little to fill a letter. I will therefore make up the deficiency by adding a few words on the Constitution proposed by our Convention.

I like much the general idea of framing a government, which should go on of itself, peaceably, without needing continual recurrence to the state legislatures. I like the organization of the government into legislative, judiciary, and executive. I like the power given the legislature to levy taxes, and for that reason solely, I approve of the greater house being chosen by the people directly. For though I think a house so chosen will be very far inferior to the present Congress, will be very illy qualified to legislate for the Union, for foreign nations, etc., yet this evil does not weigh against the good, of preserving inviolate the fundamental principle that the people are not to be taxed but by representatives chosen immediately by themselves. I am captivated by the compromise of the opposite claims of the great and little states, of the latter to equal and the former to proportional influence. I am much pleased too, with the substitution of the method of voting by person, instead of that of voting by states; and I like the negative given to the executive, conjointly with a third of either house; though I should have liked it better had the judiciary been associated for that purpose, or invested separately with a similar power. There are other good things of less moment. I will now tell you what I do not like. First, the omission of a bill of rights, providing clearly, and without the aid of sophism, for freedom of religion, freedom of the press, protection against standing armies, restriction of monopolies, the eternal and unremitting force of the habeas corpus laws, and trials by jury in all matters of fact triable by the laws of the land,

and not by the laws of nations. To say, as Mr. Wilson does, that a bill of rights was not necessary, because all is reserved in the case of the general government which is not given, while in the particular ones, all is given which is not reserved, might do for the audience to which it was addressed; but it is surely a *gratis dictum,* the reverse of which might just as well be said; and it is opposed by strong inferences from the body of the instrument, as well as from the omission of the cause of our present Confederation, which had made the reservation in express terms. It was hard to conclude, because there has been a want of uniformity among the states as to the cases triable by jury, because some have been so incautious as to dispense with this mode of trial in certain cases, therefore, the more prudent states shall be reduced to the same level of calamity. It would have been much more just and wise to have concluded the other way, that as most of the states had preserved with jealousy this sacred palladium of liberty, those who had wandered should be brought back to it; and to have established general right rather than general wrong. For I consider all the ill as established which may be established. I have a right to nothing which another has a right to take away; and Congress will have a right to take away trials by jury in all civil cases. Let me add, that a bill of rights is what the people are entitled to against every government on earth, general or particular; and what no just government should refuse, or rest on inference.

The second feature I dislike, and strongly dislike, is the abandonment, in every instance, of the principle of rotation in office, and most particularly in the case of the president. Reason and experience tell us that the first magistrate will always be reelected if he may be reelected. He is then an officer for life. This once observed, it becomes of so much consequence to certain nations to have a friend or a foe at the head of our affairs, that they will interfere with money and with arms. A Galloman, or an Angloman, will be supported by the nation he be friends. If once elected, and at a second or third election outvoted by one or two votes, he will pretend false votes, foul play, hold possession of the reigns of government, be supported by the states voting for him, especially if they be the central ones, lying in a compact body themselves, and separating their opponents; and they will be aided by one nation in Europe, while the majority are aided by another. The election of a president of America, some years hence, will be much more interesting to certain nations of Europe than ever the election of a king of Poland was. Reflect on all the instances in history, ancient and modern, of elective monarchies, and say if they do not give foundation for my fears; the Roman emperors, the popes while they were of any importance, the German emperors till they became hereditary in practice, the kings of Poland, the deys of the Ottoman dependencies. It may be said that if elections are to be attended with these disorders, the less frequently they are repeated the better. But experience says that to free them from disorder, they must be rendered less interesting by a necessity of change. No foreign power, nor domestic party, will waste their blood and money to elect a person who must go out at the end of a short period. The power of removing every fourth year by the vote of the people is a power which they will not exercise, and if they were disposed to exercise it, they would not be permitted. The king of Poland is removable every day by the Diet. But they never remove him. Nor would Russia, the emperor, etc., permit them to do it. Smaller objections are: the appeals on matters of fact as well as laws; and the binding all persons, legislative, executive, and judiciary by oath to maintain that Constitution. I do not pretend to decide what would be the best method of procuring the establishment of the manifold good things in this constitution, and of getting rid of the bad. Whether by adopting it, in hopes of future amendment; or after it shall have been duly weighed and canvassed by the people, after seeing the parts they generally dislike and those they generally approve, to say to them, "We see now what you wish. You are willing to give to your federal government such and such powers; but you wish, at the same time, to have such and such fundamental rights secured to you, and certain sources of convulsion taken away. Be it so. Send together deputies again. Let them establish your fundamental rights by a sacrosanct declaration, and let them pass the parts of the constitution you have approved. These will give powers to your federal government sufficient for your happiness."

This is what might be said, and would probable produce a speedy, more perfect, and more permanent form of government. At all events, I hope you will not be discouraged from making other trials, if the present one should fail. We are never permitted to despair of the commonwealth. I have thus told you freely what I like, and what I dislike, merely as a matter of curiosity; for I know it is not in my power to offer matter of information to your judgment, which has been formed after hearing and weighing everything which the wisdom of man could offer on these subjects. I own I am not a friend to a very energetic government. It is always oppressive. It places the governors indeed more at their ease, at the expense of the people. The late rebellion in Massachusetts has given more alarm than I think it should have done. Calculate that one rebellion in thirteen states in the course of eleven years is but one for each state in a century and a half. No country should be so long without one. Nor will any degree of power in the hands of government prevent insurrections. In England, where the hand of power is heavier than with us, there are seldom half a dozen years without an insurrection. In France, where it is still heavier, but less despotic, as Montesquieu supposes, than in some other countries, and where there are always two or three hundred thousand men ready to crush insurrections, there have been three in the course of the three years I have been here, in every one of which greater numbers were engaged than in Massachusetts, and a great deal more blood was spilt. In Turkey, where the sole nod of the despot is death, insurrections are the events of every day. Compare again the ferocious depredations of their insurgents, with the order, the moderation, and the almost self-extinguishment of ours. And say, finally, whether peace is best preserved by giving energy to the government or information to the people.

This last is the most certain and the most legitimate engine of government. Educate and inform the whole mass of the people. Enable them to see that it is their interest to preserve peace and order, and they will preserve them. And it requires no very high degree of education to convince them of this. They are the only sure reliance for the preservation of our liberty. After all, it is my principle that the will of the majority should prevail. If they approve the proposed Constitution in all its parts, I shall concur in it cheerfully, in hopes they will amend it, whenever they shall find it works wrong. This reliance cannot deceive us, as long as we remain virtuous; and I think we shall be so, as long as agriculture is our principal object, which will be the case while there remains vacant lands in any part of America. When we get piled upon one another in large cities, as in Europe, we shall become corrupt as in Europe, and go to eating one another as they do there. I have tired you by this time with disquisitions which you have already heard repeated by others a thousand and a thousand times; and therefore, shall only add assurances of the esteem and attachment with which I have the honor to be, dear sir, your affectionate friend and servant.

P. S. The instability of our laws is really an immense evil. I think it would be well to provide in our constitutions that there shall always be a twelvemonth between the engrossing a bill and passing it; that it should then be offered to its passage without changing a word; and that if circumstances should be thought to require a speedier passage, it should take two-thirds of both houses, instead of a bare majority.

LETTER TO GENERAL
GEORGE WASHINGTON

Paris, May 2, 1788

Dear Sir:

I am honored with Your Excellency's letter by the last packet, and thank you for the information it contains on the communication between the Cayahoga and Big Beaver. I have ever considered the opening a canal between those two water courses as the most important work in that line which the state of Virginia could undertake. It will infallibly turn through the Potomac all the commerce of Lake Erie, and the country west of that, except what may pass down the Mississippi; and it is important that it be soon done, lest that commerce should, in the meantime, get established in another channel. Having, in the spring of the last year, taken a journey through the southern parts of France, and particularly examined the canal of Languedoc, through its whole course, I take the liberty of sending you the notes I made on the spot, as you may find in them something, perhaps, which may be turned to account, some time or other, in the prosecution of the Potomac canal. Being merely a copy from my traveling notes, they are undigested and imperfect, but may still perhaps give hints capable of improvement in your mind.

The affairs of Europe are in such a state still that it is impossible to say what form they will take ultimately. France and Prussia, viewing the emperor as their most dangerous and common enemy, had heretofore seen their common safety as depending on a strict connection with one another. This had naturally inclined the emperor to the scale of England, and the empress also, as having views in common with the emperor, against the Turks. But these two powers would, at any time, have gladly quitted England, to coalesce with France, as being the power which they met everywhere, opposed as a barrier to all their schemes of aggrandizement. When, therefore, the present king of Prussia took the eccentric measure of bidding defiance to France by placing his brother-in-law on the throne of Holland, the two empires immediately seized the occasion of soliciting an alliance with France. The motives for this appeared so plausible that it was believed the latter would have entered into this alliance, and that thus, the whole political system of Europe would have taken a new form. What has prevented this court from coming into it, we know not. The unmeasurable ambition of the emperor, and his total want of moral principle and honor, are suspected. A great share of Turkey, the recovery of Silesia, the consolidation of his dominions by the Bavarian exchange, the liberties of the Germanic body all occupy his mind together, and his head is not well enough organized to pursue so much only of all this as is practicable. Still, it was thought that France might safely have coalesced with these powers, because Russia and herself holding close together, as their interests would naturally dictate, the emperor could never stir but with their permission. France seems, however, to have taken the worst of all parties, that is, none at all. She folds her arms, lets the two empires go to work to cut up Turkey as they can, and holds Prussia aloof, neither as a friend nor foe. This is withdrawing her opposition from the two empires, without the benefit of any condition whatever. In the meantime, England has clearly overreached herself. She excited the war between the Russians and Turks, in hopes that France, still supporting the Turks, would be embarrassed with the two empires. She did not foresee the event which has taken place, of France abandoning the Turks, and that which may take place, of her union with the two empires. She allied herself with Holland, but cannot obtain the alliance of Prussia. This latter power would be very glad to close again the breach with France, and, therefore, while there remains an opening for this, holds off from England, whose fleets could not enter into Silesia, to protect that from the emperor. Thus, you see, that the old system is unhinged, and no new one hung in its place. Probabilities are rather in favor of a connection between the two empires, France and Spain. Several symptoms show themselves of friendly dispositions between Russia and France, unfriendly ones between Russia and England, and such as are barely short of hostility between England and France. But into real hostilities this country would with difficulty be drawn. Her finances are too deranged, her internal union too much dissolved, to hazard a war. The nation is pressing on fast to a fixed constitution. Such a revolution in the public opinion has taken place that the crown already feels its powers bounded, and is obliged, by its measures, to acknowledge limits. A States General will be called at some epoch not distant; they will probably establish a civil list, and leave the government to temporary provisions of money, so as to render frequent assemblies of the national representative necessary. How that representative will be organized is yet uncertain. Among a thousand projects, the best seems to me that of dividing them into two houses, of Commons and Nobles; the Commons to be chosen by the Provincial Assemblies, who are chosen themselves by the people, and the Nobles by the body of Noblesse, as in Scotland. But there is no reason to conjecture that this is the particular scheme which will be preferred.

The war between the Russians and Turks has made an opening for our Commodore Paul Jones. The empress has invited him into her service. She insures to him the rank of rear admiral; will give him a separate command, and, it is understood, that he is never to be commanded. I think she means to oppose him to the Captain Pacha, on the Black Sea. He is by this time, probably, at St. Petersburg. The circumstances did not permit his awaiting the permission of Congress, because the season was close at hand for opening the campaign. But he has made it a condition that he shall be free at all times to return to the orders of Congress, whenever they shall please to call for him; and also, that he shall not in any case be expected to bear arms against France. I believe Congress had it in contemplation to give him the grade of admiral, from the date of his taking the Serapis. Such a measure now would greatly gratify him, second the efforts of fortune in his favor, and better the opportunities of improving him for our service, whenever the moment shall come in which we may want him.

The danger of our incurring something like a bankruptcy in Holland, which might have been long and even fatally felt in a moment of crisis, induced me to take advantage of Mr. Adams's journey to take leave at the Hague to meet him there, get him to go on to Amsterdam, and try to avert the impending danger. The moment of paying a great sum of annual interest was approaching. There was no money on hand; the board of treasury had notified that they could not remit any; and the progress of the loan which had been opened there had absolutely stopped. Our bankers there gave me notice of all this, and that a single day's failure in the payment of interest would have the most fatal effect on our credit. I am happy to inform you we were able to set the loan a going again, and that the evil is at least postponed. Indeed, I am tolerably satisfied that if the measures we proposed are ratified by Congress, all European calls for money (except the French debt) are secure enough, till the end of the year 1790; by which time, we calculated that the new government might be able to get money into their treasury. Much conversation with the bankers, brokers, and money holders gave me insight into the state of national credit there, which I had never before been able satisfactorily to get. The English credit is the first, because they never open a loan without laying and appropriating taxes for the payment of the interest, and there has never been an instance of their failing one day in that payment. The emperor and empress have good credit, because they use it little, and have hitherto been very punctual. This country is among the lowest in point of credit. Ours stands in hope only. They consider us as the surest nation on earth for the repayment of the capital; but as the punctual payment of interest is of absolute necessity in their arrangements, we cannot borrow but with difficulty and disadvantage. The monied men, however, look towards our new government with a great degree of partiality, and even anxiety. If they see that set out on the English plan, the first degree of credit will be transferred to us. A favorable occasion will arise to our new government of asserting this ground to themselves. The transfer of the French debt, public and private, to Amsterdam, is certainly desirable. An act of the new government, therefore, for opening a loan in Holland for the purpose, laying taxes at the same time, for paying annually the interest and a part of the principal, will answer the two valuable purposes, of ascertaining the degree of our credit, and of removing those causes of bickering and irritation, which should never be permitted to subsist with a nation with which it is so much our interest to be on cordial terms as with France. A very small portion of this debt, I mean that part due to the French officers, has done us an injury, of which, those in office in America cannot have an idea. The interest is unpaid for the last three years; and these creditors, highly connected, and at the same time needy, have felt and communicated hard thoughts of us. Borrowing, as we have done, three hundred thousand florins a year, to pay our interest in Holland, it would have been worth while to have added twenty thousand more to suppress those clamors. I am anxious about everything which may affect our credit. My wish would be to possess it in the highest degree, but to use it little. Were we without credit, we might be crushed by a nation of much inferior resources but possessing higher credit. The present system of war renders it necessary to make exertions far beyond the annual resources of the state, and to consume in one year the efforts of many. And this system we cannot change. It remains, then, that we cultivate our credit with the utmost attention.

I had intended to have written a word to Your Excellency on the subject of the new Constitution, but I have already spun out my letter to an immoderate length. I will just observe, therefore, that according to my ideas, there is a great deal of good in it. There are two things, however, which I dislike strongly: (1) the want of a declaration of rights; I am in hopes the opposition of Virginia will remedy this, and produce such a declaration; (2) the perpetual reeligibility of the president. This, I fear, will make that an office for life, first, and then hereditary. I was much an enemy to monarchies before I came to Europe. I am ten thousand times more so since I have seen what they are. There is scarcely an evil known in these countries which may not be traced to their king as its source, nor a good which is not derived from the small fibers of republicanism existing among them. I can further say, with safety, there is not a crowned head in Europe, whose talents or merits would entitle him to be elected a vestryman, by the people of any parish in America. However, I shall hope, that before there is danger of this change taking place in the office of president, the good sense and free spirit of our countrymen will make the changes necessary to prevent it. Under this hope, I look forward to the general adoption of the new Constitution with anxiety, as necessary for us under our present circumstances. I have so much trespassed on your patience already, by the length of this letter, that I will add nothing further than those assurances of sincere esteem and attachment with which I have the honor to be Your Excellency's most obedient and most humble servant.

LETTER TO
WILLIAM CARMICHAEL

Paris, August 12, 1788

Dear Sir:

Since my last to you, I have been honored with yours of the 18th and 29th of May, and 8th of June. My latest American intelligence is of the 24th of June, when nine certainly, and probably ten states, had accepted the new Constitution, and there was no doubt of the eleventh (North Carolina), because there was no opposition there. In New York, two-thirds of the state were against it, and certainly, if they had been called to the decision in any other stage of the business, they would have rejected it; but before they put it to the vote, they would certainly have heard that eleven states had joined in it, and they would find it safer to go with those eleven than put themselves into opposition, with Rhode Island only. Though I am much pleased with this successful issue of the new Constitution, yet I am more so to find that one of its principal defects (the want of a declaration of rights) will pretty certainly be remedied. I suppose this, because I see that both people and conventions, in almost every state, have concurred in demanding it. Another defect, the perpetual reeligibility of the same president, will probably not be cured during the life of General Washington. His merit has blinded our countrymen to the danger of making so important an officer reeligible. I presume there will not be a vote against him in the United States. It is more doubtful who will be vice president. The age of Dr. Franklin, and the doubt whether he would accept it, are the only circumstances that admit a question, but that he would be the man. After these two characters of first magnitude, there are so many which present themselves equally, on the second line, that we cannot see which of them will be singled out. John Adams, Hancock, Jay, Madison, Rutledge will all be voted for. Congress has acceded to the prayer of Kentucky to become an independent member of the Union. A committee was occupied in settling the plan of receiving them, and their government is to commence on the 1st day of January next.

You are, I daresay, pleased, as I am, with the promotion of our countryman, Paul Jones. He commanded the right wing, in the first engagement between the Russian and Turkish gallies; his absence from the second proves his superiority over the Captain Pacha, as he did not choose to bring his ships into the shoals in which the Pacha ventured, and lost those entrusted to him. I consider this officer as the principal hope of our future efforts on the ocean. You will have heard of the action between the Swedes and Russians, on the Baltic; as yet, we have only the Swedish version of it. I apprehend this war must catch from nation to nation, till it becomes general.

With respect to the internal affairs of this country, I hope they will be finally well arranged, and without having cost a drop of blood. Looking on as a bystander, no otherwise interested than as entertaining a sincere love for the nation in general and a wish to see their happiness promoted, keeping myself clear of the particular views and passions of individuals, I applaud extremely the patriotic proceedings of the present ministry. Provincial Assemblies established, the States General called, the right of taxing the nation without their consent abandoned, corvées abolished, torture abolished, the criminal code reformed are facts which will do eternal honor to their administration, in history. But were I their historian, I should not equally applaud their total abandonment of their foreign affairs. A bolder front in the beginning would have prevented the first loss, and, consequently, all the others. Holland, Prussia, Turkey, and Sweden, lost without the acquisition of a single new ally, are painful reflections for the friends of France. They may, indeed, have in their places the two empires, and perhaps Denmark; in which case, physically speaking, they will stand on as good ground as before, but not on as good moral ground. Perhaps, seeing more of the internal working of the machine, they saw, more than we do, the physical impossibility of having money to carry on a war. Their justification must depend on this, and their atonement on the internal good they are doing to their country; this makes me completely their friend.

I am, with great esteem and attachment, dear sir, your friend and servant.

LETTER TO
THOMAS PAINE

Paris, December 23, 1788

Dear Sir:

It is true that I received, very long ago, your favors of September 9 and 15, and that I have been in daily intention of answering them, fully and confidentially; but you know such a correspondence between you and me cannot pass through the post, nor even by the couriers of ambassadors. The French packet boats being discontinued, I am now obliged to watch opportunities by Americans going to London, to write my letters to America. Hence it has happened, that these, the sole opportunities by which I can write to you without fear, have been lost, by the multitude of American letters I had to write. I now determine, without foreseeing any such conveyance, to begin my letter to you, so that when a conveyance occurs, I shall only have to add recent occurrences. Notwithstanding the interval of my answer which has taken place, I must beg a continuance of your correspondence; because I have great confidence in your communications, and since Mr. Adams's departure, I am in need of authentic information from that country.

I will begin with the subject of your bridge, in which I feel myself interested; and it is with great pleasure that I learn, by your favor of the 16th, that the execution of the arch of experiment exceeds your expectations. In your former letter, you mention that instead of arranging your tubes and bolts as ordinates to the cord of the arch, you had reverted to your first idea of arranging them in the direction of the radii. I am sure it will gain, both in beauty and strength. It is true that the divergence of those radii recurs as a difficulty, in getting the rails on upon the bolts; but I thought this fully removed by the answer you first gave me, when I suggested that difficulty, to wit, that you should place the rails first and drive the bolts through them, and not, as I had imagined, place the bolts first and put the rails on them. I must doubt whether what you now suggest will be as good as your first idea; to wit, to have every rail split into two pieces longitudinally, so that there shall be but the halves of the holes in each, and then to clamp the two halves together. The solidity of this method cannot be equal to that of the solid rail, and it increases the suspicious part of the whole machine, which, in a first experiment, ought to be rendered as few as possible. But of all this, the practical iron men are much better judges than we theorists. You hesitate between the catenary and portion of a circle. I have lately received from Italy a treatise on the equilibrium of arches, by the Abbé Mascheroni. It appears to be a very scientific work. I have not yet had time to engage in it; but I find that the conclusions of his demonstrations are that every part of the catenary is in perfect equilibrium. It is a great point, then, in a new experiment, to adopt the sole arch, where the pressure will be equally borne by every point of it. If any one point is pushed with accumulated pressure, it will introduce a danger foreign to the essential part of the plan. The difficulty you suggest is that the rails being all in catenaries, the tubes must be of different lengths, as these approach nearer or recede farther from each other, and therefore, you recur to the portions of concentric circles, which are equidistant in all their parts. But I would rather propose that you make your middle rail an exact catenary, and the interior and exterior rails parallels to that. It is true they will not be exact catenaries, but they will depart very little from it, much less than portions of circles will. Nothing has been done here on the subject since you went away. There is an Abbé D'Arnal at Nismes, who has obtained an exclusive privilege for navigating the rivers of this country, by the aid of the steam engine. This interests Mr. Rumsey, who had hoped the same thing. D'Arnal's privilege was published in a paper of the 10th of November. Probably, therefore, his application for it was previous to the delivery of Mr. Rumsey's papers to the secretary of the Academy of Sciences, which was in the latter part of the month of August. However, D'Arnal is not a formidable competitor. He is not in circumstances to make any use, himself, of his privilege, and he has so illy succeeded with a steam mill he erected at Nismes that he is not likely to engage others to venture in his projects. To say another word of the catenarian arch, without caring about mathematical demonstrations, its nature proves it to be in equilibrio in every point. It is the arch formed by a string fixed at both ends, and swaying loose in all the intermediate points. Thus at liberty, they must finally take that position wherein every one will be equally pressed; for if any one was more pressed than the neighboring point, it would give way, from the flexibility of the matter of the string. . . .

I am, with sentiments of sincere esteem and attachment, dear sir, your friend and servant.

LETTER TO
FRANCIS HOPKINSON

Paris, March 13, 1789

Dear Sir:

Since my last, which was of December 21, yours of December 9 and 21 are received. Accept my thanks for the papers and pamphlets which accompanied them, and mine and my daughter's for the book of songs. I will not tell you how much they have pleased us, nor how well the last of them merits praise for its pathos, but relate a fact only, which is that while my elder daughter was playing it on the harpsichord, I happened to look towards the fire, and saw the younger one all in tears. I asked her if she was sick. She said, "No, but the tune was so mournful."

The editor of the Encyclopedia has published something as to an advanced price on his future volumes, which, I understand, alarms the subscribers. It was in a paper which I do not take, and therefore I have not yet seen it, nor can I say what it is. I hope that by this time you have ceased to make wry faces about your vinegar, and that you have received it safe and good. You say that I have been dished up to you as an Anti-Federalist, and ask me if it be just. My opinion was never worthy enough of notice to merit citing; but since you ask it, I will tell it to you. I am not a Federalist, because I never submitted the whole system of my opinions to the creed of any party of men whatever, in religion, in philosophy, in politics, or in anything else, where I was capable of thinking for myself. Such an addiction is the last degradation of a free and moral agent. If I could not go to heaven but with a party, I would not go there at all. Therefore, I am not of the party of federalists. But I am much farther from that of the Anti-Federalists. I approved, from the first moment, of the great mass of what is in the new Constitution: the consolidation of the government; the organization into executive, legislative, and judiciary; the subdivision of the legislative; the happy compromise of interests between the great and little states, by the different manner of voting in the different houses; the voting by persons instead of states; the qualified negative on laws given to the executive, which, however, I should have liked better if associated with the judiciary also, as in New York; and the power of taxation. I thought at first that the latter might have been limited. A little reflection soon convinced me it ought not to be. What I disapproved from the first moment also was the want of a bill of rights, to guard liberty against the legislative as well as the executive branches of the government; that is to say, to secure freedom in religion, freedom of the press, freedom from monopolies, freedom from unlawful imprisonment, freedom from a permanent military, and a trial by jury, in all cases determinable by the laws of the land. I disapproved, also, the perpetual reeligibility of the president. To these points of disapprobation I adhere. My first wish was that the nine first conventions might accept the Constitution, as the means of securing to us the great mass of good it contained, and that the four last might reject it, as the means of obtaining amendments. But I was corrected in this wish, the moment I saw the much better plan of Massachusetts, and which had never occurred to me. With respect to the declaration of rights, I suppose the majority of the United States are of my opinion; for I apprehend all the Anti-Federalists and a very respectable proportion of the Federalists think that such a declaration should now be annexed. The enlightened part of Europe have given us the greatest credit for inventing the instrument of security for the rights of the people, and have been not a little surprised to see us so soon give it up. With respect to the reeligibility of the president, I find myself differing from the majority of my countrymen; for I think there are but three states out of the eleven which have desired an alteration of this. And indeed, since the thing is established, I would wish it not to be altered during the life of our great leader, whose executive talents are superior to those, I believe, of any man in the world, and who alone, by the authority of his name and the confidence reposed in his perfect integrity, is fully qualified to put the new government so under way, as to secure it against the efforts of opposition. But, having derived from our error all the good there was in it, I hope we shall correct it, the moment we can no longer have the same name at the helm.

These, my dear friend, are my sentiments, by which you will see I was right in saying I am neither Federalist nor Anti-Federalist; that I am of neither party, nor yet a trimmer between parties. These, my opinions, I wrote within a few hours after I had read the Constitution, to one or two friends in America. I had not then read one single word printed on the subject. I never had an opinion in politics or religion which I was afraid to own. A costive reserve on these subjects might have procured me more esteem from some people, but less from myself. My great wish is to go on in a strict but silent performance of my duty; to avoid attracting notice, and to keep my name out of newspapers, because I find the pain of a little censure, even when it is unfounded, is more acute than the pleasure of much praise. The attaching circumstance of my present office is that I can do its duties unseen by those for whom they are done. You did not think, by so short a phrase in your letter, to have drawn on yourself such an egotistical dissertation. I beg your pardon for it, and will endeavor to merit that pardon by the constant sentiments of esteem and attachment with which I am, dear sir, your sincere friend and servant.

LETTER TO
JAMES MADISON

Paris, March 15, 1789

Dear Sir:

I wrote you last on the 12th of January; since which I have received yours of October 17, December 8 and 12. That of October 17 came to hand only February 23. How it happened to be four months on the way I cannot tell, as I never knew by what hand it came. Looking over my letter of January 12, I remark an error of the word "probable" instead of "improbable," which doubtless, however, you had been able to correct.

Your thoughts on the subject of the declaration of rights, in the letter of October 17, I have weighed with great satisfaction. Some of them had not occurred to me before, but were acknowledged just in the moment they were presented to my mind. In the arguments in favor of a declaration of rights, you omit one which has great weight with me: the legal check which it puts into the hands of the judiciary. This is a body which, if rendered independent and kept strictly to their own department, merits great confidence for their learning and integrity. In fact, what degree of confidence would be too much for a body composed of such men as Wythe, Blair, and Pendleton? On characters like these, the *"civium ardor prava jubentium"* would make no impression. I am happy to find that, on the whole, you are a friend to this amendment. The declaration of rights is, like all other human blessings, alloyed with some inconveniences, and not accomplishing fully its object. But the good in this instance vastly overweighs the evil. I cannot refrain from making short answers to the objections which your letter states to have been raised.

1. That the rights in question are reserved, by the manner in

which the federal powers are granted. *Answer:* A constitutive act may, certainly, be so formed as to need no declaration of rights. The act itself has the force of a declaration, as far as it goes; and if it goes to all material points, nothing more is wanting. In the draft of a constitution which I had once a thought of proposing in Virginia, and printed afterwards, I endeavored to reach all the great objects of public liberty, and did not mean to add a declaration of rights. Probably the object was imperfectly executed; but the deficiencies would have been supplied by others, in the course of discussion. But in a constitutive act which leaves some precious articles unnoticed, and raises implications against others, a declaration of rights becomes necessary, by way of supplement. This is the case of our new federal Constitution. This instrument forms us into one state, as to certain objects, and gives us a legislative and executive body for these objects. It should, therefore, guard us against their abuses of power, within the field submitted to them.

2. A positive declaration of some essential rights could not be obtained in the requisite latitude. *Answer:* Half a loaf is better than no bread. If we cannot secure all our rights, let us secure what we can.

3. The limited powers of the federal government, and jealousy of the subordinate governments, afford a security which exists in no other instance. *Answer:* The first member of this seems resolvable into the first objection before stated. The jealousy of the subordinate governments is a precious reliance. But observe that those governments are only agents. They must have principles furnished them, whereon to found their opposition. The declaration of rights will be the text, whereby they will try all the acts of the federal government. In this view, it is necessary to the federal government also; as by the same text, they may try the opposition of the subordinate governments.

4. Experience proves the inefficacy of a bill of rights. *True.* But though it is not absolutely efficacious under all circumstances, it is of great potency always, and rarely inefficacious. A brace the more will often keep up the building which would

have fallen, with that brace the less. There is a remarkable difference between the characters of the inconveniences which attend a declaration of rights and those which attend the want of it. The inconveniences of the declaration are that it may cramp government in its useful exertions. But the evil of this is short-lived, moderate, and reparable. The inconveniences of the want of a declaration are permanent, afflicting, and irreparable. They are in constant progression from bad to worse. The executive, in our governments, is not the sole, it is scarcely the principal object of my jealousy. The tyranny of the legislatures is the most formidable dread at present, and will be for many years. That of the executive will come in its turn; but it will be at a remote period. I know there are some among us who would now establish a monarchy. But they are inconsiderable in number and weight of character. The rising race are all republicans. We were educated in royalism; no wonder, if some of us retain that idolatry still. Our young people are educated in republicanism; an apostasy from that to royalism is unprecedented and impossible. I am much pleased with the prospect that a declaration of rights will be added; and I hope it will be done in that way which will not endanger the whole frame of government, or any essential part of it.

I have hitherto avoided public news in my letters to you, because your situation insured you a communication of my letters to Mr. Jay. This circumstance being changed, I shall, in future, indulge myself in these details to you. There had been some slight hopes that an accommodation might be effected between the Turks and two empires; but these hopes do not strengthen, and the season is approaching which will put an end to them, for another campaign, at least. The accident to the king of England has had great influence on the affairs of Europe. His mediation, joined with that of Prussia, would certainly have kept Denmark quiet, and so have left the two empires in the hands of the Turks and Swedes. But the inactivity to which England is reduced leaves Denmark more free, and she will probably go on in opposition to Sweden. The king of Prussia, too, had advanced so far that he can scarcely retire. This is rendered the more difficult by the troubles he has excited in Poland. He cannot well abandon the party he had brought forward there; so that it is very possible he may be engaged in the ensuing campaign. France will be quiet this year, because this year, at least, is necessary for settling her future constitution. The States will meet the 27th of April; and the public mind will, I think, by that time, be ripe for a just decision of the question, whether they shall vote by orders or persons. I think there is a majority of the Nobles already for the latter. If so, their affairs cannot but go on well. Besides settling for themselves a tolerably free constitution, perhaps as free a one as the nation is as yet prepared to bear, they will fund their public debts. This will give them such a credit as will enable them to borrow any money they may want and, of course, to take the field again when they think proper. And I believe they mean to take the field as soon as they can. The pride of every individual in the nation suffers under the ignominies they have lately been exposed to, and I think the States General will give money for a war to wipe off the reproach. There have arisen new bickerings between this court and that of the Hague; and the papers which have passed show the most bitter acrimony rankling at the heart of this Ministry. They have recalled their ambassador from the Hague, without appointing a successor. They have given a note to the Diet of Poland, which shows a disapprobation of their measures. The insanity of the king of England has been fortunate for them, as it gives them time to put their house in order. The English papers tell you the king is well; and even the English Ministry says so. They will naturally set the best foot foremost; and they guard his person so well that it is difficult for the public to contradict them. The king is probably better, but not well, by a great deal: (1) he has been bled, and judicious physicians say that in his exhausted state, nothing could have induced a recurrence to bleeding but symptoms of relapse; (2) the Prince of Wales tells the Irish deputation he will give them a definitive answer in some days; but if the king had been well, he could have given it at once; (3) they talk of passing a standing law for providing a regency in similar cases; they apprehend, then, they are not yet clear of the danger of wanting a regency; (4) they have carried the king to church; but it was his private chapel. If he be well, why do not they show him publicly to the nation, and raise them from that consternation into which they have been thrown, by the prospect of being delivered over to the profligate hands of the Prince of Wales. In short, judging from little facts, which are known in spite of their teeth, the king is better, but not well. Possibly he is getting well, but still, time will be wanting to satisfy even the Ministry, that it is not merely a lucid interval. Consequently, they cannot interrupt France this year in the settlement of her affairs, and after this year it will be too late.

As you will be in a situation to know when the leave of absence will be granted me, which I have asked, will you be so good as to communicate it, by a line, to Mr. Lewis and Mr. Eppes? I hope to see you in the summer, and that if you are not otherwise engaged, you will encamp with me at Monticello for awhile.

I am, with great and sincere attachment, dear sir, your affectionate friend and servant.

LETTER TO
THOMAS PAINE

Paris, July 11, 1789

Dear Sir:

Since my last, which was of May 19, I have received yours of June 17 and 18. I am struck with the idea of the geometrical wheelbarrow, and will beg of you a farther account, if it can be obtained. I have no news yet of my congé.

Though you have doubtless heard most of the proceedings of the States General since my last, I will take up the narration where that left it, that you may be able to separate the true from the false accounts you have heard. A good part of what was conjecture in that letter, is now become true history. . . . The *National Assembly* then (for that is the name they take), having shown through every stage of these transactions a coolness, wisdom, and resolution to set fire to the four corners of the kingdom and to perish with it themselves, rather than to relinquish an iota from their plan of a total change of government, are now in complete and undisputed possession of the sovereignty. The executive and aristocracy are at their feet; the mass of the nation, the mass of the clergy, and the army are with them; they have prostrated the old government, and are now beginning to build one from the foundation. A committee, charged with the arrangement of their business, gave in, two days ago, the following order of proceedings.

"1. Every government should have for its only end, the preservation of the rights of man; whence it follows, that to recall constantly the government to the end proposed, the constitution should begin by a declaration of the natural and imprescriptible rights of man.

"2. Monarchical government being proper to maintain

those rights, it has been chosen by the French nation. It suits especially a great society; it is necessary for the happiness of France. The declaration of the principles of this government, then, should follow immediately the declaration of the rights of man.

"3. It results from the principles of monarchy, that the nation, to assure its own rights, has yielded particular rights to the monarch; the constitution, then, should declare, in a precise manner, the rights of both. It should begin by declaring the rights of the French nation, and then it should declare the rights of the king.

"4. The rights of the king and nation not existing but for the happiness of the individuals who compose it, they lead to an examination of the rights of citizens.

"5. The French nation not being capable of assembling individually, to exercise all its rights, it ought to be represented. It is necessary, then, to declare the form of its representation and the rights of its representatives.

"6. From the union of the powers of the nation and king should result the enacting and execution of the laws; thus, then, it should first be determined how the laws shall be established, afterwards should be considered, how they shall be executed.

"7. Laws have for their object the general administration of the kingdom, the property, and the actions of the citizens. The execution of the laws which concern the general administration, requires Provincial and Municipal Assemblies. It is necessary to examine, therefore, what should be the organization of the Provincial Assemblies, and what of the Municipal.

"8. The execution of the laws which concern the property and actions of the citizens call for the judiciary power. It should be determined how that should be confided, and then its duties and limits.

"9. For the execution of the laws and the defense of the kingdom, there exists a public force. It is necessary, then, to determine the principles which should direct it, and how it should be employed.

"*Recapitulation*. Declaration of the rights of man. Principles of the monarchy. Rights of the nation. Rights of the king. Rights of the citizens. Organization and rights of the National Assembly. Forms necessary for the enaction of laws. Organization and functions of the Provincial and Municipal Assemblies. Duties and limits of the judiciary power. Functions and duties of the military power."

You see that these are the materials of a superb edifice, and the hands which have prepared them are perfectly capable of putting them together, and of filling up the work of which these are only the outlines. While there are some men among them of very superior abilities, the mass possess such a degree of good sense as enables them to decide well. I have always been afraid their numbers might lead to confusion. Twelve hundred men in one room are too many. I have still that fear. Another apprehension is that a majority cannot be induced to adopt the trial by jury; and I consider that as the only anchor ever yet imagined by man by which a government can be held to the principles of its constitution. Mr. Paradise is the bearer of this letter. He can supply those details which it would be too tedious to write.

I am, with great esteem, dear sir, your friend and servant.

LETTER TO
JOHN JAY

Dear Sir:

I am become very uneasy lest you should have adopted some channel for the conveyance of your letters to me which is unfaithful. I have none from you of later date than November 25, 1788, and of consequence, no acknowledgment of the receipt of any of mine, since that of August 11, 1788. Since that period, I have written to you of the following dates. 1788: August 20, September 3, 5, 24, November 14, 19, 29. 1789: January 11, 14, 21, February 4, March 1, 12, 14, 15, May 9, 11, 12, June 17, 24, 29. I know, through another person, that you have received mine of November 29, and that you have written an answer; but I have never received the answer, and it is this which suggests to me the fear of some general source of miscarriage.

The capture of three French merchant ships by the Algerines, under different pretexts, has produced great sensation in the seaports of this country, and some in its government. They have ordered some frigates to be armed at Toulon to punish them. There is a possibility that this circumstance, if not too soon set to rights by the Algerines, may furnish occasion to the States General, when they shall have leisure to attend to matters of this kind, to disavow any future tributary treaty with them. These pirates respect still less their treaty with Spain, and treat the Spaniards with an insolence greater than was usual before the treaty.

The scarcity of bread begins to lessen in the southern parts of France, where the harvest has commenced. Here it is still threatening, because we have yet three weeks to the beginning of harvest, and I think there has not been three days' provision beforehand in Paris, for two or three weeks past. Monsieur de Mirabeau, who is very hostile to Mr. Neckar, wished to find a ground for censuring him, in a proposition to have a great quantity of flour furnished from the United States, which he supposed me to have made to Mr. Neckar, and to have been refused by him; and he asked time of the States General to furnish proofs. The Marquis de Lafayette immediately gave me notice of this matter, and I wrote him a letter to disavow having ever made any such proposition to Mr. Neckar, which I desired him to communicate to the States. I waited immediately on Mr. Neckar and Monsieur de Montmorin, satisfied them that what had been suggested was absolutely without foundation from me; and indeed they had not needed this testimony. I gave them copies of my letter to the Marquis de Lafayette, which was afterwards printed. The marquis, on the receipt of my letter, showed it to Mirabeau, who turned then to a paper from which he had drawn his information, and found he had totally mistaken it. He promised immediately that he would himself declare his error to the States General, and read to them my letter, which he did. I state this matter to you, though of little consequence in itself, because it might go to you misstated in the English papers.

Our supplies to the Atlantic ports of France, during the months of March, April, and May, were only 12,220 quintals, 33 pounds of flour, and 44,115 quintals, 40 pounds of wheat, in 21 vessels.

My letter of the 29th of June brought down the proceedings of the States and government to the reunion of the orders, which took place on the 27th. Within the Assembly, matters went on well. But it was soon observed that troops, and particularly the foreign troops, were on their march towards Paris from various quarters, and that this was against the opinion of Mr. Neckar. The king was probably advised to this, under pretext of preserving peace in Paris and Versailles, and saw nothing else in the measure. That his advisers are supposed to have had in view, when he should be secured and inspirited by the presence of the troops, to take advantage of some favorable moment, and surprise him into an act of authority for establishing the declaration of the 23d of June, and perhaps dispersing the States General, is probable. The Marshal de Broglio was appointed to command all the troops within the isle of France—a high flying aristocrat, cool and capable of everything. Some of the French guards were soon arrested under other pretexts, but in reality on account of their dispositions in favor of the national cause. The people of Paris forced the prison, released them, and sent a deputation to the States General, to solicit a pardon. The States, by a most moderate and prudent *arreté*, recommended these prisoners to the king and peace to the people of Paris. Addresses came in to them from several of the great cities, expressing sincere allegiance to the king, but a determined resolution to support the States General. On the 8th of July, they voted an address to the king to remove the troops. This piece of masculine eloquence, written by Monsieur de Mirabeau, is worth attention on account of the bold matter it expresses and discovers through the whole. The king refused to remove the troops, and said they might remove themselves, if they pleased, to Noyons or Soissons. They proceeded to fix the order in which they will take up the several branches of their future constitution, from which it appears they mean to build it from the bottom, confining themselves to nothing in their ancient form but a king. A declaration of rights, which forms the first chapter of their work, was then proposed by the Marquis de Lafayette. This was on the 11th. In the meantime, troops, to the number of about twenty-five or thirty thousand, had arrived, and were posted in and between Paris and Versailles. The bridges and passes were guarded. At three o'clock in the afternoon, the Count de La Luzerne was sent to notify Mr. Neckar of his dismission, and to enjoin him to retire instantly, without saying a word of it to anybody. He went home, dined, proposed to his wife a visit to a friend, but went in fact to his country-house at St. Ouen, and at midnight, set out from thence, as is supposed, for Brussels. This was not known till the next day, when the whole ministry was changed, except Villedeuil, of the domestic department, and Barentin, Garde des Sceaux. These changes were as follows: the Baron de Breteuil, president of the Council of Finance; and de La Galaisiere, comptroller general in the room of Mr. Neckar; the Marshal de Broglio, minister of war, and Foulon under him, in the room of Puy-Segur; Monsieur de La Vauguyon, minister of foreign affairs, instead of Monsieur de Montmorin; de La Porte, minister of marine, in place of the Count de La Luzerne; St. Priest was also removed from the Council. It is to be observed, that Luzerne and Puy-Segur had been strongly of the aristocratical party in Council; but they were not considered as equal to bear their shares in the work now to be done. For this change, however sudden it may have been in the mind of the king, was, in that of his advisers, only one chapter of a great plan, of which the bringing together the foreign troops had been the first. He was now completely in the hands of men, the principal among whom had been noted through their lives for the Turkish despotism of their characters, and who were associated about the king as proper instruments for what was to be executed. The news of this change began to be known in Paris about one or two o'clock. In the afternoon, a body of about one hundred German cavalry were advanced and drawn up in the Place Louis XV and about two hundred Swiss posted at a little distance in their rear. This drew the people to that spot, who naturally formed themselves in front of the troops, at first merely to look at them. But as their numbers increased, their indignation arose; they retired a few steps, posted themselves on and behind large piles of loose stone, collected in that place for a bridge adjacent to it, and attacked the horse with stones. The horse charged, but the advantageous position of the people, and the showers of stones, obliged them to retire, and even to quit the field altogether, leaving one of their number on the ground. The Swiss in their rear were observed never to stir. This was the signal for universal insurrection, and this body of cavalry, to avoid being massacred, retired towards Versailles. The people now armed themselves with such weapons as they could find in armorers' shops and private houses, and with bludgeons, and were roaming all night through all parts of the city, without any decided practicable object. The next day, the States pressed on the king to send away the troops, to permit the bourgeoise of Paris to arm for the preservation of order in the city, and offered to send a deputation from their body to tranquillize them. He refused all their propositions. A committee of magistrates and electors of the city were appointed by their bodies to take upon them its government. The mob, now openly joined by the French guards, forced the prison of St. Lazare, released all the prisoners, and took a great store of corn, which they carried to the corn market. Here they got some arms, and the French guards began to form and train them. The committee determined to raise forty-eight thousand bourgeoise, or rather to restrain their numbers to forty-eight thousand. On the 14th, they sent one of their members (Monsieur de Corny, whom we knew in America) to the Hotel des Invalides, to ask arms for their Garde Bourgeoise. He was followed by, or he found there, a great mob. The governor of the Invalides came out and represented the impossibility of his delivering arms without the orders of those from whom he received them. De Corny advised the people then to retire, and retired himself; and the people took possession of the arms. It was remarkable that not only the Invalides themselves made no opposition but that a body of five thousand foreign troops, encamped within four hundred yards, never stirred. Monsieur de Corny and five others were then sent to ask arms of Monsieur de Launai, governor of the Bastile. They found a great collection of people already before the place, and they immediately planted a flag of truce, which was answered by a like flag hoisted on the parapet. The deputation prevailed on the people to fall back a little, advanced themselves to make their demand of the governor, and in that instant a discharge from the Bastile killed four people of those nearest to the deputies. The deputies retired; the people rushed against the place, and almost in an instant were in possession of a fortification defended by one hundred men of infinite strength, which in other times had stood several regular sieges and had never been taken. How they got in has, as yet, been impossible to discover. Those who pretend to have been of the party tell so many different stories as to destroy the credit of them all. They took all the arms, discharged the prisoners, and such of the garrison as were not killed in the first moment of fury carried the governor and lieutenant governor to the Gréve (the place of public execution), cut off their heads, and sent them through the city in triumph to the Palais Royal. About the same instant, a treacherous correspondence having been discovered in Monsieur de Flesselles, prevost des Marchands, they seized him in the Hotel de Ville, where he was in the exercise of his office, and cut off his head. These events, carried imperfectly to Versailles, were the subject of two successive deputations from the States to the king, to both of which he gave dry and hard answers; for it has transpired that it had been proposed and agitated in Council, to seize on the principal members of the States General, to march the whole army down upon Paris, and to suppress its tumults by the sword. But at night, the Duke de Liancourt forced his way into the king's bed chamber and obliged him to hear a full and animated detail of the disasters of the day in Paris. He went to bed deeply impressed. The decapitation of de Launai worked powerfully through the night on the whole aristocratical party, insomuch that in the morning those of the greatest influence on the Count d'Artois, represented to him the absolute necessity that the king should give up everything to the States. This according well enough with the dispositions of the king, he went about eleven o'clock, accompanied only by his brothers, to the States General, and there read to them a speech, in which he asked their interposition to reestablish order. Though this be couched in terms of some caution, yet the manner in which it was delivered made it evident that it was meant as a surrender at discretion. He returned to the chateau afoot, accompanied by the States. They sent off a deputation, the Marquis de Lafayette at their head, to quiet Paris. He had, the same morning, been named commandant-in-chief of the Milice Bourgeoise, and

Monsieur Bailly, former president of the States General, was called for as Prevost des Marchands. The demolition of the Bastile was now ordered, and begun. A body of the Swiss guards of the regiment of Ventimille, and the city horse guards, joined the people. The alarm at Versailles increased instead of abating. They believed that the aristocrats of Paris were under pillage and carnage, that 150,000 men were in arms, coming to Versailles to massacre the royal family, the court, the ministers, and all connected with them, their practices, and principles. The aristocrats of the Nobles and Clergy in the States General vied with each other in declaring how sincerely they were converted to the justice of voting by persons, and how determined to go with the nation all its lengths. The foreign troops were ordered off instantly. Every minister resigned. The king confirmed Bailly as prevost des Marchands, wrote to Mr. Neckar to recall him, sent his letter open to the States General, to be forwarded by them, and invited them to go with him to Paris the next day, to satisfy the city of his dispositions; and that night and the next morning, the Count d'Artois and Monsieur de Montisson (a deputy connected with him), Madame de Polignac, Madame de Guiche, and the Count de Vandreuil, favorites of the queen, the Abbé de Vermont, her confessor, the Prince of Condé and Duke de Bourbon, all fled; we know not whither. The king came to Paris, leaving the queen in consternation for his return. Omitting the less important figures of the procession, I will only observe that the king's carriage was in the center, on each side of it the States General, in two ranks, afoot, and at their head the Marquis de Lafayette, as commander-in-chief, on horseback, and bourgeoise guards before and behind. About sixty thousand citizens of all forms and colors, armed with the muskets of the Bastile and Invalides, as far as they would go, the rest with pistols, swords, pikes, pruning hooks, scythes, etc., lined all the streets through which the procession passed, and, with the crowds of people in the streets, doors, and windows, saluted them everywhere with cries of "Vive la nation," but not a single "Vive le roy" was heard. The king stopped at the Hotel de Ville.

There Monsieur Bailly presented and put into his hat the popular cockade, and addressed him. The king being unprepared and unable to answer, Bailly went to him, gathered from him some scraps of sentences, and made out an answer, which he delivered to the audience as from the king. On their return, the popular cries were *"Vive le roy et la nation."* He was conducted by a Garde Bourgeoise to his palace at Versailles, and thus concluded such an *amende honorable* as no sovereign ever made, and no people ever received. Letters written with his own hand to the Marquis de Lafayette remove the scruples of his position. Tranquillity is now restored to the capital: the shops are again opened; the people resuming their labors, and if the want of bread does not disturb our peace, we may hope a continuance of it. The demolition of the Bastile is going on, and the Milice Bourgeoise organizing and training. The ancient police of the city is abolished by the authority of the people, the introduction of the king's troops will probably be proscribed, and a watch or city guards substituted, which shall depend on the city alone. But we cannot suppose this paroxysm confined to Paris alone. The whole country must pass successively through it, and happy if they get through it as soon and as well as Paris has done.

I went yesterday to Versailles, to satisfy myself what had passed there; for nothing can be believed but what one sees, or has from an eyewitness. They believe there, still, that three thousand people have fallen victims to the tumults of Paris. Mr. Short and myself have been every day among them, in order to be sure what was passing. We cannot find, with certainty, that anybody has been killed but the three before mentioned, and those who fell in the assault or defense of the Bastile. How many of the garrison were killed nobody pretends to have ever heard. Of the assailants, accounts vary from six to six hundred. The most general belief is that there fell about thirty. There have been many reports of instantaneous executions by the mob, on such of their body as they caught in acts of theft or robbery. Some of these may perhaps be true. There was a severity of honesty observed, of which no example has been known. Bags of money offered on various occasions through fear or guilt have been uniformly refused by the mobs. The churches are now occupied in singing "De profundis" and requiems "for the repose of the souls of the brave and valiant citizens who have sealed with their blood the liberty of the nation." Monsieur de Montmorin is this day replaced in the department of foreign affairs, and Monsieur de St. Priest is named to the home department. The gazettes of France and Leyden accompany this. I send, also, a paper (called the *Point du Jour*), which will give you some idea of the proceedings of the National Assembly. It is but an indifferent thing; however, it is the best.

I have the honor to be, with great esteem and respect, sir, your most obedient and most humble servant.

P. S. *July 21.* Mr. Neckar had left Brussels for Frankfort, before the courier got there. We expect, however, to hear of him in a day or two. Monsieur le Comte de La Luzerne has resumed the department of the marine this day. Either this is an office of friendship effected by Monsieur de Montmorin (for though they had taken different sides, their friendship continued) or he comes in as a stop-gap, till somebody else can be found. Though very unequal to his office, all agree that he is an honest man. The Count d'Artois was at Valenciennes. The Prince of Condé and Duke de Bourbon had passed that place.

LETTER TO THE
MARQUIS DE LAFAYETTE

New York, April 2, 1790

Behold me, my dear friend, elected secretary of state, instead of returning to the far more agreeable position which placed me in the daily participation of your friendship. I found the appointment in the newspapers the day of my arrival in Virginia. I had indeed been asked while in France whether I would accept of any appointment at home, and I had answered that, not meaning to remain long where I was, I meant it to be the last office I should ever act in. Unfortunately this letter had not arrived at the time of arranging the new government. I expressed freely to the president my desire to return. He left me free, but still showing his own desire. This, and the concern of others, more general than I had a right to expect, induced, after three months parleying, to sacrifice my own inclinations. I have been here, then, ten days harnessed in new gear. Wherever I am, or ever shall be, I shall be sincere in my friendship to you and to your nation. I think with others that nations are to be governed with regard to their own interests, but I am convinced that it is their interest, in the long run, to be grateful, faithful to their engagements, even in the worst of circumstances, and honorable and generous always. If I had not known that the head of our government was in these sentiments, and that his national and private ethics were the same, I would never have been where I am. I am sorry to tell you his health is less firm than it used to be. However, there is nothing in it to give alarm. The opposition to our new Constitution has almost totally disappeared. Some few indeed had gone such lengths in their declarations of hostility that they feel it awkward perhaps to come over; but the amendments proposed by Congress have brought over almost all their followers. If the president can be preserved a few years till habits of authority and obedience can be established generally, we have nothing to fear. The little vautrien, Rhode Island, will come over with a little more time. Our last news from Paris is of the 8th of January. So far it seemed that your revolution had got along with a steady peace; meeting indeed occasional difficulties and dangers, but we are not to expect to be translated from despotism to liberty in a feather-bed. I have never feared for the ultimate result, though I have feared for you personally. Indeed, I hope you will never see such another 5th or 6th of October. Take care of yourself, my dear friend, for though I think your nation would in any event work out her salvation, I am persuaded, were she to lose you, it would cost her oceans of blood, and years of confusion and anarchy. Kiss and bless your dear children for me. Learn them to be as you are, a cement between our two nations. I write to Madame de Lafayette, so have only to add assurances of the respect of your affectionate friend and humble servant.

LETTER TO
EDMUND RANDOLPH

New York, May 30, 1790

Dear Sir:

I at length find myself, though not quite well, yet sufficiently so to resume business in a moderate degree. I have, therefore, to answer your two favors of April 23 and May 3, and in the first place to thank you for your attention to the Paccan, Gloucester, and European walnuts, which will be great acquisitions at Monticello. I will still ask your attention to Mr. Foster's boring machines, lest he should go away suddenly, and the opportunity of getting it be lost. I enquired of Mr. Hamilton the quantity of coal imported; but he tells me there are not returns as yet sufficient to ascertain it; but as soon as there shall be, I shall be informed. I am told there is a considerable prejudice against our coal in these Northern states. I do not know whence it proceeds; perhaps from the want of attention to the different species, and an ignorant application of them to cross purposes. I have not begun my meteorological diary, because I have not yet removed to the house I have taken. I remove tomorrow; but as far as I can judge from its aspects, there will not be one position to be had for the thermometer free from the influence of the sun both morning and evening. However, as I go into it only till I can get a better, I shall hope ere long to find a less objectionable situation. You know that during my short stay at Monticello I kept a diary of the weather. Mr. Madison has just received one comprehending the same period, kept at his father's at Orange. The hours of observation were the same, and he has the fullest confidence in the accuracy of the observer. All the morning observations in Orange are lower than those of Monticello, from one to, I believe, fifteen or sixteen degrees; the afternoon observations are near as much higher as those of Monticello. Nor will the variations permit us to ascribe them to any supposed irregularities in either tube; because, in that case, at the same point the variation would always be the same, which it is not. You have often been sensible that in the afternoon, or rather evening, the air has become warmer in ascending the mountain. The same is true in the morning. This might account for a higher station of the mercury in the morning observations at Monticello. Again, when the air is equally dry in the lower and higher situations, which may be supposed the case in the warmest part of the day, the mercury should be lower on the latter, because, all other circumstances the same, the nearer the common surface the warmer the air. So that on a mountain it ought really to be warmer in the morning and cooler in the heat of the day than on the common plain, but not in so great a degree as these observations indicate. As soon as I am well enough I intend to examine them more accurately. Your resolution to apply to the study of the law is wise in my opinion, and at the same time to mix with it a good degree of attention to the farm. The one will relieve the other. The study of the law is useful in a variety of points of view. It qualifies a man to be useful to himself, to his neighbors, and to the public. It is the most certain stepping-stone to preferment in the political line. In political economy, I think Smith's *Wealth of Nations* the best book extant; in the science of government, Montesquieu's *Spirit of Laws* is generally recommended. It contains, indeed, a great number of political truths, but also an equal number of heresies, so that the reader must be constantly on his guard. There has been lately published a letter of Helvetius, who was the intimate friend of Montesquien, and whom he consulted before the publication of his book. Helvetius advised him not to publish it; and in this letter to a friend he gives us a solution for the mixture of truth and error found in this book. He says Montesquieu was a man of immense reading; that he had commonplaced all his reading, and that his object was to throw the whole contents of his commonplace book into systematical order, and to show his ingenuity by reconciling the contradictory facts it presents. Locke's little book on government is perfect as far as it goes. Descending from theory to practice there is no better book than *The Federalist*. Burgh's *Political Disquisitions* is good also, especially after reading De Lome. Several of Hume's political essays are good. There are some excellent books of theory written by Turgot and the economists of France. For parliamentary knowledge, the *Lex Parliamentaria* is the best book. On my return to Virginia in the fall, I cannot help hoping some practicable plan may be devised for your settling in Albemarle, should your inclination lead you to it. Nothing could contribute so much to my happiness were it at the same time consistent with yours. You might get into the Assembly for that county as soon as you should please.

A motion has been made in the Senate to remove the federal government to Philadelphia. There was a trial of strength on a question for a week's postponement. On that it was found there would be eleven for the removal, and thirteen against it. The motion was therefore withdrawn and made in the other house, where it is still depending, and of very uncertain event. The question of the assumption is again brought on. The parties were so nearly equal on the former trial that it is very possible that with some modifications it may yet prevail. The tonnage bill will probably pass, and must, I believe, produce salutary effects. It is a mark of energy in our government, in a case, I believe, where it cannot be parried. The French Revolution still goes on well, though the danger of a suspension of payments is very imminent. Their appeal to the inhabitants of their colonies to say on what footing they wish to be placed will end, I hope, in our free admissions into their islands with our produce. This precedent must have consequences. It is impossible the world should continue long insensible to so evident a truth as that the right to have commerce and intercourse with our neighbors is a natural right. To suppress this neighborly intercourse is an exercise of force, which we shall have a just right to remove when the superior force. Dear sir, your affectionate friend.

LETTER TO
NOAH WEBSTER

Sir:

Your favor of October 4 came to my hands on the 20th of November. Application was made a day or two after to Mr. Dobson for the copies of your *Essays,* which were received, and one of them lodged in the office. For that intended for myself, be pleased to accept my thanks. I return you the order on Mr. Allen, that on Dobson having been made use of instead of it. I submit to your consideration whether it might not be advisable to record a second time your right to the *Grammatical Institutes,* in order to bring the lodging of the copy in my office within the six months made a condition in the law? I have not at this moment an opportunity of turning to the law to see if that may be done; but I suppose it possible that the failure to fulfill the legal condition on the first record might excite objections against the validity of that.

In mentioning me in your *Essays,* and canvassing my opinions, you have done what every man has a right to do, and it is for the good of society that that right should be freely exercised. No republic has more zeal than that of letters, and I am the last in principles, as I am the least in pretensions, to any dictatorship in it. Had I other dispositions, the philosophical and dispassionate spirit with which your have expressed your own opinions in opposition to mine would still have commanded my approbation. A desire of being set right in your opinion, which I respect too much not to entertain that desire, induces me to hazard to you the following observations. It had become a universal and almost uncontroverted position in the several states that the purposes of society do not require a surrender of all our rights to our ordinary governors; that there are certain portions of right not necessary to enable them to carry on an effective government, and which experience has nevertheless proved they will be constantly encroaching on, if submitted to them; that there are also certain fences which experience has proved peculiarly efficacious against wrong, and rarely obstructive of right, which yet the governing powers have ever shown a disposition to weaken and remove. Of the first kind, for instance, is freedom of religion; of the second, trial by jury, habeas corpus laws, free presses. These were the settled opinions of all the states—of that of Virginia, of which I was writing, as well as the others. The others had, in consequence, delineated these unceded portions of right, and these fences against wrong, which they meant to exempt from the power of their governors, in instruments called declarations of rights and constitutions; and as they did this by conventions, which they appointed for the express purpose of reserving these rights and of delegating others to their ordinary legislative, executive, and judiciary bodies, none of the reserved rights can be touched without resorting to the people to appoint another convention for the express purpose of permitting it. Where the constitutions then have been so formed by conventions named for this express purpose, they are fixed and unalterable but by a convention or other body to be specially authorized; and they have been so formed by, I believe, all the states, except Virginia. That state concurs in all these opinions, but has run into the wonderful error that her constitution, though made by the ordinary legislature, cannot yet be altered by the ordinary legislature. I had, therefore, no occasion to prove to them the expediency of a constitution alterable only by a special convention. Accordingly, I have not in my notes advocated that opinion, though it was and is mine, as it was and is theirs. I take that position as admitted by them, and only proceed to adduce arguments to prove that they were mistaken in supposing their constitution could not be altered by the common legislature. Among other arguments I urge that the convention which formed the constitution had been chosen merely for ordinary legislation; that they had no higher power than every subsequent legislature was to have; that all their acts are consequently repealable by subsequent legislatures; that their own practice at a subsequent session proved they were of this opinion themselves; that the opinion and practice of several subsequent legislatures had been the same, and so conclude "that their constitution is alterable by the common legislature." Yet these arguments urged to prove that their constitution *is* alterable, you cite as if urged to prove that it *ought not to be* alterable, and you combat them on that ground. An argument which is good to prove one thing may become ridiculous when exhibited as intended to prove another thing. I will beg the favor of you to look over again the passage in my notes, and am persuaded you will be sensible that you have misapprehended the object of my arguments, and therefore have combated them on a ground for which they were not intended. My only object in this is the rectification of your own opinion of me, which I repeat that I respect too much to neglect. I have certainly no view of entering into the contest whether it be expedient to delegate unlimited powers to our ordinary governors. My opinion is against that expediency; but my occupations do not permit me to undertake to vindicate all my opinions, nor have they importance enough to merit it. It cannot, however, but weaken my confidence in them, when I find them opposed to yours, there being no one who respects the latter more than, sir, your most obedient and most humble servant.

LETTER TO
BENJAMIN BANNEKER

Philadelphia, August 30, 1791

Sir:

I thank you sincerely for your letter of the 19th instant, and for the Almanac it contained. Nobody wishes more than I do to see such proofs as you exhibit, that nature has given to our black brethren talents equal to those of the other colors of men, and that the appearance of a want of them is owing merely to the degraded condition of their existence, both in Africa and and America. I can add with truth that nobody wishes more ardently to see a good system commenced for raising the condition both of their body and mind to what it ought to be, as fast as the imbecility of their present existence, and other circumstances which cannot be neglected, will admit. I have taken the liberty of sending your Almanac to Monsieur de Condorcet, Secretary of the Academy of Sciences at Paris, and member of the Philanthropic Society, because I considered it as a document to which your color had a right for their justification against the doubts which have been entertained of them. I am, with great esteem, sir, your most obedient humble servant.

MEMORANDUM
WRITTEN AS
SECRETARY OF STATE

March 1, 1792

CONVERSATION WITH THE PRESIDENT, FEBRUARY 28, 1792

I was to have been with him long enough before three o'clock (which was the hour and day he received visits) to have opened to him a proposition for doubling the velocity of the post riders, who now travel about fifty miles a day, and might, without difficulty, go one hundred, and for taking measures (by way bills) to know where the delay is, when there is any. I was delayed by business, so as to have scarcely time to give him the outlines. I ran over them rapidly, and observed afterwards that I had hitherto never spoken to him on the subject of the post office, not knowing whether it was considered as a revenue law or a law for the general accommodation of the citizens: that the law just passed seemed to have removed the doubt, by declaring that the whole profits of the office should be applied to extending the posts, and that even the past profits should be refunded by the treasury for the same purpose; that I therefore conceive it was now in the department of the secretary of state; that I thought it would be advantageous so to declare it for another reason, to wit: that the Department of the Treasury possessed already such an influence as to swallow up the whole executive powers, and that even the future presidents (not supported by the weight of character which himself possessed) would not be able to make head against this department. That in urging this measure I had certainly no personal interest, since, if I was supposed to have any appetite for power, yet as my career would certainly be exactly as short as his own, the intervening time was too short to be an object. My real wish was to avail the public of every occasion, during the residue of the President's period, to place things on a safe footing. He was now called on to attend his company, and he desired me to come and breakfast with him the next morning.

CONVERSATION WITH THE PRESIDENT, FEBRUARY 29, 1792

I did so; and after breakfast we retired to his room, and I unfolded my plan for the post office, and after such an approbation of it as he usually permitted himself on the first presentment of any idea, and desiring me to commit it to writing, he, during that pause of conversation which follows a business closed, said in an affectionate tone that he had felt much concern at an expression which dropped from me yesterday, and which marked my intention of retiring when he should. That as to himself, many motives obliged him to it. He had, through the whole course of the war, and most particularly at the close of it, uniformly declared his resolution to retire from public affairs, and never to act in any public office; that he had retired under that firm resolution: that the government, however, which had been formed, being found evidently too inefficacious, and it being supposed that his aid was of some consequence towards bringing the people to consent to one of sufficient efficacy for their own good, he consented to come into the Convention, and on the same motive, after much pressing, to take a part in the new government, and get it under way. That were he to continue longer, it might give room to say, that having tasted the sweets of office, he could not do without them: that he really felt himself growing old, his bodily health less firm, his memory, always bad, becoming worse, and perhaps the other faculties of his mind showing a decay to others of which he was insensible himself; that this apprehension particularly oppressed him; that he found, moreover, his activity lessened, business therefore more irksome, and tranquillity and retirement became an irresistible passion. That however he felt himself obliged, for these reasons, to retire from the government, yet he should consider it as unfortunate if that should bring on the retirement of the great officers of the government, and that this might produce a shock on the public mind of dangerous consequence.

I told him that no man had ever had less desire of entering into public offices than myself; that the circumstance of a perilous war, which brought everything into danger, and called for all the services which every citizen could render, had induced me to undertake the administration of the government of Virginia; that I had both before and after refused repeated appointments of Congress to go abroad in that sort of office, which, if I had consulted my own gratification, would almost have been the most agreeable to me; that at the end of two years, I resigned the government of Virginia, and retired with a firm resolution never more to appear in public life; that a domestic loss, however, happened, and made me fancy that absence and a change of scene for a time might be expedient for me; that I therefore accepted a foreign appointment, limited to two years; that at the close of that, Dr. Franklin having left France, I was appointed to supply his place, which I had accepted, and though I continued in it three or four years, it was under the constant idea of remaining only a year or two longer; that the revolution in France coming on, I had so interested myself in the event of that, that when obliged to bring my family home, I had still an idea of returning and awaiting the close of that, to fix the era of my final retirement; that on my arrival here I found he had appointed me to my present office; that he knew I had not come into it without some reluctance; that it was, on my part, a sacrifice of inclination to the opinion that I might be more serviceable here than in France, and with a firm resolution in my mind, to indulge my constant wish for retirement at no very distant day; that when, therefore, I had received his letter, written from Mount Vernon, on his way to Carolina and Georgia (April 1, 1791) and discovered, from an expression in that, that he meant to retire from the government ere long, and as to the precise epoch there could be no doubt, my mind was immediately made up to make that the epoch of my own retirement from those labors of which I was heartily tired. That, however, I did not believe there was any idea in any of my brethren in the administration of retiring; that on the contrary, I had perceived at a late meeting of the trustees of the sinking fund, that the secretary of the treasury had developed the plan he intended to pursue, and that it embraced years in its view.

He said that he considered the Treasury Department as a much more limited one, going only to the single object of revenue, while that of the secretary of state, embracing nearly all the objects of administration, was much more important, and the retirement of the officer, therefore, would be more noticed; that though the government had set out with a pretty general good will of the public, yet that symptoms of dissatisfaction had lately shown themselves far beyond what he could have expected, and to what height these might arise, in case of too great a change in the administration, could not be foreseen.

I told him, that in my opinion, there was only a single source of these discontents. Though they had indeed appeared to spread themselves over the War Department also, yet I considered that as an overflowing only from their real channel, which would never have taken place, if they had not first been generated in another department, to wit, that of the Treasury. That a system had there been contrived, for deluging the states with paper money instead of gold and silver, for withdrawing our citizens from the pursuits of commerce, manufactures, buildings, and other branches of useful industry, to occupy themselves and their capitals in a species of gambling, destructive of morality, and which had introduced its poison into the government itself. That it was a fact, as certainly known as that he and I were then conversing, that particular members of the legislature, while those laws were on the carpet, had feathered their nests with paper, had then voted for the laws, and constantly since lent all the energy of their talents, and instrumentality of their offices, to the establishment and enlargement of this system; that they had chained it about our necks for a great length of time, and in order to keep the game in their hands had, from time to time, aided in making such legislative constructions of the Constitution as made it a very different thing from what the people thought they had submitted to; that they had now brought forward a proposition far beyond any one ever yet advanced, and to which the eyes of many were turned, as the decision which was to let us know whether we live under a limited or an unlimited government. He asked me to what proposition I alluded. I answered, to that in the report on manufactures, which, under color of giving *bounties* for the encouragement of particular manufactures, meant to establish the doctrine that the power given by the Constitution to collect taxes to provide for the *general welfare* of the United States permitted Congress to take everything under their management which *they* should deem for the *public welfare,* and which is susceptible of the application of money; consequently, that the subsequent enumeration of their powers was not the description to which resort must be had, and did not at all constitute the limits of their authority; that this was a very different question from that of the bank, which was thought an incident to an enumerated power; that, therefore, this decision was expected with great anxiety; that, indeed, I hoped the proposition would be rejected, believing there was a majority in both houses against it, and that if it should be, it would be considered as a proof that things were returning into their true channel; and that, at any rate, I looked forward to the broad representation, which would shortly take place, for keeping the general Constitution on its true ground; and that this would remove a great deal of the discontent which had shown itself. The conversation ended with this last topic. It is here stated nearly as much at length as it really was; the expressions preserved where I could recollect them, and their substance always faithfully stated.

MEMORANDUM
WRITTEN AS
SECRETARY OF STATE

April 9, 1792

The president had wished to redeem our captives at Algiers, and to make peace with them on paying an annual tribute. The Senate was willing to approve this, but unwilling to have the lower house applied to previously to furnish the money; they wished the president to take the money from the treasury, or open a loan for it. They thought that to consult the representatives on one occasion would give them a handle always to claim it, and would let them into a participation of the power of making treaties, which the Constitution had given exclusively to the president and Senate. They said, too, that if the particular sum was voted by the representatives, it would not be a secret. The president had no confidence in the secrecy of the Senate, and did not choose to take money from the treasury or to borrow. But he agreed he would enter into provisional treaties with the Algerines, not to be binding on us till ratified here. I prepared questions for consultation with the Senate, and added that the Senate were to be apprised, that on the return of the provisional treaty, and after they should advise the ratification, he would not have the seal put to it till the two houses should vote the money. He asked me if the treaty stipulating a sum and ratified by him, with the advice of the Senate, would not be good under the Constitution, and obligatory on the representatives to furnish the money. I answered it certainly would, and that it would be the duty of the representatives to raise the money; but that they might decline to do what was their duty, and I thought it might be incautious to commit himself by a ratification with a foreign nation, where he might be left in the lurch in the execution: it was possible too, to conceive a treaty, which it would not be their duty to provide for. He said that he did not like throwing too much into democratic hands, that if they would not do what the Constitution called on them to do, the government would be at an end, and must *then assume another form.* He stopped here; and I kept silence to see whether he would say anything more in the same line, or add any qualifying expression to soften what he had said; but he did neither.

I had observed that wherever the agency of either or both houses would be requisite subsequent to a treaty, to carry it into effect, it would be prudent to consult them previously, if the occasion admitted. That thus it was, we were in the habit of consulting the Senate previously, when the occasion permitted, because their subsequent ratification would be necessary. That there was the same reason for consulting the lower House previously, where they were to be called on afterwards, and especially in the case of money, as they held the purse strings, and would be jealous of them. However, he desired me to strike out the intimation that the seal would not be put till both houses should have voted the money.

LETTER TO
THE COMMISSIONERS OF
THE CITY OF
WASHINGTON

Philadelphia, April 9, 1792

Gentlemen:

In a former letter I enclosed you an idea of Mr. Lee's for an immediate appropriation of a number of lots to raise a sum of money for erecting a national monument in the city of Washington. It was scarcely to be doubted but that you would avoid appropriations for matters of ornament till a sufficient sum should be secured out of the proceeds of your sales to accomplish the public buildings, bridges, and other such objects as are essential. Mr. Caracchi, the artist, who had proposed to execute the monument, has had hopes that a subscription set on foot for that purpose would have sufficed to effect it. That hope is now over, and he is about to return to Europe. He is unquestionably an artist of the first class. He has had the advantage of taking the model of the president's person in plaster, equal to every wish in resemblance and spirit. It is pretty certain that the equestrian statue of the president can never be executed by an equal workman, who has had equal advantages, and the question is whether a prudent caution will permit you to enter into any engagement now, taking time enough before the term of payment to have accomplished the more material objects of the public buildings, etc. He says to execute the equestrian statue, with the cost of the materials, in marble, will be worth twenty thousand guineas; that he would begin it on his return, if four or five years hence you can engage to pay him twenty thousand dollars, and the same sum annually afterwards, till the whole is paid, before which time the statue shall be ready. It is rather probable that within some time Congress would take it off your hands, in compliance with an ancient vote of that body. The questions for your considerations are whether, supposing no difficulty as to the means, you think such a work might be undertaken by you? Whether you can have so much confidence in the productiveness of your funds as to engage for a residuum of this amount, all more necessary objects being first secured, and that this may be within the time before proposed? And, in fine, which will preponderate in your minds, the hazard of undertaking this now, or that of losing the aid of this artist? The nature of this proposition will satisfy you that it has not been communicated to the president, and of course would not be, unless a previous acceptance on your part should render it necessary to obtain his sanction. Your answer is necessary for the satisfaction of Mr. Caracchi, at whose instance I submit the proposal to you, and who, I believe, will only wait here the return of that answer. I have the honor to be, with the most perfect esteem, gentlemen, your most obedient and most humble servant.

LETTER TO PRESIDENT GEORGE WASHINGTON

Monticello, September 9, 1792

Dear Sir:

I received on the 2d instant the letter of August 23, which you did me the honor to write me; but the immediate return of our post, contrary to his custom, prevented my answer by that occasion. The proceedings of Spain, mentioned in your letter, are really of a complexion to excite uneasiness, and a suspicion that their friendly overtures about the Mississippi have been merely to lull us while they should be strengthening their holds on that river. Mr. Carmichael's silence has been long my astonishment; and however it might have justified something very different from a new appointment, yet the public interest certainly called for his junction with Mr. Short, as it is impossible but that his knowledge of the ground of negotiation, of persons and characters, must be useful and even necessary to the success of the mission. That Spain and Great Britain may understand one another on our frontiers is very possible; for however opposite their interests or disposition may be in the affairs of Europe, yet while these do not call them into opposite action, they may concur as against us. I consider their keeping an agent in the Indian country as a circumstance which requires serious interference on our part; and I submit to your decision whether it does not furnish a proper occasion to us to send an additional instruction to Messrs. Carmichael and Short to insist on a mutual and formal stipulation to forbear employing agents or pensioning any persons within each other's limits; and if this be refused, to propose the contrary stipulation, to wit, that each party may freely keep agents within the Indian territories of the other, in which case we might soon sicken them of the license.

I now take the liberty of proceeding to that part of your letter wherein you notice the internal dissensions which have taken place within our government, and their disagreeable effect on its movements. That such dissensions have taken place is certain, and even among those who are nearest to you in the administration. To no one have they given deeper concern than myself; to no one equal mortification at being myself a part of them. Though I take to myself no more than my share of the general observations of your letter, yet I am so desirous ever that you should know the whole truth, and believe no more than the truth, that I am glad to seize every occasion of developing to you whatever I do or think relative to the government; and shall, therefore, ask permission to be more lengthy now than the occasion particularly calls for, or could otherwise perhaps justify.

When I embarked in the government, it was with a determination to intermeddle not at all with the legislature, and as little as possible with my co-departments. The first and only instance of variance from the former part of my resolution, I was duped into by the secretary of the treasury, and made a tool for forwarding his schemes, not then sufficiently understood by me; and of all the errors of my political life, this has occasioned me the deepest regret. It has ever been my purpose to explain this to you, when, from being actors on the scene, we shall have become uninterested spectators only. The second part of my resolution has been religiously observed with the War Department; and as to that of the Treasury, has never been further swerved from than by the mere enunciation of my sentiments in conversation, and chiefly among those who, expressing the same sentiments, drew mine from me. If it has been supposed that I have ever intrigued among the members of the legislature to defeat the plans of the secretary of the treasury, it is contrary to all truth. As I never had the desire to influence the members, so neither had I any other means than my friendships, which I valued too highly to risk by usurpation on their freedom of judgment, and the conscientious pursuit of their own sense of duty. That I have utterly, in my private conversations, disapproved of the system of the secretary of the treasury, I acknowledge and avow; and this was not merely a speculative difference. His system flowed from principles adverse to liberty, and was calculated to undermine and demolish the Republic, by creating an influence of his department over the members of the legislature. I saw this influence actually produced, and its first fruits to be the establishment of the great outlines of his project by the votes of the very persons who, having swallowed his bait, were laying themselves out to profit by his plans; and that had these persons withdrawn, as those interested in a question ever should, the vote of the disinterested majority was clearly the reverse of what they made it. These were no longer the votes then of the representatives of the people, but of deserters from the rights and interests of the people; and it was impossible to consider their decisions, which had nothing in view but to enrich themselves, as the measures of the fair majority, which ought always to be respected. If what was actually doing begat uneasiness in those who wished for virtuous government, what was further proposed was not less threatening to the friends of the Constitution. For, in a report on the subject of manufactures (still to be acted on), it was expressly assumed that the general government has a right to exercise all powers which may be for the *general welfare,* that is to say, all the legitimate powers of government; since no government has a legitimate right to do what is not for the welfare of the governed. There was, indeed, a sham limitation of the universality of this power *to cases where money is to be employed.* But about what is it that money cannot be employed? Thus the object of these plans, taken together, is to draw all the powers of government into the hands of the general legislature, to establish means for corrupting a sufficient corps in that legislature to divide the honest votes, and preponderate, by their own, the scale which suited, and to have the corps under the command of the secretary of the treasury, for the purpose of subverting, step by step, the principles of the Constitution, which he has so often declared to be a thing of nothing, which must be changed. Such views might have justified something more than mere expressions of dissent, beyond which, nevertheless, I never went. Has abstinence from the department, committed to me, been equally observed by him? To say nothing of other interferences equally known, in the case of the two nations, with which we have the most intimate connections, France and England, my system was to give some satisfactory distinctions to the former, of little cost to us, in return for the solid advantages yielded us by them; and to have met the English with some restrictions which might induce them to abate their severities against our commerce. I have always supposed this coincided with your sentiments. Yet the secretary of the treasury, by his cabals with members of the legislature, and by high-toned declamations on other occasions, has forced down his own system, which was exactly the reverse. He undertook, of his own authority, the conferences with the ministers of those two nations, and was, on every consultation, provided with some report of a conversation with the one or the other of them, adapted to his views. These views thus made to prevail, their execution fell, of course, to me; and I can safely appeal to you, who have seen all my letters and proceedings, whether I have not carried them into execution as sincerely as if they had been my own, though I ever considered them as inconsistent with the honor and interest of our country. That they have been inconsistent with our interest is but too fatally proved by the stab to our navigation given by the French. So that if the question be by whose fault is it that Colonel Hamilton and myself have not drawn together, the answer will depend on that to two other questions: Whose principles of administration best justify, by their purity, conscientious adherence? And which of us has, notwithstanding, stepped farthest into the control of the department of the other?

To this justification of opinions, expressed in the way of conversation, against the views of Colonel Hamilton, I beg leave to add some notice of his late charges against me in Fenno's *Gazette;* for neither the style, matter, nor venom of the pieces alluded to can leave a doubt of their author. Spelling my name and character at full length to the public, while he conceals his own under the signature of "An American," he charges me: (1) with having written letters from Europe to my friends to oppose the present Constitution, while depending; (2) with a desire of not paying the public debt; (3) with setting up a paper to decry and slander the government.

1. The first charge is most false. No man in the United States, I suppose, approved of every title in the Constitution: no one, I believe, approved more of it than I did, and more of it was certainly disapproved by my accuser than by me, and of its parts most vitally republican. Of this the few letters I wrote on the subject (not half a dozen I believe) will be a proof; and for my own satisfaction and justification, I must tax you with the reading of them when I return to where they are. You will there see that my objection to the Constitution was that it wanted a bill of rights securing freedom of religion, freedom of the press, freedom from standing armies, trial by jury, and a constant habeas corpus act. Colonel Hamilton's was that it wanted a king and house of lords. The sense of America has approved my objection and added the bill of rights, not the king and lords. I also thought a longer term of service, insusceptible of renewal, would have made a president more independent. My country has thought otherwise; I have acquiesced implicitly. He wishes the general government should have power to make laws binding the states in all cases whatsoever. Our country has thought otherwise; has he acquiesced? Notwithstanding my wish for a bill of rights, my letters strongly urged the adoption of the Constitution, by nine states at least, to secure the good it contained. I at first thought that the best method of securing the bill of rights would be for four states to hold off till such a bill should be agreed to. But the moment I saw Mr. Hancock's proposition to pass the Constitution as it stood, and give perpetual instructions to the representatives of every state to insist on a bill of rights, I acknowledged the superiority of his plan, and advocated universal adoption.

2. The second charge is equally untrue. My whole correspondence while in France, and every word, letter, and act on the subject, since my return, prove that no man is more ardently intent to see the public debt soon and sacredly paid off than I am. This exactly marks the difference between Colonel Hamilton's views and mine, that I would wish the debt paid tomorrow; he wishes it never to be paid, but always to be a thing wherewith to corrupt and manage the legislature.

3. I have never inquired what number of sons, relatives, and friends of senators, representatives, printers, or other useful partisans Colonel Hamilton has provided for among the hundred clerks of his department, the thousand excisemen, at his nod, and spread over the Union; nor could ever have imagined that the man who has the shuffling of millions backwards and forwards from paper into money and money into paper, from Europe to America, and America to Europe, the dealing out of treasury secrets among his friends in what time and measure he pleases, and who never slips an occasion of making friends with his means, that such a one, I say, would have brought forward a charge against me for having appointed the poet Freneau translating clerk to my office, with a salary of $250 a year. That fact stands thus. While the government was at New York I was applied to on behalf of Freneau to know if there was any place within my department to which he could be appointed. I answered there were but four clerkships, all of which I found full, and continued without any change. When we removed to Philadelphia, Mr. Pintard, the translating clerk, did not choose to remove with us. His office then became vacant. I was again applied to there for Freneau, and had no hesitation to promise the clerkship for him. I cannot recollect whether it was at the same time, or afterwards, that I was told he had a thought of setting up a newspaper there. But whether then, or afterwards, I considered it a circumstance of some value, as it might enable me to do what I had long wished to have done, that is, to have the material parts of the *Leyden Gazette* brought under your eye, and that of the public, in order to possess yourself and them

of a juster view of the affairs of Europe than could be obtained
from any other public source. This I had ineffectually attempted
through the press of Mr. Fenno, while in New York, selecting
and translating passages myself at first, then having it done by
Mr. Pintard, the translating clerk, but they found their way too
slowly into Mr. Fenno's papers. Mr. Bache essayed it for me in
Philadelphia, but his being a daily paper, did not circulate sufficiently in the other states. He even tried, at my request, the plan
of a weekly paper of recapitulation from his daily paper, in
hopes that that might go into the other states, but in this too we
failed. Freneau, as translating clerk, and the printer of a periodical paper likely to circulate through the states (uniting in one
person the parts of Pintard and Fenno), revived my hopes that
the thing could at length be effected. On the establishment of his
paper, therefore, I furnished him with the *Leyden Gazette,* with
an expression of my wish that he could always translate and
publish the material intelligence they contained, and have continued to furnish them from time to time, as regularly as I
received them. But as to any other direction or indication of my
wish how his press should be conducted, what sort of intelligence he should give, what essays encourage, I can protest, in
the presence of heaven, that I never did by myself, or any other,
or indirectly, say a syllable, nor attempt any kind of influence.
I can further protest, in the same awful presence, that I never
did, by myself, or any other, directly or indirectly, write, dictate
or procure any one sentence or sentiment to be inserted *in his,
or any other gazette,* to which my name was not affixed or that
of my office. I surely need not exce[r]pt here a thing so foreign
to the present subject as a little paragraph about our Algerine
captives, which I put once into Fenno's paper. Freneau's proposition to publish a paper, having been about the time that the
writings of Publicola, and the discourses on Davila, had a good
deal excited the public attention, I took for granted from Freneau's character, which had been marked as that of a good
whig, that he would give free place to pieces written against
the aristocratical and monarchical principles these papers had

inculcated. This having been in my mind, it is likely enough I may have expressed it in conversation with others, though I do not recollect that I did. To Freneau I think I could not, because I had still seen him but once, and that was at a public table, at breakfast, at Mrs. Elsworth's, as I passed through New York the last year. And I can safely declare that my expectations looked only to the chastisement of the aristocratical and monarchical writers, and not to any criticisms on the proceedings of government. Colonel Hamilton can see no motive for any appointment but that of making a convenient partisan. But you, sir, who have received from me recommendations of a Rittenhouse, Barlow, Paine, will believe that talents and science are sufficient motives with me in appointments to which they are fitted; and that Freneau, as a man of genius, might find a preference in my eye to be a translating clerk, and make good title to the little aids I could give him as the editor of a gazette, by procuring subscriptions to his paper, as I did some before it appeared, and as I have with pleasure done for the labors of other men of genius. I hold it to be one of the distinguishing excellences of elective over hereditary successions that the talents which nature has provided in sufficient proportion should be selected by the society for the government of their affairs, rather than that this should be transmitted through the loins of knaves and fools, passing from the debauches of the table to those of the bed. Colonel Hamilton, alias Plain Facts, says, that Freneau's salary began before he resided in Philadelphia. I do not know what quibble he may have in reserve on the word *residence*. He may mean to include under that idea the removal of his family; for I believe he removed himself, before his family did, to Philadelphia. But no act of mine gave commencement to his salary before he so far took up his abode in Philadelphia as to be sufficiently in readiness for the duties of the office. As to the merits or demerits of his paper, they certainly concern me not. He and Fenno are rivals for the public favor. The one courts them by flattery, the other by censure, and I believe it will be admitted that the one has been as servile as the other severe. But is not the dignity and even decency of government committed, when one of its principal ministers enlists himself as an anonymous writer or paragraphist for either the one or the other of them? No government ought to be without censors; and where the press is free, no one ever will. If virtuous, it need not fear the fair operation of attack and defense. Nature has given to man no other means of sifting out the truth, either in religion, law, or politics. I think it as honorable to the government neither to know, nor notice, its sycophants or censors as it would be undignified and criminal to pamper the former and persecute the latter. So much for the past, a word now of the future.

When I came into this office, it was with a resolution to retire from it as soon as I could with decency. It pretty early appeared to me that the proper moment would be the first of those epochs at which the Constitution seems to have contemplated a periodical change or renewal of the public servants. In this I was confirmed by your resolution respecting the same period; from which, however, I am happy in hoping you have departed. I look to that period with the longing of a wave-worn mariner, who has at length the land in view, and shall count the days and hours which still lie between me and it. In the meanwhile, my main object will be to wind up the business of my office, avoiding as much as possible all new enterprise. With the affairs of the legislature, as I never did intermeddle, so I certainly shall not now begin. I am more desirous to predispose everything for the repose to which I am withdrawing than expose it to be disturbed by newspaper contests. If these however cannot be avoided altogether, yet a regard for your quiet will be a sufficient motive for my deferring it till I become merely a private citizen, when the propriety or impropriety of what I may say or do may fall on myself alone. I may then, too, avoid the charge of misapplying that time which now, belonging to those who employ me, should be wholly devoted to their service. If my own justification, or the interests of the Republic shall require it, I reserve to myself the right of then appealing to my country, subscribing my name to whatever I write, and using with freedom and truth the facts and names necessary to place the cause in its just form before that tribunal. To a thorough disregard of the honors and emoluments of office, I join as great a value for the esteem of my countrymen, and conscious of having merited it by an integrity which cannot be reproached, and by an enthusiastic devotion to their rights and liberty, I will not suffer my retirement to be clouded by the slanders of a man whose history, from the moment at which history can stoop to notice him, is a tissue of machinations against the liberty of the country which has not only received and given him bread but heaped its honors on his head. Still, however, I repeat the hope that it will not be necessary to make such an appeal. Though little known to the people of America, I believe, that as far as I am known, it is not as an enemy to the Republic, nor an intriguer against it, nor a waster of its revenue, nor prostitutor of it to the purposes of corruption, as the "American" represents me; and I confide that yourself are satisfied that as to dissensions in the newspapers, not a syllable of them has ever proceeded from me, and that no cabals or intrigues of mine have produced those in the legislature, and I hope I may promise both to you and myself that none will receive aliment from me during the short space I have to remain in office, which will find ample employment in closing the present business of the department.

Observing that letters written at Mount Vernon on the Monday, and arriving at Richmond on the Wednesday, reach me on Saturday, I have now the honor to mention that the 22d instant will be the last of our post days that I shall be here, and consequently that no letter from you after the 17th will find me here. Soon after that I shall have the honor of receiving at Mount Vernon your orders for Philadelphia, and of there also delivering you the little matter which occurs to me as proper for the opening of Congress, exclusive of what has been recommended in former speeches, and not yet acted on. In the meantime and ever I am, with great and sincere affection and respect, dear sir, your most obedient and most humble servant.

MEMORANDUM
WRITTEN AS
SECRETARY OF STATE

October 1, 1792

This morning, at Mount Vernon, I had the following conversation with the president. He opened it by expressing his regret at the resolution in which I appeared so fixed, in the letter I had written him, of retiring from public affairs. He said that he should be extremely sorry that I should do it, as long as he was in office, and that he could not see where he should find another character to fill my office; that, as yet, he was quite undecided whether to retire in March or not. His inclinations led him strongly to do it. Nobody disliked more the ceremonies of his office, and he had not the least taste or gratification in the execution of its functions. That he was happy at home alone, and that his presence there was now peculiarly called for by the situation of Major Washington, whom he thought irrecoverable, and should he get well, he would remove into another part of the country, which might better agree with him. That he did not believe his presence necessary; that there were other characters who would do the business as well or better. Still, however, if his aid was thought necessary to save the cause to which he had devoted his life principally, he would make the sacrifice of a longer continuance. That he therefore reserved himself for future decision, as his declaration would be in time if made a month before the day of election. He had desired Mr. Lear to find out from conversation, without appearing to make the inquiry, whether any other person would be desired by anybody. He had informed him he judged from conversations that it was the universal desire he should continue, and he believed that those who expressed a doubt of his continuance did it in the language of apprehension, and not of desire. But this, says he, is only from the North; it may be very different in the South. I thought this meant as an opening to me to say what was the sentiment in the South, from which quarter I came. I told him that as far as I knew, there was but one voice there, which was for his continuance. That as to myself, I had ever preferred the pursuits of private life to those of public, which had nothing in them agreeable to me. I explained to him the circumstances of the war which had first called me into public life, and those following the war, which had called me from a retirement on which I had determined. That I had constantly kept my eye on my own home, and could no longer refrain from returning to it. As to himself, his presence was important; that he was the only man in the United States who possessed the confidence of the whole; that government was founded in opinion and confidence, and that the longer he remained, the stronger would become the habits of the people in submitting to the government, and in thinking it a thing to be maintained; that there was no other person who would be thought anything more than the head of a party. He then expressed his concern at the difference which he found to subsist between the secretary of the treasury and myself, of which he said he had not been aware. He knew, indeed, that there was a marked difference in our political senti-ments, but he had never suspected it had gone so far in produc-ing a personal difference, and he wished he could be the mediator to put an end to it. That he thought it important to preserve the check of my opinions in the administration, in order to keep things in their proper channel, and prevent them from going too far. That as to the idea of transforming this government into a monarchy, he did not believe there were ten men in the United States whose opinions were worth attention who entertained such a thought. I told him there were many more than he imagined. I recalled to his memory a dispute at his own table, a little before we left Philadelphia, between General Schuyler on one side and Pinckney and myself on the other, wherein the former maintained the position that hereditary descent was as likely to produce good magistrates as election. I told him that though the people were sound, there were a numerous sect who had monarchy in contemplation; that the secretary of the treasury was one of these. That I had heard him say that this Constitution was a shilly-shally thing, of mere milk and water, which could not last, and was only good as a step to something better. That when we reflected, that he had endeavored in the Convention to make an English constitution of it; and when failing in that, we saw all his measures tending to bring it to the same thing, it was natural for us to be jealous; and particularly, when we saw that these measures had established corruption in the legislature, where there was a squadron devoted to the nod of the Treasury, doing whatever he had directed, and ready to do what he should direct. That if the equilibrium of the three great bodies, legislative, executive, and judiciary, could be preserved, if the legislature could be kept independent, I should never fear the result of such a government; but that I could not but be uneasy when I saw that the executive had swallowed up the legislative branch. He said that as to that interested spirit in the legislature, it was what could not be avoided in any government, unless we were to exclude particular descriptions of men, such as the holders of the funds, from all office. I told him there was great difference between the little accidental schemes of self-interest, which would take place in every body of men and influence their votes, and a regular system for forming a corps of interested persons, who should be steadily at the orders of the Treasury. He touched on the merits of the funding system, observed there was a difference of opinion about it, some thinking it very bad, others very good; that experience was the only criterion of right which he knew, and this alone would decide which opinion was right. That for himself, he had seen our affairs desperate and our credit lost, and that this was in a sudden and extraordinary degree raised to the highest pitch. I told him all that was ever necessary to establish our credit was an efficient government and an honest one, declaring it would sacredly pay our debts, laying taxes for this purpose, and applying them to it. I avoided going further into the subject. He finished by another exhortation to me not to decide too positively on retirement, and here we were called to breakfast.

LETTER TO PRESIDENT GEORGE WASHINGTON

Philadelphia, July 31, 1793

Dear Sir:

When you did me the honor of appointing me to the office I now hold, I engaged in it without a view of continuing any length of time, and I pretty early concluded on the close of the first four years of our Republic as a proper period for withdrawing; which I had the honor of communicating to you. When the period, however, arrived, circumstances had arisen, which, in the opinion of some of my friends, rendered it proper to postpone my purpose for awhile. These circumstances have now ceased in such a degree as to leave me free to think again of a day on which I may withdraw without its exciting disadvantageous opinions or conjectures of any kind. The close of the present quarter seems to be a convenient period, because the quarterly accounts of the domestic department are then settled of course, and by that time, also, I may hope to receive from abroad the materials for bringing up the foreign account to the end of its third year. At the close, therefore, of the ensuing month of September, I shall beg leave to retire to scenes of greater tranquillity, from those which I am every day more and more convinced that neither my talents, tone of mind, nor time of life fit me. I have thought it my duty to mention the matter thus early, that there may be time for the arrival of a successor, from any part of the Union from which you may think proper to call one. That you may find one more able to lighten the burden of your labors, I most sincerely wish; for no man living more sincerely wishes that your administration could be rendered as pleasant to yourself as it is useful and necessary to our country, nor feels for you a more rational or cordial attachment and respect than, dear sir, your most obedient and most humble servant.

MEMORANDUM
WRITTEN AS
SECRETARY OF STATE

August 2, 1793

Met again. Hamilton spoke again three-quarters of an hour. I answered on these topics. *Object of the appeal*—The democratic society; this the great circumstance of alarm; afraid it would extend its connections over the continent; chiefly meant for the local object of the ensuing election of governor. If left alone, would die away after that is over. If opposed, if proscribed, would give it importance and vigor; would give it a new object, and multitudes would join it merely to assert the right of voluntary associations. That the measure was calculated to make the president assume the station of the head of a party, instead of the head of the nation. *Plan of the appeal*—To consist of *facts* and the *decisions* of the president. As to facts we are agreed; but as to decisions, there have been great differences of opinion among us. Sometimes as many opinions as persons. This proves there will be ground to attack the decisions. Genet will appeal also; it will become a contest between the president and Genet—anonymous writers—will be same difference of opinion in *public,* as in our cabinet—will be same difference in *Congress,* for it must be laid before them—would, therefore, work very unpleasantly *at home.* How would it work *abroad?* France—unkind—after such proofs of her friendship, should rely on that friendship, and her justice. Why appeal to the world? Friendly nations always negotiate little differences in private. Never appeal to the world, but when they appeal to the sword. Confederacy of Pilnitz was to overthrow the government of France. The interference of France to disturb other governments and excite insurrections was a measure of reprisal.

Yet these princes have been able to make it believed to be the system of France. Colonel Hamilton supposes Mr. Genet's proceedings here are in pursuance of that system; and we are so to declare it to the world, and to add our testimony to this base calumny of the princes. What a triumph to them to be backed by our testimony. What a fatal stroke at the cause of liberty; *et tu Brute*. We indispose the French government, and they will retract their offer of the treaty of commerce. The president manifestly inclined to the appeal to the people.* Knox, in a foolish, incoherent sort of a speech, introduced the pasquinade lately printed, called the "Funeral of George W——n, and James W——n, King and Judge, etc.," where the president was placed on a guillotine. The president was much inflamed; got into one of those passions when he cannot command himself; ran on much on the personal abuse which had been bestowed on him; defied any man on earth to produce one single act of his since he had been in the government which was not done on the purest motives; that he had never repented but once the having slipped the moment of resigning his office, and that was every moment since; that *by God* he had rather be in his grave than in his present situation; that he had rather be on his farm than to be made *emperor of the world;* and yet that they were charging him with wanting to be a king. That *that rascal Freneau* sent him three of his papers every day, as if he thought he would become the distributor of his papers; that he could see in this nothing but an impudent design to insult him: he ended in this high tone. There was a pause. Some difficulty in resuming our question; it was, however, after a little while, presented again, and he said there seemed to be no necessity for deciding it now;

*He said that Mr. Morris, taking a family dinner with him the other day, went largely, and of his own accord, into this subject; advised this appeal, and promised, if the president adopted it, that he would support it himself, and engage for all his connections. The president repeated this twice, and with an air of importance. Now, Mr. Morris has no family connections: he engaged then for his political friends. This shows that the president has not confidence enough in the virtue and good sense of mankind to confide in a government bottomed on them, and thinks other props necessary.

the propositions before agreed on might be put into a train of execution, and perhaps events would show whether the appeal would be necessary or not. He desired we would meet at my office the next day, to consider what should be done with the vessels armed in our ports by Mr. Genet, and their prizes.

MEMORANDUM
WRITTEN AS
SECRETARY OF STATE

August 6, 1793

The president calls on me at my house in the country, and introduces my letter of July 31, announcing that I should resign at the close of the next month. He again expressed his repentance at not having resigned himself, and how much it was increased by seeing that he was to be deserted by those on whose aid he had counted; that he did not know where he should look to find characters to fill up the offices; that mere talents did not suffice for the Department of State, but it required a person conversant in foreign affairs, perhaps acquainted with foreign courts; that without this, the best talents would be awkward and at a loss. He told me that Colonel Hamilton had three or four weeks ago written to him, informing him that private as well as public reasons had brought him to the determination to retire, and that he should do it towards the close of the next session. He said he had often before intimated dispositions to resign, but never as decisively before; that he supposed he had fixed on the latter part of next session, to give an opportunity to Congress to examine into his conduct; that our going out at times so different increased his difficulty; for if he had both places to fill at once, he might consult both the particular talents and geographical situation of our successors. He expressed great apprehensions at the fermentation which seemed to be working in the mind of the public; that many descriptions of persons, actuated by different causes, appeared to be uniting; what it would end in he knew not; a new Congress was to assemble, more numerous, perhaps of a different spirit; the first expressions of their sentiments would be important; if I would only stay to the end of that, it would relieve him considerably.

I expressed to him my excessive repugnance to public life, the particular uneasiness of my situation in this place, where the laws of society oblige me always to move exactly in the circle which I know to bear me peculiar hatred; that is to say, the wealthy aristocrats, the merchants connected closely with England, the new created paper fortunes; that thus surrounded, my words were caught, multiplied, misconstrued, and even fabricated and spread abroad to my injury; that he saw also that there was such an opposition of views between myself and another part of the administration as to render it peculiarly unpleasing and to destroy the necessary harmony. Without knowing the views of what is called the republican party here, or having any communication with them, I could undertake to assure him, from my intimacy with that party in the late Congress, that there was not a view in the Republican party, as spread over the United States, which went to the frame of the government; that I believed the next Congress would attempt nothing material, but to render their own body independent; that that party were firm in their dispositions to support the government; that the maneuvers of Mr. Genet might produce some little embarrassment, but that he would be abandoned by the Republicans the moment they knew the nature of his conduct; and on the whole, no crisis existed which threatened anything.

He said he believed the views of the Republican party were perfectly pure, but when men put a machine into motion, it is impossible for them to stop it exactly where they would choose, or to say where it will stop. That the Constitution we have is an excellent one, if we can keep it where it is; that it was, indeed, supposed there was a party disposed to change it into a monarchical form, but that he could conscientiously declare there was not a man in the United States who would set his face more decidedly against it than himself. Here I interrupted him, by saying, "No rational man in the United States suspects you of any other disposition; but there does not pass a week in which we cannot prove declarations dropping from the monarchical party that our government is good for nothing, is a milk and water thing which cannot support itself, we must knock it down, and set up something of more energy." He said if that was the case, he thought it a proof of their insanity, for that the republican spirit of the Union was so manifest and so solid that it was astonishing how anyone could expect to move it.

He returned to the difficulty of naming my successor; he said Mr. Madison would be his first choice, but that he had always expressed to him such a decision against public office that he could not expect he would undertake it. Mr. Jay would prefer his present office. He said that Mr. Jay had a great opinion of the talents of Mr. King; that there was also Mr. Smith of South Carolina, and E. Rutledge; but he observed, that name whom he would, some objections would be made, some would be called speculators, some one thing, some another; and he asked me to mention any characters occurring to me. I asked him if Governor Johnson of Maryland had occurred to him. He said he had; that he was a man of great good sense, an honest man, and, he believed, clear of speculations; but this, says he, is an instance of what I was observing; with all these qualifications, Governor Johnson, from a want of familiarity with foreign affairs, would be in them like a fish out of water; everything would be new to him, and he awkward in everything. I confessed to him that I had considered Johnson rather as fit for the Treasury Department. Yes, says he, for that he would be the fittest appointment that could be made; he is a man acquainted with figures, and having as good a knowledge of the resources of this country as any man. I asked him if Chancellor Livingston had occurred to him? He said yes; but he was from New York, and to appoint him while Hamilton was in, and before it should be known he was going out, would excite a newspaper conflagration, as the ultimate arrangement would not be known. He said McLurg had occurred to him as a man of first-rate abilities, but it is said that he is a speculator. He asked me what sort of a man Wolcott was. I told him I knew nothing of him myself; I had heard him characterized as a cunning man. I asked him whether some person could not take my office *par interim,* till he should make an appointment, as Mr. Randolph, for instance. Yes, says he, but there you would raise the expectation of keeping it, and I do not know that he is fit for it, nor what is thought of Mr. Randolph. I avoided noticing the last observation, and he put the question to me directly. I then told him I went into society so little as to be unable to answer it: I knew that the embarrassments in his private affairs had obliged him to use expedients, which had injured him with the merchants and shopkeepers, and affected his character of independence; that these embarrassments were serious, and not likely to cease soon. He said if I would only stay in till the end of another quarter (the last of December) it would get us through the difficulties of this year, and he was satisfied that the affairs of Europe would be settled with this campaign; for that either France would be overwhelmed by it, or the confederacy would give up the contest. By that time, too, Congress will have manifested its character and view. I told him that I had set my private affairs in motion in a line which had powerfully called for my presence the last spring, and that they had suffered immensely from my not going home; that I had now calculated them to my return in the fall, and to fail in going then would be the loss of another year, and prejudicial beyond measure. I asked him whether he could not name Governor Johnson to my office, under an express arrangement that at the close of the session he should take that of the Treasury. He said that men never chose to descend; that being once in a higher department, he would not like to go into a lower one. He asked me whether I could not arrange my affairs by going home. I told him I did not think the public business would admit of it; that there never was a day now in which the absence of the secretary of state would not be inconvenient to the public. And he concluded by desiring that I would take two or three days to consider whether I could not stay in till the end of another quarter, for that like a man going to the gallows, he was willing to put it off as long as he could; but if I persisted, he must then look about him and make up his mind to do the best he could; and so he took leave.

MEMORANDUM
WRITTEN AS
SECRETARY OF STATE

August 20, 1793

We met at the president's to examine by paragraphs the draft of a letter I had prepared to Gouverneur Morris on the conduct of Mr. Genet. There was no difference of opinion on any part of it, except on this expression: "An attempt to embroil both, to add still another nation to the enemies of his country, and to draw on both a reproach which it is hoped will never stain the history of either, that of *liberty warring on herself.*" Hamilton moved to strike out these words, that of "liberty warring on herself." He urged generally that it would give offense to the combined powers; that it amounted to a declaration that they were warring on liberty; that we were not called on to declare that the cause of France was that of liberty; that he had at first been with them with all his heart, but that he had long since left them, and was not for encouraging the idea here that the cause of France was the cause of liberty in general, or could have either connection or influence in our affairs. Knox, according to custom, jumped plump into all his opinions. The president, with a good deal of positiveness, declared in favor of the expression; that he considered the pursuit of France to be that of liberty, however they might sometimes fail of the best means of obtaining it; that he had never at any time entertained a doubt of their ultimate success, if they hung well together; and that as to their dissensions, there were such contradictory accounts given that no one could tell what to believe. I observed that it had been supposed among us all along that the present letter might become public; that we had therefore three parties to attend to—(1) France; (2) her enemies; (3) the people of the United States; that as to the enemies of France, it ought not to offend them, because the passage objected to only spoke of an attempt to make the United States, a *free nation,* war on France, a *free nation,* which would be liberty warring against liberty; that as to France, we were taking so harsh a measure (desiring her to recall her minister) that a precedent for it could scarcely be found; that we knew that minister would represent to his government that our executive was hostile to liberty, leaning to monarchy, and would endeavor to parry the charges on himself by rendering suspicions the source from which they flowed; that, therefore, it was essential to satisfy France, not only of our friendship to her, but our attachment to the general cause of liberty, and to hers in particular; that as to the people of the United States, we knew there were suspicions abroad that the executive, in some of its parts, was tainted with a hankering after monarchy, an indisposition towards liberty, and towards the French cause; and that it was important, by an explicit declaration, to remove these suspicions, and restore the confidence of the people in their government. Randolph opposed the passage on nearly the same ground with Hamilton. He added that he thought it had been agreed that this correspondence should contain no expressions which could give offense to either party. I replied that it had been my opinion in the beginning of the correspondence that while we were censuring the conduct of the French minister, we should make the most cordial declarations of friendship to them; that in the first letter or two of the correspondence, I had inserted expressions of that kind, but that himself and the other two gentlemen had struck them out; that I thereupon conformed to their opinions in my subsequent letters, and had carefully avoided the insertion of a single term of friendship to the French nation, and the letters were as dry and husky as if written between the generals of two enemy nations; that on the present occasion, however, it had been agreed that such expressions ought to be inserted in the letter now under consideration, and I had accordingly charged it pretty well with them; that I had further thought it essential to satisfy the French and our own citizens of the light in which we viewed their cause, and of our fellow feeling for the general cause of liberty, and had ventured only four words on the subject; that there was not from beginning to end of the letter one other expression or word in favor of liberty, and I should think it singular, at least, if the single passage of that character should be struck out.

The president again spoke. He came into the idea that attention was due to the two parties who had been mentioned, France and the United States; that as to the former, thinking it certain their affairs would issue in a government of some sort—of considerable freedom—it was the only nation with whom our relations could be counted on; that as to the United States, there could be no doubt of their universal attachment to the cause of France, and of the solidity of their republicanism. He declared his strong attachment to the expression, but finally left it to us to accommodate. It was struck out, of course, and the expressions of affection in the context were a good deal taken down.

LETTER TO PRESIDENT
GEORGE WASHINGTON

Philadelphia, December 31, 1793

Dear Sir:

Having had the honor of communicating to you in my letter of the last of July, my purpose of returning from the office of secretary of state, at the end of the month of September, you were pleased, for particular reasons, to wish its postponement to the close of the year. That term being now arrived, and my propensities to retirement becoming daily more and more irresistible, I now take the liberty of resigning the office into your hands. Be pleased to accept with it my sincere thanks for all the indulgences which you have been so good as to exercise towards me in the discharge of its duties. Conscious that my need of them has been great, I have still ever found them greater, without any other claim on my part, than a firm pursuit of what has appeared to me to be right, and a thorough disdain of all means which were not as open and honorable as their object was pure. I carry into my retirement a lively sense of your goodness, and shall continue gratefully to remember it. With very sincere prayers for your life, health and tranquility, I pray you to accept the homage of the great and constant respect and attachment with which I have the honor to be, dear sir, your most obedient and most humble servant.

LETTER TO
JAMES MADISON

Monticello, January 1, 1797

Dear Sir:

Yours of December the 19th is safely received. I never entertained a doubt of the event of the election. I knew that the eastern troops were trained in the schools of their town meetings to sacrifice little differences of opinion to the solid advantages of operating in phalanx, and that the more free and moral agency of the other states would fully supply their deficiency. I had no expectation, indeed, that the vote would have approached so near an equality. It is difficult to obtain full credit to declarations of disinclination to honors, and most so with those who still remain in the world. But never was there a more solid unwillingness, founded on rigorous calculation, formed in the mind of any man, short of peremptory refusal. No arguments, therefore, were necessary to reconcile me to a relinquishment of the first office, or acceptance of the second. No motive could have induced me to undertake the first but that of putting our vessel upon her republican tack, and preventing her being driven too far to leeward of her true principles. And the second is the only office in the world about which I cannot decide in my own mind whether I had rather have it or not have it. Pride does not enter into the estimate. For I think with the Romans of old, that the general of today should be a common soldier tomorrow, if necessary. But as to Mr. Adams, particularly, I could have no feelings which would revolt at being placed in a secondary station to him. I am his junior in life, I was his junior in Congress, his junior in the diplomatic line, and lately his junior in our civil government. I had written him the enclosed letter before the receipt of yours. I had intended it for some time, but had put it off, from time to time, from the discouragement of despair to make him believe me sincere. As the information by the last post does not make it necessary to change anything in the letter, I enclose it open for your perusal, as well that you may be possessed of the true state of dispositions between us, as that if there be any circumstance which might render its delivery ineligible, you may return it to me. If Mr. Adams could be induced to administer the government on its true principles, quitting his bias for an English constitution, it would be worthy consideration whether it would not for the public good to come to a good understanding with him as to his future elections. He is the only sure barrier against Hamilton's getting in. . . .

The *Political Progress* is a work of value and of a singular complexion. The author's eye seems to be a natural achromatic, divesting every object of the glare of color. The former work of the same title possessed the same kind of merit. They disgust one, indeed, by opening to his view the ulcerated state of the human mind. But to cure an ulcer you must go to the bottom of it, which no author does more radically than this. The reflections into which it leads us are not very flattering to the human species. In the whole animal kingdom I recollect no family but man steadily and systematically employed in the destruction of itself. Nor does what is called civilization produce any other effect than to teach him to pursue the principle of the *bellum omnium in omnia* on a greater scale and, instead of the little contest between tribe and tribe, to comprehend all the quarters of the earth in the same work of destruction. If to this we add that as to other animals, the lions and tigers are mere lambs compared with man as a destroyer, we must conclude that nature has been able to find in man alone a sufficient barrier against the too great multiplication of other animals and of man himself, an equilibrating power against the fecundity of generation. While in making these observations my situation points my attention to the warfare of man in the physical world, yours may perhaps present him as equally warring in the moral one. Adieu. Yours affectionately.

LETTER TO
JAMES SULLIVAN

Dear Sir:

I have many acknowledgments to make for the friendly anxiety you are pleased to express in your letter of January 12 for my undertaking the office to which I have been elected. The idea that I would accept the office of president, but not that of vice president of the United States, had not its origin with me. I never thought of questioning the free exercise of the right of my fellow citizens to marshal those whom they call into their service according to their fitness, nor ever presumed that they were not the best judges of that. Had I indulged a wish in what manner they should dispose of me, it would precisely have coincided with what they have done. Neither the splendor, nor the power, nor the difficulties, nor the fame or defamation, as may happen, attached to the first magistracy, have any attractions for me. The helm of a free government is always arduous, and never was ours moreso than at a moment when two friendly people[s] are like to be committed in war by the ill temper of their administrations. I am so much attached to my domestic situation that I would not have wished to leave it at all. However, if I am to be called from it, the shortest absences and most tranquil station suit me best. I value highly, indeed, the part my fellow citizens gave me in their late vote, as an evidence of their esteem, and I am happy in the information you are so kind as to give, that many in the eastern quarter entertain the same sentiment.

Where a Constitution, like ours, wears a mixed aspect of monarchy and republicanism, its citizens will naturally divide into two classes of sentiment, according as their tone of body or mind; their habits, connections, and callings induce them to wish to strengthen either the monarchial or the republican features of the Constitution. Some will consider it as an elective monarchy, which had better be made hereditary, and therefore endeavor to lead towards that all the forms and principles of its administration. Others will view it as an energetic republic, turning in all its points on the pivot of free and frequent elections. The great body of our native citizens are unquestionably of the republican sentiment. Foreign education, and foreign connections of interest, have produced some exceptions in every part of the Union, North and South, and perhaps other circumstances in your quarter, better known to you, may have thrown into the scale of exceptions a greater number of the rich. Still there, I believe, and here, I am sure, the great mass is republican. Nor do any of the forms in which the public disposition has been pronounced in the last half dozen years evince the contrary. All of them, when traced to their true source, have only been evidences of the preponderant popularity of a particular great character. That influence once withdrawn, and our countrymen left to the operation of their own unbiased good sense, I have no doubt we shall see a pretty rapid return of general harmony, and our citizens moving in phalanx in the paths of regular liberty, order, and a sacrosanct adherence to the Constitution. Thus I think it will be, if war with France can be avoided. But if that untoward event comes athwart us in our present point of deviation, nobody, I believe, can foresee into what port it will drive us.

I am always glad of an opportunity of inquiring after my most ancient and respected friend Mr. Samuel Adams. His principles, founded on the immovable basis of equal right and reason, have continued pure and unchanged. Permit me to place here my sincere veneration for him, and wishes for his health and happiness; and to assure yourself of the sentiments of esteem and respect with which I am, dear sir, your most obedient and most humble servant.

LETTER TO
ELBRIDGE GERRY

Philadelphia, May 13, 1797

My dear Friend:

Your favor of the 4th instant came to hand yesterday. That of the 4th of April, with the one for Monroe, has never been received. The first, of March 27, did not reach me till April 21, when I was within a few days of setting out for this place, and I put off acknowledging it till I should come here. I entirely commend your dispositions towards Mr. Adams, knowing his worth as intimately and esteeming it as much as anyone, and acknowledging the preference of his claims, if any I could have had, to the high office conferred on him. But in truth, I had neither claims nor wishes on the subject, though I know it will be difficult to obtain belief of this. When I retired from this place and the office of secretary of state, it was in the firmest contemplation of never more returning here. There had indeed been suggestions in the public papers that I was looking towards a succession to the president's chair, but feeling a consciousness of their falsehood, and observing that the suggestions came from hostile quarters, I considered them as intended merely to excite public odium against me. I never in my life exchanged a word with any person on the subject till I found my name brought forward generally, in competition with that of Mr. Adams. Those with whom I then communicated could say, if it were necessary, whether I met the call with desire, or even with a ready acquiescence, and whether from the moment of my first acquiescence I did not devoutly pray that the very thing might happen which has happened. The second office of the government is honorable and easy, the first is but a splendid misery.

You express apprehensions that stratagems will be used to

produce a misunderstanding between the President and myself. Though not a word having this tendency has ever been hazarded to me by anyone, yet I consider as a certainty that nothing will be left untried to alienate him from me. These machinations will proceed from the Hamiltonians by whom he is surrounded, and who are only a little less hostile to him than to me. It cannot but damp the pleasure of cordiality when we suspect that it is suspected. I cannot help thinking that it is impossible for Mr. Adams to believe that the state of my mind is what it really is; that he may think I view him as an obstacle in my way. I have no supernatural power to impress truth on the mind of another, nor he any to discover that the estimate which he may form, on a just view of the human mind as generally constituted, may not be just in its application to a special constitution. This may be a source of private uneasiness to us; I honestly confess that it is so to me at this time. But neither of us is capable of letting it have effect on our public duties. Those who may endeavor to separate us are probably excited by the fear that I might have influence on the executive councils; but when they shall know that I consider my office as constitutionally confined to legislative functions, and that I could not take any part whatever in executive consultations, even were it proposed, their fears may perhaps subside, and their object he found not worth a machination.

I do sincerely wish with you that we could take our stand on a ground perfectly neutral and independent towards all nations. It has been my constant object through my public life; and with respect to the English and French, particularly, I have too often expressed to the former my wishes, and made to them propositions verbally and in writing, officially and privately, to official and private characters, for them to doubt of my views, if they would be content with equality. Of this they are in possession of several written and formal proofs in my own handwriting. But they have wished a monopoly of commerce and influence with us; and they have in fact obtained it. When we take notice that theirs is the workshop to which we go for all we want; that with them center either immediately or ultimately all the labors of our hands and lands; that to them belongs either openly or secretly the great mass of our navigation; that even the factorage of their affairs here is kept to themselves by factitious citizenships; that these foreign and false citizens now constitute the great body of what are called our merchants, fill our seaports, are planted in every little town and district of the interior country, sway everything in the former places by their own votes, and those of their dependants, in the latter, by their insinuations and the influence of their ledgers; that they are advancing fast to a monopoly of our banks and public funds, and thereby placing our public finances under their control; that they have in their alliance the most influential characters in and out of office; when they have shown that by all these bearings on the different branches of the government, they can force it to proceed in whatever direction they dictate, and bend the interests of this country entirely to the will of another; when all this, I say, is attended to, it is impossible for us to say we stand on independent ground, impossible for a free mind not to see and to groan under the bondage in which it is bound. If anything after this could excite surprise, it would be that they have been able so far to throw dust in the eyes of our own citizens, as to fix on those who wish merely to recover self-government the charge of subserving one foreign influence, because they resist submission to another. But they possess our printing presses, a powerful engine in their government of us. At this very moment, they would have drawn us into a war on the side of England, had it not been for the failure of her bank. Such was their open and loud cry, and that of their gazettes till this event. After plunging us in all the broils of the European nations, there would remain but one act to close our tragedy, that is, to break up our Union; and even this they have ventured seriously and solemnly to propose and maintain by arguments in a Connecticut paper. I have been happy, however, in believing, from the stifling of this effort, that that dose was found too strong, and excited as much repugnance there as it did horror in other parts of our country, and that whatever follies we may be led into as to foreign nations, we shall never give up our Union, the last anchor of our hope, and that alone which is to prevent this heavenly country from becoming an arena of gladiators. Much as I abhor war, and view it as the greatest scourge of mankind, and anxiously as I wish to keep out of the broils of Europe, I would yet go with my brethren into these rather than separate from them. But I hope we may still keep clear of them, notwithstanding our present thralldom, and that time may be given us to reflect on the awful crisis we have passed through, and to find some means of shielding ourselves in future from foreign influence, political, commercial, or in whatever other form it may be attempted. I can scarcely withhold myself from joining in the wish of Silas Deane that there were an ocean of fire between us and the old world.

A perfect confidence that you are as much attached to peace and union as myself, that you equally prize independence of all nations, and the blessings of self-government, has induced me freely to unbosom myself to you, and let you see the light in which I have viewed what has been passing among us from the beginning of the war. And I shall be happy, at all times, in an intercommunication of sentiments with you, believing that the dispositions of the different parts of our country have been considerably misrepresented and misunderstood in each part, as to the other, and that nothing but good can result from an exchange of information and opinions between those whose circumstances and morals admit no doubt of the integrity of their views.

I remain, with constant and sincere esteem, dear sir, your affectionate friend and servant.

THE KENTUCKY
RESOLUTIONS

1798

I. *Resolved,* That the several states composing the United States of America are not united on the principle of unlimited submission to their general government; but that by compact under the style and title of a Constitution for the United States and of amendments thereto, they constituted a general government for special purposes, delegated to that government certain definite powers, reserving each state to itself, the residuary mass of right to their own self-government; and that whensoever the general government assumes undelegated powers, its acts are unauthoritative, void, and of no force: That to this compact each state acceded as a state, and is an integral party, its co-states forming, as to itself, the other party: That the government created by this compact was not made the exclusive or final judge of the extent of the powers delegated to itself; since that would have made its discretion, and not the Constitution, the measure of its powers; but that as in all other cases of compact among parties having no common judge, *each party has an equal right to judge for itself, as well as infractions as of the mode and measure of redress.*

II. *Resolved,* That the Constitution of the United States having delegated to Congress a power to punish treason, counterfeiting the securities and current coin of the United States, piracies and felonies committed on the high seas, and offenses against the laws of nations, and no other crimes whatever, and it being true as a general principle, and one of the amendments to the Constitution having also declared "that the powers not delegated to the United States by the Constitution, nor prohibited by it to the states, are reserved to the states respectively, or to the people," therefore also [the 1798 Sedition Act], as also the act passed by them on the 27th day of June, 1798, entitled "An Act to Punish Frauds Committed on the Bank of the United States" (and all other their acts which assume to create, define, or punish crimes other than those enumerated in the Constitution), are altogether void and of no force, and that the power to create, define, and punish such other crimes is reserved, and of right appertains solely and exclusively to the respective states, each within its own territory.

III. *Resolved,* That it is true as a general principle, and is also expressly declared by one of the amendments to the Constitution, that "the powers not delegated to the United States by the Constitution, nor prohibited by it to the states, are reserved to the states respectively or to the people"; and that no power over the freedom of religion, freedom of speech, or freedom of the press being delegated to the United States by the Constitution, nor prohibited by it to the states, all lawful powers respecting the same did of right remain, and were reserved to the states, or to the people: That thus was manifested their determination to retain to themselves the right of judging how far the licentiousness of speech and of the press may be abridged without lessening their useful freedom, and how far those abuses which cannot be separated from their use should be tolerated rather than the use be destroyed; and thus also they guarded against all abridgment by the United States of the freedom of religious opinions and exercises, and retained to themselves the right of protecting the same, as this state, by a law passed on the general demand of its citizens, had already protected them from all human restraint or interference: And that in addition to this general principle and express declaration, another and more special provision has been made by one of the amendments to the Constitution which expressly declares that "Congress shall make no law respecting an establishment of religion, or prohibiting the free exercise thereof, or abridging the freedom of speech, or of the press," thereby guarding in the same sentence, and under the same words, the freedom of religion, of speech, and of the press, insomuch that whatever violates either throws down the sanctuary which covers the others, and that libels, falsehoods, defamation equally with heresy and false religion, are withheld from the cognizance of federal tribunals. That therefore [the Sedition Act], which does abridge the freedom of the press, is not law, but is altogether void and of no effect.

IV. *Resolved,* That alien friends are under the jurisdiction and protection of the laws of the state wherein they are; that no power over them has been delegated to the United States, nor prohibited to the individual states distinct from their power over citizens; and it being true as a general principle, and one of the amendments to the Constitution having also declared that "the powers not delegated to the United States by the Constitution, nor prohibited by it to the states, are reserved to the states respectively, or to the people," the [1798 Alien Act], which assumes power over alien friends not delegated by the Constitution, is not law, but is altogether void and of no force.

V. *Resolved,* That in addition to the general principle, as well as the express declaration, that powers not delegated are reserved, another and more special provision inserted in the Constitution from abundant caution has declared, "that the migration or importation of such persons as any of the states now existing shall think proper to admit, shall not be prohibited by the Congress prior to the year 1808." That this commonwealth does admit the migration of alien friends described as the subject of the said act concerning aliens; that a provision against prohibiting their migration is a provision against all acts equivalent thereto, or it would be nugatory; that to remove them when migrated is equivalent to a prohibition of their migration, and is therefore contrary to the said provision of the Constitution, and void.

VI. *Resolved,* That the imprisonment of a person under the protection of the laws of this commonwealth on his failure to obey the simple order of the president to depart out of the United States, as is undertaken by the said act entitled "An Act Concerning Aliens," is contrary to the Constitution, one amendment to which has provided that "no person shall be deprived of liberty without due process of law," and that another having provided "that in all criminal prosecutions, the accused shall enjoy the right to a public trial by an impartial jury, to be informed of the nature and cause of the accusation, to be confronted with the witnesses against him, to have compulsory process for obtaining witnesses in his favor and to have the assistance of counsel for his defense," the same act undertaking to authorize the president to remove a person out of the United States who is under the protection of the law, on his own suspicion, without accusation, without jury, without public trial, without confrontation of the witnesses against him, without having witnesses in his favor, without defense, without counsel, is contrary to these provisions also of the Constitution, is therefore not law, but utterly void and of no force. That transferring the power of judging any person who is under the protection of the laws, from the courts to the president of the United States, as is undertaken by the same act concerning aliens, is against the article of the Constitution which provides that "the judicial power of the United States shall be vested in courts, the judges of which shall hold their offices during good behavior," and that the said act is void for that reason also; and it is further to be noted that this transfer of judiciary power is to that magistrate of the general government who already possesses all the executive, and a qualified negative in all the legislative powers.

VII. *Resolved,* That the construction applied by the general government (as is evinced by sundry of their proceedings) to those parts of the Constitution of the United States which delegate to Congress a power to lay and collect taxes, duties, imposts, and excises; to pay the debts, and provide for the common defense and general welfare of the United States, and to make all laws which shall be necessary and proper for carrying into execution the powers vested by the Constitution in the government of the United States, or any department thereof, goes to the destruction of all the limits prescribed to their power by the Constitution: That words meant by that instrument to be subsidiary only to the execution of the limited powers ought not to be so construed as themselves to give unlimited powers, nor a part so to be taken as to destroy the whole residue of the instrument: That the proceedings of the general government under color of these articles will be a fit and necessary subject for revisal and correction at a time of greater tranquillity, while those specified in the preceding resolutions call for immediate redress.

VIII. *Resolved,* That the preceding resolutions be transmitted to the senators and representatives in Congress from this commonwealth, who are hereby enjoined to present the same to their respective houses, and to use their best endeavors to procure, at the next session of Congress, a repeal of the aforesaid unconstitutional and obnoxious acts.

IX. *Resolved,* lastly, That the governor of this commonwealth be, and is hereby, authorized and requested to communicate the preceding resolutions to the legislatures of the several states, to assure them that this commonwealth considers union for specified national purposes, and particularly for those specified in their late federal compact, to be friendly to the peace, happiness, and prosperity of all the states: That faithful to that compact according to the plain intent and meaning in which it was understood and acceded to by the several parties, it is sincerely anxious for its preservation: That it does also believe, that to take from the states all the powers of self-government, and transfer them to a general and consolidated government, without regard to the special delegations and reservations solemnly agreed to in that compact, is not for the peace, happiness, or prosperity of these states: And that, therefore, this commonwealth is determined, as it doubts not its co-states are, tamely to submit to undelegated and consequently unlimited powers in no man or body of men on earth: That if the acts before specified should stand, these conclusions would flow from them: That the general government may place any act they think proper on the list of crimes and punish it themselves, whether enumerated or not enumerated by the Constitution as cognizable by them: That they may transfer its cognizance to the president or any other person, who may himself be the accuser, counsel, judge, and jury, whose suspicions may be the evidence, his order the sentence, his officer the executioner, and his breast the sole record of the transaction: That a very numerous and valuable description of the inhabitants of these states being by this precedent reduced as outlaws to the absolute dominion of one man, and the barrier of the Constitution thus swept away from us all, no rampart now remains against the passions and the powers of a majority of Congress, to protect from a like exportation or other more grievous punishment the minority of the same body, the legislatures, judges, governors, and counselors of the states, nor their other peaceable inhabitants who may venture to reclaim the constitutional rights and liberties of the state and people, or who for other causes, good or bad, may be obnoxious to the views or marked by the suspicions of the president, or be thought dangerous to his or their elections or other interests, public or personal: That the friendless alien has indeed been selected as the safest subject of a first experiment, but the citizen will soon follow, or rather has already followed, for already has a Sedition Act marked him as its prey: That these and successive acts of the same character, unless arrested on the threshold, may tend to drive these states into revolution and blood, and will furnish new calumnies against republican governments, and new pretexts for those who wish it to be believed that man cannot be governed but by a rod of iron: That it would be a dangerous delusion were a confidence in the men of our choice to silence our fears for the safety of our rights: That confidence is everywhere the parent of despotism; free government is founded in jealousy and not in confidence; it is jealousy and not confidence which prescribes limited Constitutions to bind down those whom we are obliged to trust with power: That our Constitution has accordingly fixed the limits to which and no further our confidence may go; and let the honest advocate of confidence read the Alien and Sedition Acts, and say if the Constitution has not been wise in fixing limits to the government it created, and whether we should be wise in destroying those limits; let him say what the government is if it be not a tyranny, which the men of our choice have conferred on the president, and the president of our choice has assented to and accepted over the friendly strangers, to whom the mild spirit of our country and its laws had pledged hospitality and protection: That the men of our choice have more respected the bare suspicions of the president than the solid rights of innocence, the claims of justification, the sacred force of truth, and the forms and substance of law and justice. In questions of power then let no more be heard of confidence in man, but bind him down from mischief by the claims of the Constitution. That this commonwealth does therefore call on its co-states for an expression of their sentiments on the acts concerning aliens, and for the punishment of certain crimes herein before specified, plainly declaring whether these acts are or are not authorized by the federal compact. And it doubts not that their sense will be so announced as to prove their attachment unaltered to limited government, whether general or particular, and that the rights and liberties of their co-states will be exposed to no dangers by remaining embarked on a common bottom with their own: That they will concur with this commonwealth in considering the said acts so palpably against the Constitution as to amount to an undisguised declaration, that the compact is not meant to be the measure of the powers of the general government, but that it will proceed in the exercise over these states of all powers whatsoever: That they will view this as seizing the rights of the states and consolidating them in the hands of the general government with a power assumed to bind the states (not merely in cases made federal) but in all cases whatsoever, by laws made, not with their consent, but by others against their consent: That this would be to surrender the form of government we have chosen, and to live under one deriving its powers from its own will, and not from our authority; and that the co-states, recurring to their natural right in cases not made federal, will concur in declaring these acts void and of no force, and will each unite with this commonwealth in requesting their repeal at the next session of Congress.

MEMORANDUM
WRITTEN AS
VICE PRESIDENT

February 15, 1798

I dined this day with Mr. Adams (the president). The company was large. After dinner I was sitting next to him, and our conversation was first on the enormous price of labor,* house rent, and other things. We both concurred in ascribing it chiefly to the floods of bank paper now afloat, and in condemning those institutions. We then got on the Constitution; and in the course of our conversation he said that no republic could ever last which had not a Senate, and a Senate deeply and strongly rooted, strong enough to bear up against all popular storms and passions; that he thought our Senate as well constituted as it could have been, being chosen by the legislatures; for if these could not support them, he did not know what could do it; that perhaps it might have been as well for them to be chosen by the state at large, as that would insure a choice of distinguished men, since none but such could be known to a whole people; that the only fault in our Senate was that it was not durable enough; that hitherto, it had behaved very well; however, he was afraid they would give way in the end. That as to trusting to a popular assembly for the preservation of our liberties, it was the merest chimera imaginable; they never had any rule of decision but their own will; that he would as lieve be again in the hands of our old committees of safety, who made the law and executed it at the same time; that it had been observed by some writer (I forget whom he named) that anarchy did more

*He observed that eight or ten years ago, he gave only $50 to a common laborer for his farm, finding him food and lodging. Now he gives $150, and even $200 to one.

mischief in one night than tyranny in an age; and that in modern times we might say, with truth, that in France, anarchy had done more harm in one night than all the despotism of their kings had ever done in twenty or thirty years. The point in which he views our Senate, as the colossus of the Constitution, serves as a key to the politics of the Senate, who are two-thirds of them in his sentiments, and accounts for the bold line of conduct they pursue.

LETTER TO
JAMES MADISON

Philadelphia, April 6, 1798

Dear Sir:

So much of the communications from our envoys has got abroad, and so partially, that there can now be no ground for reconsideration with the Senate. I may therefore, consistently with duty, do what every member of the body is doing. Still, I would rather you would use the communication with reserve till you see the whole papers. The first impressions from them are very disagreeable and confused. Reflection, however, and analysis resolve them into this. Mr. Adams's speech to Congress in May is deemed such a national affront that no explanation on other topics can be entered on till that, as a preliminary, is wiped away by humiliating disavowals or acknowledgments. This working hard with our envoys, and indeed seeming impracticable for want of that sort of authority, submission to a heavy amendment (upwards of a million sterling), was, at an after-meeting, suggested as an alternative, which might be admitted if proposed by us. These overtures had been through informal agents; and both the alternatives bringing the envoys to their *ne plus,* they resolve to have no more communication through unofficial characters, but to address a letter directly to the government, to bring forward their pretensions. This letter had not yet, however, been prepared. There were, interwoven with these overtures, some base propositions on the part of Talleyrand, through one of his agents, to sell his interest and influence with the Directory towards soothing difficulties with them, in consideration of a large sum (fifty thousand pounds sterling); and the arguments to which his agent resorted to induce compliance with this demand were very unworthy of a great nation (could they be imputed to them), and calculated to excite disgust and indignation in Americans generally, and alienation in the republicans particularly, whom they so far mistake as to presume an attachment to France and hatred to the federal party, and not the love of their country, to be their first passion. No difficulty was expressed towards an adjustment of all differences and misunderstandings, or even ultimately a payment for spoliations, if the insult from our executive should be first wiped away. Observe that I state all this from only a single hearing of the papers, and therefore it may not be rigorously correct. The little slanderous imputation before mentioned has been the bait which hurried the opposite party into this publication. The first impressions with the people will be disagreeable, but the last and permanent one will be that the speech in May is now the only obstacle to accommodation, and the real cause of war, if war takes place. And how much will be added to this by the speech of November is yet to be learned. It is evident, however, on reflection, that these papers do not offer one motive the more for our going to war. Yet such is their effect on the minds of wavering characters, that I fear that to wipe off the imputation of being French partisans, they will go over to the war measures so furiously pushed by the other party. It seems, indeed, as if they were afraid they should not be able to get into war till Great Britain shall be blown up, and the prudence of our countrymen from that circumstance, have influence enough to prevent it. The most artful misrepresentations of the contents of these papers were published yesterday, and produced such a shock in the republican mind as had never been seen since our independence. We are to dread the effects of this dismay till their fuller information. Adieu.

LETTER TO
JOHN TAYLOR

Monticello, November 26, 1798

Dear Sir:

We formerly had a debtor and creditor account of letters on farming; but the high price of tobacco, which is likely to continue for some short time, has tempted me to go entirely into that culture, and in the meantime, my farming schemes are in abeyance, and my farming fields at nurse against the time of my resuming them. But I owe you a political letter. Yet the infidelities of the post office and the circumstances of the times are against my writing fully and freely, whilst my own dispositions are as much against mysteries, innuendos and half-confidences. I know not which mortifies me most, that I should fear to write what I think, or my country bear such a state of things. Yet Lyon's judges, and a jury of all nations, are objects of national fear. We agree in all the essential ideas of your letter. We agree particularly in the necessity of some reform, and of some better security for civil liberty. But perhaps we do not see the existing circumstances in the same point of view. There are many consideration *dehors* of the state, which will occur to you without enumeration. I should not apprehend them, if all was sound within. But there is a most respectable part of our state who have been enveloped in the XYZ delusion, and who destroy our unanimity for the present moment. This disease of the imagination will pass over, because the patients are essentially republicans. Indeed, the doctor is now on his way to cure it, in the guise of a tax gatherer. But give time for the medicine to work, and for the repetition of stronger doses, which must be administered. The principle of the present majority is *excessive expense,* money enough to fill all their maws, or it will not be worth the risk of their supporting. They cannot borrow a dollar in Europe, or above two or three millions in America. This is not the fourth of the expenses of this year, unprovided for. Paper money would be perilous even to the paper men. Nothing then but excessive taxation can get us along; and this will carry reason and reflection to every man's door, and particularly in the hour of election.

I wish it were possible to obtain a single amendment to our Constitution. I would be willing to depend on that alone for the reduction of the administration of our government to the genuine principles of its Constitution; I mean an additional article, taking from the federal government the power of borrowing. I now deny their power of making paper money or anything else a legal tender. I know that to pay all proper expenses within the year, would, in case of war, be hard on us. But not so hard as ten wars instead of one. For wars would be reduced in that proportion; besides that the state governments would be free to lend *their credit* in borrowing quotas. For the present, I should be for resolving the alien and sedition laws to be against the Constitution and merely void, and for addressing the other states to obtain similar declarations; and I would not do anything at this moment which should commit us further, but reserve ourselves to shape our future measures or no measures by the events which may happen. It is a singular phenomenon that while our state governments are the very *best in the world,* without exception or comparison, our general government has, in the rapid course of nine or ten years, become more arbitrary, and has swallowed more of the public liberty than even that of England. I enclose you a column, cut out of a London paper, to show you that the English, though charmed with our making their enemies our enemies, yet blush and weep over our sedition law. But I enclose you something more important. It is a petition for a reformation in the manner of appointing our juries, and a remedy against the *jury of all nations,* which is handing about here for signature, and will be presented to your House. I know it will require but little ingenuity to make objections to the details of its execution; but do not be discouraged by small difficulties; make it as perfect as you can at a first essay, and depend on amending its defects as they develop themselves in practice. I hope it will meet with your approbation and patronage. It is the only thing which can yield us a little present protection against the dominion of a faction, while circumstances are maturing for bringing and keeping the government in real unison with the spirit of their constituents. I am aware that the act of Congress has directed that juries shall be appointed by lot or otherwise, as the laws *now* (at the date of the act) in force in the several states provide. The New England states have always had them elected by their select men, who are elected by the people. Several or most of the other states have a large number appointed (I do not know how) to attend, out of whom twelve for each cause are taken by lot. This provision of Congress will render it necessary for our senators or delegates to apply for an amendatory law, accommodated to that prayed for in the petition. In the meantime, I would pass the law as if the amendatory one existed, in reliance, that our select jurors attending, the federal judge will, under a sense of right, direct the juries to be taken from among them. If he does not, or if Congress refuses to pass the amendatory law, it will serve as eyewater for their constituents. Health, happiness, *safety,* and esteem to yourself and my ever-honored and ancient friend, Mr. Pendleton. Adieu.

LETTER TO
SAMUEL ADAMS

Philadelphia, February 26, 1800

Dear Sir:

Mr. Erving delivered me your favor of January 31, and I thank you for making me acquainted with him. You will always do me a favor in giving me an opportunity of knowing gentlemen as estimable in their principles and talents as I find Mr. Erving to be. I have not yet seen Mr. Winthrop. A letter from you, my respectable friend, after three and twenty years of separation, has given me a pleasure I cannot express. It recalls to my mind the anxious days we then passed in struggling for the cause of mankind. Your principles have been tested in the crucible of time, and have come out pure. You have proved that it was monarchy, and not merely British monarchy, you opposed. A government by representatives, elected by the people at *short* periods, was our object; and our maxim at that day was, "Where annual election ends, tyranny begins"; nor have our departures from it been sanctioned by the happiness of their effects. A debt of a hundred millions growing by usurious interest, and an artificial paper phalanx overruling the agricultural mass of our country, with other et ceteras, have a portentous aspect.

I fear our friends on the other side of the water, laboring in the same cause, have yet a great deal of crime and misery to wade through. My confidence has been placed in the head, not in the heart, of Bonaparte. I hoped he would calculate truly the difference between the fame of a Washington and a Cromwell. Whatever his views may be, he has at least transferred the destinies of the republic from the civil to the military arm. Some will use this as a lesson against the practicability of republican government. I read it as a lesson against the danger of standing armies.

Adieu, my ever respected and venerable friend. May that kind overruling Providence which has so long spared you to our country, still foster your remaining years with whatever may make them comfortable to yourself and soothing to your friends. Accept the cordial salutations of your affectionate friend.

LETTER TO
GIDEON GRANGER

Monticello, August 13, 1800

Dear Sir:

I received with great pleasure your favor of June 4, and am much comforted by the appearance of a change of opinion in your state; for though we may obtain, and I believe shall obtain, a majority in the legislature of the United States, attached to the preservation of the federal Constitution according to its obvious principles, and those on which it was known to be received; attached equally to the preservation to the states of those rights unquestionably remaining with them; friends to the freedom of religion, freedom of the press, trial by jury and to economical government; opposed to standing armies, paper systems, war, and all connection, other than commerce, with any foreign nation; in short, a majority firm in all those principles which we have espoused and the Federalists have opposed uniformly; still, should the whole body of New England continue in opposition to these principles of government, either knowingly or through delusion, our government will be a very uneasy one. It can never be harmonious and solid, while so respectable a portion of its citizens support principles which go directly to a change of the federal Constitution, to sink the state governments, consolidate them into one, and to monarchize that. Our country is too large to have all its affairs directed by a single government. Public servants at such a distance, and from under the eye of their constituents, must, from the circumstance of distance, be unable to administer and overlook all the details necessary for the good government of the citizens, and the same circumstance, by rendering detection impossible to their constituents, will invite the public agents to corruption, plunder, and waste. And I do verily believe that if the principle were to prevail of a common law being in force in the United States (which principle possesses the general government at once of all the powers of the state governments, and reduces us to a single consolidated government), it would become the most corrupt government on the earth. You have seen the practices by which the public servants have been able to cover their conduct, or, where that could not be done, delusions by which they have varnished it for the eye of their constituents. What an augmentation of the field for jobbing, speculating, plundering, office-building, and office-hunting would be produced by an assumption of all the state powers into the hands of the general government. The true theory of our Constitution is surely the wisest and best, that the states are independent as to everything within themselves, and united as to everything respecting foreign nations. Let the general government be reduced to foreign concerns only, and let our affairs be disentangled from those of all other nations, except as to commerce, which the merchants will manage the better the more they are left free to manage for themselves, and our general government may be reduced to a very simple organization, and a very unexpensive one; a few plain duties to be performed by a few servants. But I repeat, that this simple and economical mode of government can never be secured if the New England states continue to support the contrary system. I rejoice, therefore, in every appearance of their returning to those principles which I had always imagined to be almost innate in them. In this state, a few persons were deluded by the XYZ duperies. You saw the effect of it in our last congressional representatives, chosen under their influence. This experiment on their credulity is now seen into, and our next representation will be as republican as it has heretofore been. On the whole, we hope that by a part of the Union having held on to the principles of the Constitution, time has been given to the states to recover from the temporary frenzy into which they had been decoyed, to rally round the Constitution, and to rescue it from the destruction with which it had been threatened even at their own hands. I see copied from the *American Magazine* two numbers of a paper signed "Don Quixotte," most excellently adapted to introduce the real truth to the minds even of the most prejudiced.

I would, with great pleasure, have written the letter you desired in behalf of your friend, but there are existing circumstances which render a letter from me to that magistrate as improper as it would be unavailing. I shall be happy, on some more fortunate occasion, to prove to you my desire of serving your wishes.

I sometime ago received a letter from a Mr. McGregory of Derby, in your state; it is written with such a degree of good sense and appearance of candor as entitles it to an answer. Yet the writer being entirely unknown to me, and the stratagems of the times very multifarious, I have thought it best to avail myself of your friendship, and enclose the answer to you. You will see its nature. If you find from the character of the person to whom it is addressed, that no improper use would probably be made of it, be so good as to seal and send it. Otherwise suppress it.

How will the vote of your state and Rhode Island be as to A. and P.?

I am, with great and sincere esteem, dear sir, your friend and servant.

LETTER TO COLONEL AARON BURR

Washington, December 15, 1800

Dear Sir:

Although we have not official information of the votes for president and vice president, and cannot have until the first week in February, yet the state of the votes is given on such evidence as satisfies both parties that the two Republican candidates stand highest. From South Carolina we have not even heard of the actual vote; but we have learned who were appointed electors, and with sufficient certainty how they would vote. It is said they would withdraw from yourself one vote. It has also been said that a General Smith, of Tennessee, had declared that he would give his second vote to Mr. Gallatin, not from any indisposition towards you, but extreme reverence to the character of Mr. Gallatin. It is also surmised that the vote of Georgia will not be entire. Yet nobody pretends to know these things of a certainty, and we know enough to be certain that what it is surmised will be withheld, will still leave you four or five votes at least above Mr. Adams. However, it was badly managed not to have arranged with certainty what seems to have been left to hazard. It was the more material, because I understand several of the high-flying Federalists have expressed their hope that the two Republican tickets may be equal, and their determination in that case to prevent a choice by the House of Representatives (which they are strong enough to do), and let the government devolve on a president of the Senate. Decency required that I should be so entirely passive during the late contest that I never once asked whether arrangements had been made to prevent so many from dropping votes intentionally, as might frustrate half the Republican wish; nor did I doubt, till lately, that such had been made.

While I must congratulate you, my dear sir, on the issue of this contest, because it is more honorable, and doubtless more grateful to you than any station within the competence of the chief magistrate, yet for myself, and for the substantial service of the public, I feel most sensibly the loss we sustain of your aid in our new administration. It leaves a chasm in my arrangements which cannot be adequately filled up. I had endeavored to compose an administration whose talents, integrity, names, and dispositions should at once inspire unbounded confidence in the public mind, and insure a perfect harmony in the conduct of the public business. I lose you from the list, and am not sure of all the others. Should the gentlemen who possess the public confidence decline taking a part in their affairs, and force us to take persons unknown to the people, the evil genius of this country may realize his avowal that "he will beat down the administration." The return of Mr. Van Benthuysen, one of your electors, furnishes me a confidential opportunity of writing this much to you, which I should not have ventured through the post office at this prying season. We shall of course see you before the 4th of March. Accept my respectful and affectionate salutations.

LETTER TO
JAMES MADISON

Washington, December 19, 1800

Dear Sir:

Mr. Brown's departure for Virginia enables me to write confidentially what I could not have ventured by the post at this prying season. The election in South Carolina has in some measure decided the great contest. Though as yet we do not know the actual votes of Tennessee, Kentucky, and Vermont, yet we believe the votes to be, on the whole: J., 73; B., 73; A., 65; P., 64. Rhode Island withdrew one from P. There is a possibility that Tennessee may withdraw one from B., and Burr writes that there may be one vote in Vermont for J. But I hold the latter impossible, and the former not probable; and that there will be an absolute parity between the two Republican candidates. This has produced great dismay and gloom on the Republican gentlemen here, and exultation in the Federalists, who openly declare they will prevent an election, and will name a president of the Senate, pro tem, by what they say would only be a *stretch* of the Constitution. The prospect of preventing this, is as follows: Georgia, North Carolina, Tennessee, Kentucky, Vermont, Pennsylvania, and New York can be counted on for their vote in the House of Representatives, and it is thought by some that Baer of Maryland, and Linn of New Jersey will come over. Some even count on Morris of Vermont. But you must know the uncertainty of such a dependence under the operation of caucuses and other federal engines. The month of February, therefore, will present us storms of a new character. Should they have a particular issue, I hope you will be here a day or two, at least, before the 4th of March. I know that your appearance on the scene before the departure of Congress would assuage the minority, and inspire in the majority confidence and joy unbounded, which they would spread far and wide on their journey home. Let me beseech you then to come with a view of staying perhaps a couple of weeks, within which time things might be put into such a train, as would permit us both to go home for a short time, for removal. I wrote to R.R.L. by a confidential hand three days ago. The person proposed for the Treasury has not come yet.

Davie is here with the convention, as it is called; but it is a real treaty, and without limitation of time. It has some disagreeable features, and will endanger the compromising us with Great Britain. I am not at liberty to mention its contents, but I believe it will meet with opposition from both sides of the House. It has been a bungling negotiation. Ellsworth remains in France for the benefit of his health. He has resigned his office of chief justice. Putting these two things together, we cannot misconstrue his views. He must have had great confidence in Mr. Adams's continuance to risk such a certainty as he held. Jay was yesterday nominated chief justice. We were afraid of something worse. A scheme of government for the territory is cooking by a committee of each house, under separate authorities, but probably a voluntary harmony. They let out no hints. It is believed that the judiciary system will not be pushed, as the appointments, if made by the present administration, could not fall on those who create them. But I very much fear the road system will be urged. The mines of Peru would not supply the moneys which would be wasted on this object, nor the patience of any people stand the abuses which would be incontrolably committed under it. I propose, as soon as the state of the election is perfectly ascertained, to aim at a candid understanding with Mr. Adams. I do not expect that either his feelings or his views of interest will oppose it. I hope to induce in him dispositions liberal and accommodating. Accept my affectionate salutations.

LETTER TO
JAMES MADISON

Washington, February 18, 1801

Dear Sir:

Notwithstanding the suspected infidelity of the post, I must hazard this communication. The minority in the House of Representatives, after seeing the impossibility of electing Burr, the certainty that a legislative usurpation would be resisted by arms, and a recourse to a convention to reorganize and amend the government, held a consultation on this dilemma, whether it would be better for them to come over in a body and go with the tide of the times, or by a negative conduct suffer the election to be made by a bare majority, keeping their body entire and unbroken, to act in phalanx on such ground of opposition as circumstances shall offer; and I know their determination on this question only by their vote of yesterday. Morris of Vermont withdrew, which made Lyon's vote that of his state. The Maryland Federalists put in four blanks, which made the positive ticket of their colleagues the vote of the state. South Carolina and Delaware put in six blanks. So there were ten states for one candidate, four for another, and two blanks. We consider this, therefore, as a declaration of war on the part of this band. But their conduct appears to have brought over to us the whole body of Federalists, who, being alarmed with the danger of a dissolution of the government, had been made most anxiously to wish the very administration they had opposed, and to view it when obtained, as a child of their own. . . . Mr. A. embarrasses us. He keeps the offices of State and War vacant, but has named Bayard minister plenipotentiary to France, and has called an unorganized Senate to meet the fourth of March. As you do not like to be here on that day, I wish you would come within a day or two after. I think that between that and the middle of the month we can so far put things under way, as that we may go home to make arrangements for our final removal. Come to Conrad's, where I will bespeak lodgings for you. Yesterday Mr. A. nominated Bayard to be minister plenipotentiary of the United States to the French republic; today, Theophilus Parsons, attorney general of the United States in the room of C. Lee, who, with Keith Taylor *cum multis aliis,* are appointed judges under the new system. H. G. Otis is nominated a district attorney. A vessel has been waiting for some time in readiness to carry the new minister to France. My affectionate salutations to Mrs. Madison.

FIRST INAUGURAL
ADDRESS

March 4, 1801

Friends and Fellow Citizens: Called upon to undertake the duties of the first executive office of our country, I avail myself of the presence of that portion of my fellow citizens which is here assembled, to express my grateful thanks for the favor with which they have been pleased to look toward me, to declare a sincere consciousness that the task is above my talents, and that I approach it with those anxious and awful presentiments which the greatness of the charge and the weakness of my powers so justly inspire. A rising nation, spread over a wide and fruitful land, traversing all the seas with the rich productions of their industry, engaged in commerce with nations who feel power and forget right, advancing rapidly to destinies beyond the reach of mortal eye—when I contemplate these transcendent objects, and see the honor, the happiness, and the hopes of this beloved country committed to the issue and the auspices of this day, I shrink from the contemplation, and humble myself before the magnitude of the undertaking. Utterly indeed, should I despair, did not the presence of many whom I here see remind me that in the other high authorities provided by our Constitution, I shall find resources of wisdom, of virtue, and of zeal on which to rely under all difficulties. To you, then, gentlemen, who are charged with the sovereign functions of legislation, and to those associated with you, I look with encouragement for that guidance and support which may enable us to steer with safety the vessel in which we are all embarked amid the conflicting elements of a troubled world.

During the contest of opinion through which we have passed, the animation of discussion and of exertions has sometimes worn an aspect which might impose on strangers unused to think freely and to speak and to write what they think; but this being now decided by the voice of the nation, announced according to the rules of the Constitution, all will, of course, arrange themselves under the will of the law, and unite in common efforts for the common good. All, too, will bear in mind this sacred principle, that though the will of the majority is in all cases to prevail, that will, to be rightful, must be reasonable; that the minority possess their equal rights, which equal laws must protect, and to violate which would be oppression. Let us, then, fellow citizens, unite with one heart and one mind. Let us restore to social intercourse that harmony and affection without which liberty and even life itself are but dreary things. And let us reflect that having banished from our land that religious intolerance under which mankind so long bled and suffered, we have yet gained little if we countenance a political intolerance as despotic, as wicked, and capable of as bitter and bloody persecutions. During the throes and convulsions of the ancient world, during the agonizing spasms of infuriated man, seeking through blood and slaughter his long-lost liberty, it was not wonderful that the agitation of the billows should reach even this distant and peaceful shore; that this should be more felt and feared by some and less by others; that this should divide opinions as to measures of safety. But every difference of opinion is not a difference of principle. We have called by different names brethren of the same principle. We are all republicans—we are all federalists. If there be any among us who would wish to dissolve this Union or to change its republican form, let them stand undisturbed as monuments of the safety with which error of opinion may be tolerated where reason is left free to combat it. I know, indeed, that some honest men fear that a republican government cannot be strong; that this government is not strong enough. But would the honest patriot, in the full tide of successful experiment, abandon a government which has so far kept us free and firm, on the theoretic and visionary fear that this government, the world's best hope, may by possibility want energy to preserve itself? I trust not. I believe this, on the contrary, the strongest government on earth. I believe it is the only one where every man, at the call of the laws, would fly to the standard of the law, and would meet invasions of the public order as his own personal concern. Sometimes it is said that man cannot be trusted with the government of himself. Can he, then, be trusted with the government of others? Or have we found angels in the forms of kings to govern him? Let history answer this question.

Let us, then, with courage and confidence pursue our own federal and republican principles, our attachment to our Union and representative government. Kindly separated by nature and a wide ocean from the exterminating havoc of one quarter of the globe; too high-minded to endure the degradations of the others; possessing a chosen country, with room enough for our descendants to the hundredth and thousandth generation; entertaining a due sense of our equal right to the use of our own faculties, to the acquisitions of our industry, to honor and confidence from our fellow citizens, resulting not from birth but from our actions and their sense of them; enlightened by a benign religion, professed, indeed, and practiced in various forms, yet all of them including honesty, truth, temperance, gratitude, and the love of man; acknowledging and adoring an overruling Providence, which by all its dispensations proves that it delights in the happiness of man here and his greater happiness hereafter: with all these blessings, what more is necessary to make us a happy and prosperous people? Still one thing more, fellow citizens—a wise and frugal government, which shall restrain men from injuring one another, which shall leave them otherwise free to regulate their own pursuits of industry and improvement, and shall not take from the mouth of labor the bread it has earned. This is the sum of good government, and this is necessary to close the circle of our felicities.

About to enter, fellow citizens, on the exercise of duties which comprehend everything dear and valuable to you, it is proper that you should understand what I deem the essential principles of our government, and consequently those which ought to shape its administration. I will compress them within the narrowest compass they will bear, stating the general principle, but not all its limitations. Equal and exact justice to all men, of whatever state or persuasion, religious or political; peace, commerce, and honest friendship, with all nations—entangling alliances with none; the support of the state governments in all their rights, as the most competent administrations for our domestic concerns and the surest bulwarks against anti-republican tendencies; the preservation of the general government in its whole constitutional vigor, as the sheet anchor of our peace at home and safety abroad; a jealous care of the right of election by the people—a mild and safe corrective of abuses which are lopped by the sword of the revolution where peaceable remedies are unprovided; absolute acquiescence in the decisions of the majority—the vital principle of republics, from which there is no appeal but to force, the vital principle and immediate parent of despotism; a well-disciplined militia—our best reliance in peace and for the first moments of war, till regulars may relieve them; the supremacy of the civil over the military authority; economy in the public expense, that labor may be lightly burdened; the honest payment of our debts and sacred preservation of the public faith; encouragement of agriculture, and of commerce as its handmaid; the diffusion of information and the arraignment of all abuses at the bar of public reason; freedom of religion; freedom of the press; freedom of person under the protection of the habeas corpus; and trial by juries impartially selected—these principles form the bright constellation which has gone before us and guided our steps through an age of revolution and reformation. The wisdom of our sages and the blood of our heroes have been devoted to their attainment. They should be the creed of our political faith—the text of civil instruction—the touchstone by which to try the services of those we trust; and should we wander from them in moments of error or alarm, let us hasten to retrace our steps and to regain the road which alone leads to peace, liberty, and safety.

I repair, then, fellow citizens, to the post you have assigned me. With experience enough in subordinate offices to have seen the difficulties of this, the greatest of all, I have learned to expect that it will rarely fall to the lot of imperfect man to retire from this station with the reputation and the favor which bring him into it. Without pretensions to that high confidence reposed in our first and great revolutionary character, whose preeminent services had entitled him to the first place in his country's love, and destined for him the fairest page in the volume of faithful history, I ask so much confidence only as may give firmness and effect to the legal administration of your affairs. I shall often go wrong through defect of judgment. When right, I shall often be thought wrong by those whose positions will not command a view of the whole ground. I ask your indulgence for my own errors, which will never be intentional; and your support against the errors of others, who may condemn what they would not if seen in all its parts. The approbation implied by your suffrage is a consolation to me for the past; and my future solicitude will be to retain the good opinion of those who have bestowed it in advance, to conciliate that of others by doing them all the good in my power, and to be instrumental to the happiness and freedom of all.

Relying, then, on the patronage of your good will, I advance with obedience to the work, ready to retire from it whenever you become sensible how much better choice it is in your power to make. And may that Infinite Power which rules the destinies of the universe lead our councils to what is best, and give them a favorable issue for your peace and prosperity.

LETTER TO
ROBERT R. LIVINGSTON

Washington, April 18, 1802

Dear Sir:

A favorable and confidential opportunity offering by M. Dupont de Nemours, who is revisiting his native country, gives me an opportunity of sending you a cipher to be used between us, which will give you some trouble to understand, but once understood, is the easiest to use, the most indecipherable, and varied by a new key with the greatest facility, of any I have ever known. I am in hopes the explanation enclosed will be sufficient. . . .

But writing by Mr. Dupont, I need use no cipher. I require from him to put this into your own and no other hand, let the delay occasioned by that be what it will.

The cession of Louisiana and the Floridas by Spain to France works most sorely on the United States. On this subject the secretary of state has written to you fully, yet I cannot forbear recurring to it personally, so deep is the impression it makes on my mind. It completely reverses all the political relations of the United States, and will form a new epoch in our political course. Of all nations of any consideration, France is the one which, hitherto, has offered the fewest points on which we could have any conflict of right, and the most points of a communion of interests. From these causes, we have ever looked to her as our *natural friend,* as one with which we never could have an occasion of difference. Her growth, therefore, we viewed as our own, her misfortunes ours. There is on the globe one single spot the possessor of which is our natural and habitual enemy. It is New Orleans, through which the produce of three-eighths of our territory must pass to market, and from its

fertility it will ere long yield more than half of our whole produce, and contain more than half of our inhabitants. France,
placing herself in that door, assumes to us the attitude of defiance. Spain might have retained it quietly for years. Her pacific
dispositions, her feeble state, would induce her to increase our
facilities there, so that her possession of the place would be
hardly felt by us, and it would not, perhaps, be very long before
some circumstance might arise which might make the cession of
it to us the price of something of more worth to her. Not so can
it ever be in the hands of France: the impetuosity of her temper,
the energy and restlessness of her character, placed in a point of
eternal friction with us, and our character, which, though quiet
and loving peace and the pursuit of wealth, is high-minded,
despising wealth in competition with insult or injury, enterpris-
ing and energetic as any nation on earth; these circumstances
render it impossible that France and the United States can continue long friends, when they meet in so irritable a position.
They, as well as we, must be blind if they do not see this; and
we must be very improvident if we do not begin to make arrangements on that hypothesis. The day that France takes possession of New Orleans fixes the sentence which is to restrain
her forever within her low-water mark. It seals the union of two
nations, who, in conjunction, can maintain exclusive possession
of the ocean. From that moment, we must marry ourselves to
the British fleet and nation. We must turn all our attention to a
maritime force, for which our resources place us on very high
ground; and having formed and connected together a power
which may render reinforcement of her settlements here impossible to France, make the first cannon which shall be fired in
Europe the signal for the tearing up any settlement she may have
made, and for holding the two continents of America in seques-
tration for the common purposes of the United British and
American nations. This is not a state of things we seek or desire.
It is one which this measure, if adopted by France, forces on us
as necessarily, as any other cause, by the laws of nature, brings
on its necessary effect. It is not from a fear of France that we

deprecate this measure proposed by her. For however greater her force is than ours, compared in the abstract, it is nothing in comparison of ours, when to be exerted on our soil. But it is from a sincere love of peace, and a firm persuasion, that bound to France by the interests and the strong sympathies still existing in the minds of our citizens, and holding relative positions which insure their continuance, we are secure of a long course of peace. Whereas, the change of friends, which will be rendered necessary if France changes that position, embarks us necessarily as a belligerent power in the first war of Europe. In that case, France will have held possession of New Orleans during the interval of a peace, long or short, at the end of which it will be wrested from her. Will this short-lived possession have been an equivalent to her for the transfer of such a weight into the scale of her enemy? Will not the amalgamation of a young, thriving nation continue to that enemy the health and force which are at present so evidently on the decline? And will a few years' possession of New Orleans add equally to the strength of France? She may say she needs Louisiana for the supply of her West Indies. She does not need it in time of peace, and in war she could not depend on them, because they would be so easily intercepted. I should suppose that all these considerations might, in some proper form, be brought into view of the government of France. Though stated by us, it ought not to give offense; because we do not bring them forward as a menace, but as consequences not controllable by us, but inevitable from the course of things. We mention them not as things which we desire by any means, but as things we deprecate; and we beseech a friend to look forward and to prevent them for our common interest.

If France considers Louisiana, however, as indispensable for her views, she might perhaps be willing to look about for arrangements which might reconcile it to our interests. If anything could do this, it would be the ceding to us the island of New Orleans and the Floridas. This would certainly, in a great degree, remove the causes of jarring and irritation between us, and perhaps for such a length of time as might produce other means of making the measure permanently conciliatory to our interests and friendships. It would, at any rate, relieve us from the necessity of taking immediate measures for countervailing such an operation by arrangements in another quarter. But still we should consider New Orleans and the Florida as no equivalent for the risk of a quarrel with France, produced by her vicinage.

I have no doubt you have urged these considerations, on every proper occasion, with the government where you are. They are such as must have effect, if you can find means of producing thorough reflection on them by that government. The idea here is that the troops sent to St. Domingo, were to proceed to Louisiana after finishing their work in that island. If this were the arrangement, it will give you time to return again and again to the charge. For the conquest of St. Domingo will not be a short work. It will take considerable time, and wear down a great number of soldiers. Every eye in the United States is now fixed on the affairs of Louisiana. Perhaps nothing since the Revolutionary War has produced more uneasy sensations through the body of the nation. Notwithstanding temporary bickerings have taken place with France, she has still a strong hold on the affections of our citizens generally. I have thought it not amiss, by way of supplement to the letters of the secretary of state, to write you this private one, to impress you with the importance we affix to this transaction. I pray you to cherish Dupont. He has the best disposition for the continuance of friendship between the two nations, and perhaps you may be able to make a good use of him.

Accept assurances of my affectionate esteem and high consideration.

MESSAGE TO CONGRESS RECOMMENDING A WESTERN EXPLORING EXPEDITION

January 18, 1803

Gentlemen of the Senate and of the House of Representatives:
As the continuance of the act for establishing trading-houses
with the Indian tribes will be under the consideration of the
legislature at its present session, I think it my duty to communicate the views which have guided me in the execution of that act,
in order that you may decide on the policy of continuing it, in
the present or any other form, or discontinue it altogether, if
that shall, on the whole, seem most for the public good.

The Indian tribes residing within the limits of the United
States have, for a considerable time, been growing more and
more uneasy at the constant diminution of the territory they
occupy, although effected by their own voluntary sales; and the
policy has long been gaining strength with them, of refusing
absolutely all further sale, on any conditions; insomuch that, at
this time, it hazards their friendship, and excites dangerous
jealousies and perturbations in their minds to make any over-
ture for the purchase of the smallest portions of their land. A
very few tribes only are not yet obstinately in these dispositions.
In order peaceably to counteract this policy of theirs, and to
provide an extension of territory which the rapid increase of our
numbers will call for, two measures are deemed expedient. First:
to encourage them to abandon hunting, to apply to the raising
stock, to agriculture and domestic manufactures, and thereby
prove to themselves that less land and labor will maintain them

in this, better than in their former mode of living. The extensive forests necessary in the hunting life will then become useless, and they will see advantage in exchanging them for the means of improving their farms and of increasing their domestic comforts. Secondly: to multiply trading-houses among them, and place within their reach those things which will contribute more to their domestic comfort than the possession of extensive but uncultivated wilds. Experience and reflection will develop to them the wisdom of exchanging what they can spare and we want, for what we can spare and they want. In leading them thus to agriculture, to manufactures, and civilization, in bringing together their and our settlements, and in preparing them ultimately to participate in the benefits of our government, I trust and believe we are acting for their greatest good. At these trading-houses we have pursued the principles of the act of Congress, which directs that the commerce shall be carried on liberally, and requires only that the capital stock shall not be diminished. We consequently undersell private traders, foreign and domestic; drive them from the competition; and thus, with the good will of the Indians, rid ourselves of a description of men who are constantly endeavoring to excite in the Indian mind suspicions, fears, and irritations toward us. A letter now enclosed shows the effect of our competition on the operations of the traders, while the Indians, perceiving the advantage of purchasing from us, are soliciting generally our establishment of trading-houses among them. In one quarter this is particularly interesting. The legislature, reflecting on the late occurrences on the Mississippi, must be sensible how desirable it is to possess a respectable breadth of country on that river, from our southern limit to the Illinois at least, so that we may present as firm a front on that as on our eastern border. We possess what is below the Yazoo, and can probably acquire a certain breadth from the Illinois and Wabash to the Ohio; but between the Ohio and Yazoo, the country all belongs to the Chickasaws, the most friendly tribe within our limits, but the most decided against the alienation of lands. The portion of their country most important for us is exactly that which they do not inhabit. Their settlements are not on the Mississippi, but in the interior country. They have lately shown a desire to become agricultural, and this leads to the desire of buying implements and comforts. In the strengthening and gratifying of these wants, I see the only prospect of planting on the Mississippi itself the means of its own safety. Duty has required me to submit these views to the judgment of the legislature; but as their disclosure might embarrass and defeat their effect, they are committed to the special confidence of the two houses.

While the extension of the public commerce among the Indian tribes may deprive of that source of profit such of our citizens as are engaged in it, it might be worthy the attention of Congress, in their care of individual as well as of the general interest, to point in another direction the enterprise of these citizens, as profitably for themselves, and more usefully for the public. The river Missouri, and the Indians inhabiting it, are not as well known as is rendered desirable by their connection with the Mississippi, and consequently with us. It is, however, understood that the country on that river is inhabited by numerous tribes, who furnish great supplies of furs and peltry to the trade of another nation, carried on in a high latitude, through an infinite number of portages and lakes, shut up by ice through a long season. The commerce on that line could bear no competition with that of the Missouri, traversing a moderate climate, offering, according to the best accounts, a continued navigation from its source, and possibly with a single portage, from the western ocean, and finding to the Atlantic a choice of channels through the Illinois or Wabash, the lakes and Hudson, through the Ohio and Susquehanna, or Potomac or James rivers, and through the Tennessee and Savannah rivers. An intelligent officer, with ten or twelve chosen men, fit for the enterprise, and willing to undertake it, taken from our posts, where they may be spared without inconvenience, might explore the whole line, even to the western ocean; have conferences with the natives on the subject of commercial intercourse; get admission among them for our traders, as others are admitted; agree on convenient deposits for an interchange of articles; and return with the information acquired, in the course of two summers. Their arms and accoutrements, some instruments of observation, and light and cheap presents for the Indians, would be all the apparatus they could carry, and with an expectation of a soldier's portion of land on their return, would constitute the whole expense. Their pay would be going on, whether here or there. While other civilized nations have encountered great expense to enlarge the boundaries of knowledge, by undertaking voyages of discovery, and for other literary purposes, in various parts and directions, our nation seems to owe to the same object, as well as to its own interests, to explore this, the only line of easy communication across the continent, and so directly traversing our own part of it. The interests of commerce place the principal object within the constitutional powers and care of Congress, and that it should incidentally advance the geographical knowledge of our own continent cannot but be an additional gratification. The nation claiming the territory, regarding this as a literary pursuit, which it is in the habit of permitting within its own dominions, would not be disposed to view it with jealousy, even if the expiring state of its interests there did not render it a matter of indifference. The appropriation of $2,500, "for the purpose of extending the external commerce of the United States," while understood and considered by the executive as giving the legislative sanction, would cover the undertaking from notice, and prevent the obstructions which interested individuals might otherwise previously prepare in its way.

LETTER TO CAPTAIN MERIWETHER LEWIS

Washington, United States of America,
July 4, 1803

Dear Sir:

In the journey which you are about to undertake, for the discovery of the course and source of the Missouri, and of the most convenient water communication from thence to the Pacific Ocean, your party being small, it is to be expected that you will encounter considerable dangers from the Indian inhabitants. Should you escape those dangers, and reach the Pacific Ocean, you may find it imprudent to hazard a return the same way, and be forced to seek a passage round by sea, in such vessels as you may find on the western coast; but you will be without money, without clothes and other necessaries, as a sufficient supply cannot be carried from hence. Your resource, in that case, can only be in the credit of the United States; for which purpose I hereby authorize you to draw on the secretaries of state, of the treasury, of war, and of the navy of the United States, according as you may find your drafts will be most negotiable, for the purpose of obtaining money or necessaries for yourself and men; and I solemnly pledge the faith of the United States, that these drafts shall be paid punctually at the date at which they are made payable. I also ask of the consuls, agents, merchants, and citizens of any nation with which we have intercourse or amity to furnish you with those supplies which your necessities may call for, assuring them of honorable and prompt retribution; and our own consuls in foreign parts, where you may happen to be, are hereby instructed and required to be aiding and assisting to you in whatsoever may be necessary for procuring your return back to the United States. And to give more entire satisfaction and confidence to those who may be disposed to aid you, I, Thomas Jefferson, President of the United States of America, have written this letter of general credit for you with my own hand, and signed it with my name.

THIRD ANNUAL MESSAGE TO CONGRESS

October 17, 1803

To the Senate and House of Representatives of the United States: In calling you together, fellow citizens, at an earlier day than was contemplated by the act of the last session of Congress, I have not been insensible to the personal inconveniences necessarily resulting from an unexpected change in your arrangements. But matters of great public concernment have rendered this call necessary, and the interest you feel in these will supersede in your minds all private considerations.

Congress witnessed, at their last session, the extraordinary agitation produced in the public mind by the suspension of our right of deposit at the port of New Orleans, no assignment of another place having been made according to treaty. They were sensible that the continuance of that privation would be more injurious to our nation than any consequences which could flow from any mode of redress, but reposing just confidence in the good faith of the government whose officer had committed the wrong, friendly and reasonable representations were resorted to, and the right of deposit was restored.

Previous, however, to this period, we had not been unaware of the danger to which our peace would be perpetually exposed while so important a key to the commerce of the western country remained under foreign power. Difficulties, too, were presenting themselves as to the navigation of other streams, which, arising within our territories, pass through those adjacent. Propositions had, therefore, been authorized for obtaining, on fair conditions, the sovereignty of New Orleans, and of other possessions in that quarter interesting to our quiet, to such extent as was deemed practicable; and the provisional appropriation of two millions of dollars, to be applied and accounted for by the president of the United States, intended as part of the price, was considered as conveying the sanction of Congress to the acquisition proposed. The enlightened government of France saw, with just discernment, the importance to both nations of such liberal arrangements as might best and permanently promote the peace, friendship, and interests of both; and the property and sovereignty of all Louisiana, which had been restored to them, have on certain conditions been transferred to the United States by instruments bearing date the 30th of April last. When these shall have received the constitutional sanction of the Senate, they will without delay be communicated to the representatives also, for the exercise of their functions, as to those conditions which are within the powers vested by the constitution in Congress. While the property and sovereignty of the Mississippi and its waters secure an independent outlet for the produce of the western states, and an uncontrolled navigation through their whole course, free from collision with other powers and the dangers to our peace from that source, the fertility of the country, its climate, and extent promise in due season important aids to our treasury, an ample provision for our posterity, and a widespread field for the blessings of freedom and equal laws.

With the wisdom of Congress it will rest to take those ulterior measures which may be necessary for the immediate occupation and temporary government of the country; for its incorporation into our Union; for rendering the change of government a blessing to our newly adopted brethren; for securing to them the rights of conscience and of property; for confirming to the Indian inhabitants their occupancy and self-government, establishing friendly and commercial relations with them, and for ascertaining the geography of the country acquired. Such materials for your information, relative to its affairs in general, as the short space of time has permitted me to collect, will be laid before you when the subject shall be in a state for your consideration.

Another important acquisition of territory has also been made since the last session of Congress. The friendly tribe of Kaskaskia Indians with which we have never had a difference, reduced by the wars and wants of savage life to a few individuals unable to defend themselves against the neighboring tribes, has transferred its country to the United States, reserving only for its members what is sufficient to maintain them in an agricultural way. The considerations stipulated are that we shall extend to them our patronage and protection, and give them certain annual aids in money, in implements of agriculture and other articles of their choice. This country, among the most fertile within our limits, extending along the Mississippi from the mouth of the Illinois to and up the Ohio, though not so necessary as a barrier since the acquisition of the other bank, may yet be well worthy of being laid open to immediate settlement, as its inhabitants may descend with rapidity in support of the lower country should future circumstances expose that to foreign enterprize. As the stipulations in this treaty also involve matters within the competence of both houses only, it will be laid before Congress as soon as the senate shall have advised its ratification.

With many other Indian tribes, improvements in agriculture and household manufacture are advancing, and with all our peace and friendship are established on grounds much firmer than heretofore. The measure adopted of establishing trading-houses among them, and of furnishing them necessaries in exchange for their commodities, at such moderated prices as leave no gain but cover us from loss, has the most conciliatory and useful effect upon them, and is that which will best secure their peace and good will.

The small vessels authorized by Congress with a view to the Mediterranean service have been sent into that sea and will be able more effectually to confine the Tripoline cruisers within their harbors, and supersede the necessity of convoy to our commerce in that quarter. They will sensibly lessen the expenses of that service the ensuing year.

A further knowledge of the ground in the northeastern and northwestern angles of the United States has evinced that the boundaries established by the Treaty of Paris, between the British territories and ours in those parts, were too imperfectly described to be susceptible of execution. It has therefore been thought worthy of attention, for preserving and cherishing the harmony and useful intercourse subsisting between the two nations, to remove by timely arrangements what unfavorable incidents might otherwise render a ground of future misunderstanding. A convention has therefore been entered into, which provides for a practicable demarkation of those limits to the satisfaction of both parties.

An account of the receipts and expenditures of the year ending 30th September last, with the estimates for the service of the ensuing year, will be laid before you by the secretary of the treasury so soon as the receipts of the last quarter shall be returned from the more distant states. It is already ascertained that the amount paid into the treasury for that year has been between eleven and twelve millions of dollars, and that the revenue accrued during the same term exceeds the sum counted on as sufficient for our current expenses and to extinguish the public debt within the period heretofore proposed.

The amount of debt paid for the same year is about three millions one hundred thousand dollars, exclusive of interest, and making, with the payment of the preceding year, a discharge of more than eight millions and a half of dollars of the principal of that debt, besides the accruing interest; and there remain in the treasury nearly six millions of dollars. Of these, eight hundred and eighty thousand have been reserved for payment of the first installment due under the British convention of January 8, 1802, and two millions are what have been before mentioned as placed by Congress under the power and accountability of the president toward the price of New Orleans and other territories acquired, which, remaining untouched, are still applicable to that object, and go in diminution of the sum to be funded for it.

Should the acquisition of Louisiana be constitutionally

confirmed and carried into effect, a sum of nearly thirteen millions of dollars will then be added to our public debt, most of which is payable after fifteen years; before which term the present existing debts will all be discharged by the established operation of the sinking fund. When we contemplate the ordinary annual augmentation of imposts from increasing population and wealth, the augmentation of the same revenue by its extension to the new acquisition, and the economies which may still be introduced into our public expenditures, I cannot but hope that Congress in reviewing their resources will find means to meet the intermediate interests of this additional debt without recurring to new taxes, and applying to this object only the ordinary progression of our revenue. Its extraordinary increase in times of foreign war will be the proper and sufficient fund for any measures of safety or precaution which that state of things may render necessary in our neutral position.

Remittances for the installments of our foreign debt having been found practicable without loss, it has not been thought expedient to use the power given by a former act of Congress of continuing them by reloans, and of redeeming instead thereof equal sums of domestic debt, although no difficulty was found in obtaining that accommodation.

The sum of fifty thousand dollars appropriated by Congress for providing gunboats remains unexpended. The favorable and peaceful turn of affairs on the Mississippi rendered an immediate execution of that law unnecessary, and time was desirable in order that the institution of that branch of our force might begin on models the most approved by experience. The same issue of events dispensed with a resort to the appropriation of a million and a half of dollars contemplated for purposes which were effected by happier means.

We have seen with sincere concern the flames of war lighted up again in Europe, and nations with which we have the most friendly and useful relations engaged in mutual destruction. While we regret the miseries in which we see others involved, let us bow with gratitude to that kind Providence which, inspiring with wisdom and moderation our late legislative councils while placed under the urgency of the greatest wrongs, guarded us from hastily entering into the sanguinary contest, and left us only to look on and to pity its ravages. These will be heaviest on those immediately engaged. Yet the nations pursuing peace will not be exempt from all evil. In the course of this conflict, let it be our endeavor, as it is our interest and desire, to cultivate the friendship of the belligerent nations by every act of justice and of incessant kindness; to receive their armed vessels with hospitality from the distresses of the sea, but to administer the means of annoyance to none; to establish in our harbors such a police as may maintain law and order; to restrain our citizens from embarking individually in a war in which their country takes no part; to punish severely those persons, citizen or alien, who shall usurp the cover of our flag for vessels not entitled to it, infecting thereby with suspicion those of real Americans, and committing us into controversies for the redress of wrongs not our own; to exact from every nation the observance, toward our vessels and citizens, of those principles and practices which all civilized people acknowledge; to merit the character of a just nation, and maintain that of an independent one, preferring every consequence to insult and habitual wrong. Congress will consider whether the existing laws enable us efficaciously to maintain this course with our citizens in all places, and with others while within the limits of our jurisdiction, and will give them the new modifications necessary for these objects. Some contraventions of right have already taken place, both within our jurisdictional limits and on the high seas. The friendly disposition of the governments from whose agents they have proceeded, as well as their wisdom and regard for justice, leave us in reasonable expectation that they will be rectified and prevented in future; and that no act will be countenanced by them which threatens to disturb our friendly intercourse. Separated by a wide ocean from the nations of Europe, and from the political interests which entangle them together, with productions and wants which render our commerce and friendship useful to them and theirs to us, it cannot be the interest of any to assail us, nor ours to disturb them. We should be most unwise, indeed, were we to cast away the singular blessings of the position in which nature has placed us, the opportunity she has endowed us with of pursuing, at a distance from foreign contentions, the paths of industry, peace, and happiness; of cultivating general friendship, and of bringing collisions of interest to the umpirage of reason rather than of force. How desirable then must it be, in a government like ours, to see its citizens adopt individually the views, the interests, and the conduct which their country should pursue, divesting themselves of those passions and partialities which tend to lessen useful friendships, and to embarrass and embroil us in the calamitous scenes of Europe. Confident, fellow citizens, that you will duly estimate the importance of neutral dispositions toward the observance of neutral conduct, that you will be sensible how much it is our duty to look on the bloody arena spread before us with commiseration indeed, but with no other wish than to see it closed, I am persuaded you will cordially cherish these dispositions in all discussions among yourselves, and in all communications with your constituents; and I anticipate with satisfaction the measures of wisdom which the great interests now committed to *you* will give you an opportunity of providing, and *myself* that of approving and carrying into execution with the fidelity I owe to my country.

LETTER TO CAPTAIN
MERIWETHER LEWIS

Washington, November 16, 1803

Dear Sir:

I have not written to you since the 11th and 15th of July, since which yours of July 18, 22, 25, September 8, 13, and October 3 have been received. The present has been long delayed by an expectation daily of getting the enclosed account of Louisiana through the press. The materials are received from different persons, of good authority. I enclose you also copies of the treaties for Louisiana, the act for taking possession, a letter from Dr. Wistar, and some information obtained by myself from Truteau's journal in MS., all of which may be useful to you. The act for taking possession passed with only some small verbal variations from that enclosed, of no consequence. Orders went from hence signed by the king of Spain and the first consul of France, so as to arrive at Natchez yesterday evening, and we expect the delivery of the province at New Orleans will take place about the close of the ensuing week, say about the 26th instant. Governor Claiborne is appointed to execute the powers of commandant and intendant, until a regular government shall be organized here. At the moment of delivering over the ports in the vicinity of New Orleans, orders will be dispatched from thence to those in upper Louisiana to evacuate and deliver them immediately. You can judge better than I can when they may be expected to arrive at these ports, considering how much you have been detained by the low waters, how late it will be before you can leave Cahokia, how little progress up the Missouri you can make before the freezing of the river; that your winter might be passed in gaining much information, by making Cahokia or Caskaskia your headquarters, and going to St. Louis and the other Spanish forts, that your stores, etc., would thereby be spared for the winter, as your men would draw their military rations. All danger of Spanish opposition avoided, we are strongly of opinion here that you had better not enter the Missouri till the spring. But as you have a view of all circumstances on the spot, we do not pretend to enjoin it, but leave it to your own judgment, in which we have entire confidence. One thing, however, we are decided in: that you must not undertake the winter excursion which you propose in yours of October 3d. Such an excursion will be more dangerous than the main expedition up the Missouri, and would by an accident to you hazard our main object, which, since the acquisition of Louisiana, interests everybody in the highest degree. The object of your mission is single, the direct water communication from sea to sea formed by the bed of the Missouri, and perhaps the Oregon; by having Mr. Clark with you we consider the expedition as double manned, and therefore the less liable to failure; for which reason neither of you should be exposed to risks by going off of your line. I have proposed in conversation, and it seems generally assented to, that Congress shall appropriate ten or twelve thousand dollars for exploring the principal waters of the Mississippi and Missouri. In that case, I should send a party up the Red River to its head, then to cross over to the head of the Arkansas, and come down that. A second party for the Pani and Padouca rivers, and a third, perhaps, for the Morsigona and St. Peter's. As the boundaries of interior Louisiana are the highlands enclosing all the waters which run into the Mississippi or Missouri directly or indirectly, with a quarter breadth on the Gulf of Mexico, it becomes interesting to fix with precision by celestial observations the longitude and latitude of the sources of these rivers, so providing points in the contour of our new limits. This will be attempted distinctly from your mission, which we consider as of major importance, and therefore, not to be delayed or hazarded by any episodes whatever.

The votes of both houses on ratifying and carrying the treaties into execution have been precisely party votes, except that General Dayton has separated from his friends on these questions, and voted for the treaties. I will direct the Aurora *National Intelligencer* to be forwarded to you for six months at Cadokie or Kaskaskia, on the presumption you will be there. Your friends and acquaintances here, and in Albermarle, are all well, so far as I have heard; and I recollect no other small news worth communicating. Present my friendly salutations to Mr. Clark, and accept them affectionately yourself.

ADDRESS TO
THE CHOCTAW NATION

December 17, 1803

Brothers of the Choctaw Nation: We have long heard of your nation as a numerous, peaceable, and friendly people; but this is the first visit we have had from its great men at the seat of our government. I welcome you here; am glad to take you by the hand, and to assure you, for your nation, that we are their friends. Born in the same land, we ought to live as brothers, doing to each other all the good we can, and not listening to wicked men who may endeavor to make us enemies. By living in peace, we can help and prosper one another; by waging war, we can kill and destroy many on both sides; but those who survive will not be the happier for that. Then, brothers, let it forever be peace and good neighborhood between us. Our seventeen states compose a great and growing nation. Their children are as the leaves of the trees, which the winds are spreading over the forest. But we are just also. We take from no nation what belongs to it. Our growing numbers make us always willing to buy lands from our red brethren, when they are willing to sell. But be assured we never mean to disturb them in their possessions. On the contrary, the lines established between us by mutual consent shall be sacredly preserved, and will protect your lands from all encroachments by our own people or any others. We will give you a copy of the law, made by our great council, for punishing our people, who may encroach on your lands, or injure you otherwise. Carry it with you to your homes, and preserve it, as the shield which we spread over you, to protect your land, your property and persons.

It is at the request which you sent me in September, signed by Puckshanublee and other chiefs, and which you now repeat, that I listen to your proposition to sell us lands. You say you owe a great debt to your merchants, that you have nothing to pay it with but lands, and you pray us to take lands, and pay your debt. The sum you have occasion for, brothers, is a very great one. We have never yet paid as much to any of our red brethren for the purchase of lands. You propose to us some on the Tombigbee, and some on the Mississippi. Those on the Mississippi suit us well. We wish to have establishments on that river, as resting places for our boats, to furnish them provisions, and to receive our people who fall sick on the way to or from New Orleans, which is now ours. In that quarter, therefore, we are willing to purchase as much as you will spare. But as to the manner in which the line shall be run, we are not judges of it here, nor qualified to make any bargain. But we will appoint persons hereafter to treat with you on the spot, who, knowing the country and quality of the lands, will be better able to agree with you on a line which will give us a just equivalent for the sum of money you want paid.

You have spoken, brothers, of the lands which your fathers formerly sold and marked off to the English, and which they ceded to us with the rest of the country they held here; and you say that, though you do not know whether your fathers were paid for them, you have marked the line over again for us, and do not ask repayment. It has always been the custom, brothers, when lands were bought of the red men, to pay for them immediately, and none of us have ever seen an example of such a debt remaining unpaid. It is to satisfy their immediate wants that the red men have usually sold lands; and in such a case, they would not let the debt be unpaid. The presumption from custom then is strong; so it is also from the great length of time since your fathers sold these lands. But we have, moreover, been informed by persons now living, and who assisted the English in making the purchase, that the price was paid at the time. Were it otherwise, as it was their contract, it would be their debt, not ours.

I rejoice, brothers, to hear you propose to become cultivators of the earth for the maintenance of your families. Be assured you will support them better and with less labor by raising stock and bread, and by spinning and weaving clothes, than by hunting. A little land cultivated, and a little labor, will procure more provisions than the most successful hunt; and a woman will clothe more by spinning and weaving than a man by hunting. Compared with you, we are but as of yesterday in this land. Yet see how much more we have multiplied by industry, and the exercise of that reason which you possess in common with us. Follow then our example, brethren, and we will aid you with great pleasure.

The clothes and other necessaries which we sent you the last year, were, as you supposed, a present from us. We never meant to ask land or any other payment for them; and the store which we sent on was at your request also; and to accommodate you with necessaries at a reasonable price, you wished of course to have it on your land; but the land would continue yours, not ours.

As to the removal of the store, the interpreter, and the agent, and any other matters you may wish to speak about, the secretary at war will enter into explanations with you, and whatever he says you may consider as said by myself, and what he promises you will be faithfully performed.

I am glad, brothers, you are willing to go and visit some other parts of our country. Carriages shall be ready to convey you, and you shall be taken care of on your journey; and when you shall have returned here and rested yourselves to your own mind, you shall be sent home by land. We had provided for your coming by land, and were sorry for the mistake which carried you to Savannah instead of Augusta, and exposed you to the risks of a voyage by sea. Had any accident happened to you, though we could not help it, it would have been a cause of great mourning to us. But we thank the Great Spirit who took care of you on the ocean, and brought you safe and in good health to the seat of our great council; and we hope His care will accompany and protect you on your journey and return home, and that He will preserve and prosper your nation in all its just pursuits.

LETTER TO
BENJAMIN H. LATROBE

Washington, February 28, 1804

Dear Sir:

I am sorry the explanations attempted between Dr. Thornton and yourself, on the manner of finishing the chamber of the House of Representatives, have not succeeded. At the original establishment of this place advertisements were published many months offering premiums for the best plans for a Capitol and a president's house. Many were sent in. A council was held by General Washington with the Board of Commissioners, and after very mature examination two were preferred, and the premiums given to their authors, Dr. Thornton and Hobens, and the plans were decided on. Hobens's has been executed. On Dr. Thornton's plan of the Capitol the north wing has been extended, and the south raised one story. In order to get along with any public undertaking it is necessary that some stability of plan be observed—nothing impedes progress so much as perpetual changes of design. I yield to this principle in the present case more willingly because the plan begun for the Representative room will, in my opinion, be more handsome and commodious than anything which can now be proposed on the same area. And though the spheroidical dome presents difficulties to the executor, yet they are not beyond his art; and it is to overcome difficulties that we employ men of genius. While, however, I express my opinion that we had better go through with this wing of the Capitol on the plan which has been settled, I would not be understood to suppose there does exist sufficient authority to control the original plan in any of its parts, and to accommodate it to changes of circumstances. I only mean that it is not advisable to change that of this wing in its present stage.

Though I have spoken of a spheroidical roof, that will not be correct by the figure. Every rib will be a portion of a circle of which the radius will be determined by the span and rise of each rib. Would it not be best to make the internal columns of well-burnt brick, molded in portions of circles adapted to the diminution of the columns? 2d. Burlington, in his notes on Palladio, tells us that he found most of the buildings erected under Palladio's direction, and described in his architecture, to have their columns made of brick in this way and covered over with stucco. I know an instance of a range of six or eight columns in Virginia, twenty feet high, well proportioned and properly diminished, executed by a common bricklayer. The bases and capitols would of course be of hewn stone. I suggest this for your consideration, and tender you my friendly salutations.

LETTER TO
ABIGAIL ADAMS

Washington, June 13, 1804

Dear Madam:

The affectionate sentiments which you have had the good-ness to express in your letter of May 20, towards my dear departed daughter, have awakened in me sensibilities natural to the occasion, and recalled your kindnesses to her, which I shall ever remember with gratitude and friendship. I can assure you with truth, they had made an indelible impression on her mind, and that to the last, on our meetings after long separations, whether I had heard lately of you, and how you did, were among the earliest of her inquiries. In giving you this assurance I perform a sacred duty for her, and, at the same time, am thankful for the occasion furnished me, of expressing my regret that circumstances should have arisen, which have seemed to draw a line of separation between us. The friendship with which you honored me has ever been valued, and fully reciprocated; and although events have been passing which might be trying to some minds, I never believed yours to be of that kind, nor felt that my own was. Neither my estimate of your character, nor the esteem founded in that, has ever been lessened for a single moment, although doubts whether it would be acceptable may have forbidden manifestations of it.

Mr. Adams's friendship and mine began at an earlier date. It accompanied us through long and important scenes. The different conclusions we had drawn from our political reading and reflections were not permitted to lessen personal esteem, each party being conscious they were the result of an honest conviction in the other. Like differences of opinion existing among our fellow citizens attached them to one or the other of

us, and produced a rivalship in their minds which did not exist
in ours. We never stood in one another's way; for if either had
been withdrawn at any time, his favorers would not have gone
over to the other, but would have sought for some one of
homogeneous opinions. This consideration was sufficient to
keep down all jealousy between us, and to guard our friendship from any disturbance by sentiments of rivalship; and I
can say with truth that one act of Mr. Adams's life, and one
only, ever gave me a moment's personal displeasure. I did consider his last appointments to office as personally unkind.
They were from among my most ardent political enemies,
from whom no faithful cooperation could ever be expected;
and laid me under the embarrassment of acting through men
whose views were to defeat mine, or to encounter the odium
of putting others in their places. It seems but common justice
to leave a successor free to act by instruments of his own
choice. If my respect for him did not permit me to ascribe the
whole blame to the influence of others, it left something for
friendship to forgive, and after brooding over it for some little
time, and not always resisting the expression of it, I forgave it
cordially, and returned to the same state of esteem and respect
for him which had so long subsisted. Having come into life a
little later than Mr. Adams, his career has preceded mine, as
mine is followed by some other; and it will probably be closed
at the same distance after him which time originally placed
between us. I maintain for him, and shall carry into private
life, a uniform and high measure of respect and good will, and
for yourself a sincere attachment.

I have thus, my dear madam, opened myself to you without
reserve, which I have long wished an opportunity of doing; and
without knowing how it will be received, I feel relief from being
unbosomed. And I have now only to entreat your forgiveness for
this transition from a subject of domestic affliction to one which
seems of a different aspect. But though connected with political
events, it has been viewed by me most strongly in its unfortunate
bearings on my private friendships. The injury these have

sustained has been a heavy price for what has never given me equal pleasure. That you may both be favored with health, tranquillity, and long life is the prayer of one who tenders you the assurance of his highest consideration and esteem.

LETTER TO
PHILLIP MAZZEI

Washington, July 18, 1804

My dear Sir:

It is very long, I know, since I wrote you. So constant is the pressure of business that there is never a moment, scarcely, that something of public importance is not waiting for me. I have, therefore, on a principle of conscience, thought it my duty to withdraw almost entirely from all private correspondence, and chiefly the transatlantic; I scarcely write a letter a year to any friend beyond sea. Another consideration has led to this, which is the liability of my letters to miscarry, be opened, and made ill use of. Although the great body of our country are perfectly returned to their ancient principles, yet there remains a phalanx of old tories and monarchists, more envenomed as all their hopes become more desperate. Every word of mine which they can get hold of, however innocent, however orthodox even, is twisted, tormented, perverted, and, like the words of holy writ, are made to mean everything but what they were intended to mean. I trust little, therefore, unnecessarily in their way, and especially on political subjects. I shall not, therefore, be free to answer all the several articles of your letters.

On the subject of treaties, our system is to have none with any nation, as far as can be avoided. The treaty with England has therefore not been renewed, and all overtures for treaty with other nations have been declined. We believe that with nations, as with individuals, dealings may be carried on as advantageously, perhaps moreso, while their continuance depends on a voluntary good treatment, as if fixed by a contract, which, when it becomes injurious to either, is made, by forced constructions, to mean what suits them, and becomes a cause of war instead of a bond of peace. We wish to be on the closest terms of friendship with Naples, and we will prove it by giving to her citizens vessels and goods all the privileges of the most favored nation; and while we do this voluntarily, we cannot doubt they will voluntarily do the same for us. Our interests against the Barbaresques being also the same, we have little doubt she will give us every facility to insure them which our situation may ask and hers admit. It is not, then, from a want of friendship that we do not propose a treaty with Naples, but because it is against our system to embarrass ourselves with treaties, or to entangle ourselves at all with the affairs of Europe. The kind offices we receive from that government are more sensibly felt, as such, than they would be if rendered only as due to us by treaty.

Five fine frigates left the Chesapeake the 1st instant for Tripoli, which, in addition to the force now there, will, I trust, recover the credit which Commodore Morris's two years' sleep lost us, and for which he has been broke. I think they will make Tripoli sensible, that they mistake their interest in choosing war with us; and Tunis also, should she have declared war as we expect, and almost wish.

Notwithstanding this little diversion, we pay seven or eight millions of dollars annually of our public debt, and shall completely discharge it in twelve years more. That done, our annual revenue, now thirteen millions of dollars, which by that time will be twenty-five, will pay the expenses of any war we may be forced into, without new taxes or loans. The spirit of republicanism is now in almost all its ancient vigor, five-sixths of the people being with us. Fourteen of the seventeen states are completely with us, and two of the other three will be in one year. We have now got back to the ground on which you left us. I should have retired at the end of the first four years, but that the immense load of tory calumnies which have been manufactured respecting me, and have filled the European market, have obliged me to appeal once more to my country for a justification. I have no fear but that I shall receive honorable testimony by their verdict on those calumnies. At the end of the next four years I shall certainly retire. Age, inclination, and principle all dictate this. My health, which at one time threatened an unfavorable turn, is now firm. The acquisition of Louisiana, besides doubling our extent, and trebling our quantity of fertile country, is of incalculable value, as relieving us from the danger of war. It has enabled us to do a handsome thing for Fayette. He had received a grant of between eleven and twelve thousand acres north of Ohio, worth, perhaps, a dollar an acre. We have obtained permission of Congress to locate it in Louisiana. Locations can be found adjacent to the city of New Orleans, in the island of New Orleans and in its vicinity, the value of which cannot be calculated. I hope it will induce him to come over and settle there with his family. Mr. Livingston having asked leave to return, General Armstrong, his brother-in-law, goes in his place: he is of the first order of talents. . . .

Remarkable deaths lately are Samuel Adams, Edmund Pendleton, Alexander Hamilton, Stephens Thompson Mason, Mann Page, Bellini, and Parson Andrews. To these I have the inexpressible grief of adding the name of my youngest daughter, who had married a son of Mr. Eppes, and has left two children. My eldest daughter alone remains to me, and has six children. This loss has increased my anxiety to retire, while it has dreadfully lessened the comfort of doing it. Wythe, Dickinson, and Charles Thompson are all living, and are firm republicans. You informed me formerly of your marriage, and your having a daughter, but have said nothing in your late letters on that subject. Yet whatever concerns your happiness is sincerely interesting to me, and is a subject of anxiety, retaining as I do, cordial sentiments of esteem and affection for you. Accept, I pray you, my sincere assurances of this, with my most friendly salutations.

LETTER TO
ABIGAIL ADAMS

Monticello, September 11, 1804

Your letter, madam, of the 18th of August has been some days received, but a press of business has prevented the acknowledgment of it: perhaps, indeed, I may have already trespassed too far on your attention. With those who wish to think amiss of me, I have learned to be perfectly indifferent; but where I know a mind to be ingenuous, and to need only truth to set it to rights, I cannot be as passive. The act of personal unkindness alluded to in your former letter is said in your last to have been the removal of your eldest son from some office to which the judges had appointed him. I conclude then he must have been a commissioner of bankruptcy. But I declare to you, on my honor, that this is the first knowledge I have ever had that he was so. It may be thought, perhaps, that I ought to have inquired who were such, before I appointed others. But it is to be observed that the former law permitted the judges to name commissioners occasionally only, for every case as it arose, and not to make them permanent officers. Nobody, therefore, being in office, there could be no removal. The judges, you well know, have been considered as highly federal; and it was noted that they confined their nominations exclusively to Federalists. The legislature, dissatisfied with this, transferred the nomination to the president, and made the offices permanent. The very object in passing the law was, that he should correct, not confirm, what was deemed the partiality of the judges. I thought it therefore proper to inquire, not whom they had employed, but whom I ought to appoint to fulfill the intentions of the law. In making these appointments, I put in a proportion of Federalists, equal, I believe, to the proportion they bear in numbers through the Union generally. Had I known that your son had acted, it would have been a real pleasure to me to have preferred him to some who were named in Boston, in what was deemed the same line of politics. To this I should have been led by my knowledge of his integrity, as well as my sincere dispositions towards yourself and Mr. Adams.

You seem to think it devolved on the judges to decide on the validity of the sedition law. But nothing in the Constitution has given them a right to decide for the executive, more than to the executive to decide for them. Both magistrates are equally independent in the sphere of action assigned to them. The judges, believing the law constitutional, had a right to pass a sentence of fine and imprisonment, because the power was placed in their hands by the Constitution. But the executive, believing the law to be unconstitutional, were bound to remit the execution of it, because that power has been confided to them by the Constitution. That instrument meant that its coordinate branches should be checks on each other. But the opinion which gives to the judges the right to decide what laws are constitutional, and what not, not only for themselves in their own sphere of action but for the legislature and executive also, in their spheres, would make the judiciary a despotic branch. Nor does the opinion of the unconstitutionality, and consequent nullity of that law remove all restraint from the overwhelming torrent of slander which is confounding all vice and virtue, all truth and falsehood, in the United States. The power to do that is fully possessed by the several state legislatures. It was reserved to them, and was denied to the general government, by the Constitution, according to our construction of it. While we deny that Congress have a right to control the freedom of the press, we have ever asserted the right of the states, and their exclusive right, to do so. They have accordingly, all of them, made provisions for punishing slander, which those who have time and inclination resort to for the vindication of their characters. In general, the state laws appear to have made the presses responsible for slander as far as is consistent with its useful freedom. In those states where they do not admit even the truth of allegations to protect the printer, they have gone too far.

The candor manifested in your letter, and which I ever believed you to possess, has alone inspired the desire of calling your attention, once more, to those circumstances of fact and motive by which I claim to be judged. I hope you will see these intrusions on your time to be what they really are—proofs of my great respect for you. I tolerate with the utmost latitude the right of others to differ from me in opinion without imputing to them criminality. I know too well the weakness and uncertainty of human reason to wonder at its different results. Both of our political parties, at least the honest part of them, agree conscientiously in the same object—the public good; but they differ essentially in what they deem the means of promoting that good. One side believes it best done by one composition of the governing powers; the other, by a different one. One fears most the ignorance of the people; the other, the selfishness of rulers independent of them. Which is right, time and experience will prove. We think that one side of this experiment has been long enough tried, and proved not to promote the good of the many; and that the other has not been fairly and sufficiently tried. Our opponents think the reverse. With whichever opinion the body of the nation concurs, that must prevail. My anxieties on this subject will never carry me beyond the use of fair and honorable means, of truth and reason; nor have they ever lessened my esteem for moral worth, nor alienated my affections from a single friend, who did not first withdraw himself. Whenever this has happened, I confess I have not been insensible to it; yet have ever kept myself open to a return of their justice. I conclude with sincere prayers for your health and happiness, that yourself and Mr. Adams may long enjoy the tranquillity you desire and merit, and see in the prosperity of your family what is the consummation of the last and warmest of human wishes.

SECOND INAUGURAL ADDRESS

March 4, 1805

Proceeding, fellow citizens, to that qualification which the Constitution requires, before my entrance on the charge again conferred upon me, it is my duty to express the deep sense I entertain of this new proof of confidence from my fellow citizens at large, and the zeal with which it inspires me, so to conduct myself as may best satisfy their just expectations.

On taking this station on a former occasion, I declared the principles on which I believed it my duty to administer the affairs of our commonwealth. My conscience tells me that I have, on every occasion, acted up to that declaration, according to its obvious import, and to the understanding of every candid mind.

In the transaction of your foreign affairs, we have endeavored to cultivate the friendship of all nations, and especially of those with which we have the most important relations. We have done them justice on all occasions, favored where favor was lawful, and cherished mutual interests and intercourse on fair and equal terms. We are firmly convinced, and we act on that conviction, that with nations, as with individuals, our interests soundly calculated will ever be found inseparable from our moral duties; and history bears witness to the fact that a just nation is taken on its word, when recourse is had to armaments and wars to bridle others.

At home, fellow citizens, you best know whether we have done well or ill. The suppression of unnecessary offices, of useless establishments and expenses, enabled us to discontinue our internal taxes. These covering our land with officers, and opening our doors to their intrusions, had already begun that process of domiciliary vexation which, once entered, is scarcely to be restrained from reaching successively every article of produce and property. If among these taxes some minor ones fell which had not been inconvenient, it was because their amount would not have paid the officers who collected them, and because, if they had any merit, the state authorities might adopt them, instead of others less approved.

The remaining revenue on the consumption of foreign articles is paid cheerfully by those who can afford to add foreign luxuries to domestic comforts, being collected on our seaboards and frontiers only, and incorporated with the transactions of our mercantile citizens. It may be the pleasure and pride of an American to ask, What farmer, what mechanic, what laborer ever sees a tax-gatherer of the United States? These contributions enable us to support the current expenses of the government, to fulfill contracts with foreign nations, to extinguish the native right of soil within our limits, to extend those limits, and to apply such a surplus to our public debts as places at a short day their final redemption; and that redemption once effected, the revenue thereby liberated may, by a just repartition among the states, and a corresponding amendment of the Constitution, be applied, *in time of peace,* to rivers, canals, roads, arts, manufactures, education, and other great objects within each state. *In time of war,* if injustice, by ourselves or others, must sometimes produce war, increased as the same revenue will be increased by population and consumption, and aided by other resources reserved for that crisis, it may meet within the year all the expenses of the year, without encroaching on the rights of future generations, by burdening them with the debts of the past. War will then be but a suspension of useful works, and a return to a state of peace a return to the progress of improvement.

I have said, fellow citizens, that the income reserved had enabled us to extend our limits; but that extension may possibly pay for itself before we are called on, and in the meantime keep down the accruing interest; in all events, it will repay the advances we have made. I know that the acquisition of Louisiana has been disapproved by some, from a candid apprehension that the enlargement of our territory would endanger its union. But who can limit the extent to which the federative principle may operate effectively? The larger our association, the less will it be shaken by local passions; and in any view, is it not better that the opposite bank of the Mississippi should be settled by our own brethren and children than by strangers of another family? With which shall we be most likely to live in harmony and friendly intercourse?

In matters of religion, I have considered that its free exercise is placed by the Constitution independent of the powers of the general government. I have therefore undertaken, on no occasion, to prescribe the religious exercises suited to it; but have left them, as the Constitution found them, under the direction and discipline of state or church authorities acknowledged by the several religious societies.

The aboriginal inhabitants of these countries I have regarded with the commiseration their history inspires. Endowed with the faculties and the rights of men, breathing an ardent love of liberty and independence, and occupying a country which left them no desire but to be undisturbed, the stream of overflowing population from other regions directed itself on these shores; without power to divert, or habits to contend against, they have been overwhelmed by the current, or driven before it; now reduced within limits too narrow for the hunter's state, humanity enjoins us to teach them agriculture and the domestic arts; to encourage them to that industry which alone can enable them to maintain their place in existence; and to prepare them in time for that state of society which to bodily comforts adds the improvement of the mind and morals. We have therefore liberally furnished them with the implements of husbandry and household use; we have placed among them instructors in the arts of first necessity; and they are covered with the aegis of the law against aggressors from among ourselves.

But the endeavors to enlighten them on the fate which awaits their present course of life, to induce them to exercise their reason, follow its dictates, and change their pursuits with the change of circumstances, have powerful obstacles to encounter; they are combated by the habits of their bodies, prejudice of their minds, ignorance, pride, and the influence of interested and crafty individuals among them, who feel themselves something in the present order of things, and fear to become nothing in any other. These persons inculcate a sanctimonious reverence for the customs of their ancestors; that whatsoever they did must be done through all time; that reason is a false guide, and to advance under its counsel, in their physical, moral, or political condition, is perilous innovation; that their duty is to remain as their Creator made them, ignorance being safety, and knowledge full of danger; in short, my friends, among them is seen the action and counteraction of good sense and bigotry; they, too, have their antiphilosophers, who find an interest in keeping things in their present state, who dread reformation, and exert all their faculties to maintain the ascendency of habit over the duty of improving our reason and obeying its mandates.

In giving these outlines, I do not mean, fellow citizens, to arrogate to myself the merit of the measures; that is due, in the first place, to the reflecting character of our citizens at large, who, by the weight of public opinion, influence and strengthen the public measures; it is due to the sound discretion with which they select from among themselves those to whom they confide the legislative duties; it is due to the zeal and wisdom of the characters thus selected, who lay the foundations of public happiness in wholesome laws, the execution of which alone remains for others; and it is due to the able and faithful auxiliaries, whose patriotism has associated with me in the executive functions.

During this course of administration, and in order to disturb it, the artillery of the press has been leveled against us, charged with whatsoever its licentiousness could devise or dare. These abuses of an institution so important to freedom and science are deeply to be regretted, inasmuch as they tend to lessen its usefulness, and to sap its safety; they might, indeed, have been corrected by the wholesome punishments reserved and provided by the laws of the several states against falsehood and defamation; but public duties more urgent press on the time of public servants, and the offenders have therefore been left to find their punishment in the public indignation.

Nor was it uninteresting to the world that an experiment should be fairly and fully made, whether freedom of discussion, unaided by power, is not sufficient for the propagation and protection of truth—whether a government, conducting itself in the true spirit of its Constitution, with zeal and purity, and doing no act which it would be unwilling the whole world should witness, can be written down by falsehood and defamation. The experiment has been tried; you have witnessed the scene; our fellow citizens have looked on, cool and collected; they saw the latent source from which these outrages proceeded; they gathered around their public functionaries, and when the Constitution called them to the decision by suffrage, they pronounced their verdict, honorable to those who had served them, and consolatory to the friend of man, who believes he may be entrusted with his own affairs.

No inference is here intended that the laws, provided by the state against false and defamatory publications, should not be enforced; he who has time renders a service to public morals and public tranquillity in reforming these abuses by the salutary coercions of the law; but the experiment is noted to prove that, since truth and reason have maintained their ground against false opinions in league with false facts, the press, confined to truth, needs no other legal restraint; the public judgment will correct false reasonings and opinions, on a full hearing of all parties; and no other definite line can be drawn between the inestimable liberty of the press and its demoralizing licentiousness. If there be still improprieties which this rule would not restrain, its supplement must be sought in the censorship of public opinion.

Contemplating the union of sentiment now manifested so generally as auguring harmony and happiness to our future course, I offer to our country sincere congratulations. With those, too, not yet rallied to the same point, the disposition to do so is gaining strength; facts are piercing through the veil drawn over them; and our doubting brethren will at length see that the mass of their fellow citizens, with whom they cannot yet resolve to act, as to principles and measures, think as they think, and desire what they desire; that our wish, as well as theirs, is that the public efforts may be directed honestly to the public good, that peace be cultivated, civil and religious liberty unassailed, law and order preserved, equality of rights maintained, and that state of property, equal or unequal, which results to every man from his own industry, or that of his fathers. When satisfied of these views, it is not in human nature that they should not approve and support them; in the meantime, let us cherish them with patient affection; let us do them justice, and more than justice, in all competitions of interest; and we need not doubt that truth, reason, and their own interests will at length prevail, will gather them into the fold of their country, and will complete their entire union of opinion, which gives to a nation the blessing of harmony and the benefit of all its strength.

I shall now enter on the duties to which my fellow citizens have again called me, and shall proceed in the spirit of those principles which they have approved. I fear not that any motives of interest may lead me astray; I am sensible of no passion which could seduce me knowingly from the path of justice; but the weakness of human nature, and the limits of my own understanding, will produce errors of judgment sometimes injurious to your interests. I shall need, therefore, all the indulgence I have heretofore experienced—the want of it will certainly not lessen with increasing years. I shall need, too, the favor of that Being in whose hands we are, who led our forefathers, as Israel of old, from their native land, and planted them in a country flowing with all the necessaries and comforts of life; who has covered our infancy with his providence, and our riper years with his wisdom and power; and to whose goodness I ask you to join with me in supplications, that he will so enlighten the minds of your servants, guide their councils, and prosper their measures that whatsoever they do shall result in your good, and shall secure to you the peace, friendship, and approbation of all nations.

MEMORANDUM
WRITTEN AS
PRESIDENT

April 15, 1806

About a month ago, Colonel Burr called on me, and entered into
a conversation in which he mentioned that a little before my
coming into office, I had written to him a letter intimating that
I had destined him for a high employ, had he not been placed
by the people in a different one; that he had signified his willing-
ness to resign as vice president, to give aid to the administration
in any other place; that he had never asked an office, however;
he asked aid of nobody, but could walk on his own legs and take
care of himself; that I had always used him with politeness, but
nothing more; that he aided in bringing on the present order of
things; that he had supported the administration; and that he
could do me much harm; he wished, however, to be on different
ground; he was now disengaged from all particular business—
willing to engage in something—should be in town some days,
if I should have anything to propose to him. I observed to him
that I had always been sensible that he possessed talents which
might be employed greatly to the advantage of the public, and
that as to myself, I had a confidence that if he were employed,
he would use his talents for the public good; but that he must
be sensible the public had withdrawn their confidence from him,
and that in a government like ours it was necessary to embrace
in its administration as great a mass of public confidence as
possible, by employing those who had a character with the
public of their own, and not merely a secondary one through the
executive. He observed that if we believed a few newspapers, it
might be supposed he had lost the public confidence, but that I

knew how easy it was to engage newspapers in anything. I observed that I did not refer to that kind of evidence of his having lost the public confidence, but to the late presidential election, when, though in possession of the office of vice president, there was not a single voice heard for his retaining it. That as to any harm he could do me, I knew no cause why he should desire it, but, at the same time, I feared no injury which any man could do me; that I never had done a single act, or been concerned in any transaction, which I feared to have fully laid open, or which could do me any hurt, if truly stated; that I had never done a single thing with a view to my personal interest, or that of any friend, or with any other view than that of the greatest public good; that, therefore, no threat or fear on that head would ever be a motive of action with me. He has continued in town to this time; dined with me this day week [*sic*], and called on me to take leave two or three days ago.

I did not commit these things to writing at the time, but I do it now, because in a suit between him and Cheetham, he has had a deposition of Mr. Bayard taken, which seems to have no relation to the suit, nor to any other object than to calumniate me. Bayard pretends to have addressed to me, during the pending of the presidential election in February 1801, through General Samuel Smith, certain conditions on which my election might be obtained, and that General Smith, after conversing with me, gave answers from me. This is absolutely false. No proposition of any kind was ever made to me on that occasion by General Smith, nor any answer authorized by me. And this fact General Smith affirms at this moment.

For some matters connected with this, see my notes of February 12 and 14, 1801, made at the moment. But the following transactions took place about the same time, that is to say, while the presidential election was in suspense in Congress, which, though I did not enter at the time, they made such an impression on my mind, that they are now as fresh, as to their principal circumstances, as if they had happened yesterday. Coming out of the Senate chamber one day, I found Gouverneur Morris on the steps. He stopped me and began a conversation on the strange and portentous state of things then existing, and went on to observe that the reasons why the minority of states was so opposed to my being elected were that they apprehended that (1) I would turn all Federalists out of office; (2) put down the navy; (3) wipe off the public debt. That I need only to declare, or authorize my friends to declare, that I would not take these steps, and instantly the event of the election would be fixed. I told him that I should leave the world to judge of the course I meant to pursue by that which I had pursued hitherto, believing it to be my duty to be passive and silent during the present scene; that I should certainly make no terms; should never go into the office of president by capitulation, nor with my hands tied by any conditions which should hinder me from pursuing the measures which I should deem for the public good. It was understood that Gouverneur Morris had entirely the direction of the vote of Lewis Morris of Vermont, who, by coming over to Matthew Lyon, would have added another vote, and decided the election. About the same time, I called on Mr. Adams. We conversed on the state of things. I observed to him that a very dangerous experiment was then in contemplation, to defeat the presidential election by an act of Congress declaring the right of the Senate to name a president of the Senate, to devolve on him the government during any interregnum; that such a measure would probably produce resistance by force, and incalculable consequences, which it would be in his power to prevent by negativing such an act. He seemed to think such an act justifiable, and observed it was in my power to fix the election by a word in an instant, by declaring I would not turn out the federal officers, nor put down the navy, nor spunge the national debt. Finding his mind made up as to the usurpation of the government by the president of the Senate, I urged it no further, observed the world must judge as to myself of the future by the past, and turned the conversation to something else. About the same time, Dwight Foster of Massachusetts called on me in my room one night, and went into a very long conversation on the state of affairs, the drift of which was to let me understand that the fears above mentioned were the only obstacle to my election, to all of which I avoided giving any answer the one way or the other. From this moment he became most bitterly and personally opposed to me, and so has ever continued. I do not recollect that I ever had any particular conversation with General Samuel Smith on this subject. Very possibly I had, however, as the general subject and all its parts were the constant themes of conversation in the private tête à têtes with our friends. But certain I am that neither he nor any other Republican ever uttered the most distant hint to me about submitting to any conditions, or giving any assurances to anybody; and still more certainly, was neither he nor any other person ever authorized by me to say what I would or would not do. . . .

SIXTH ANNUAL MESSAGE
TO CONGRESS

December 2, 1806

To the Senate and House of Representatives of the United States in Congress Assembled: It would have given me, fellow citizens, great satisfaction to announce in the moment of your meeting that the difficulties in our foreign relations, existing at the time of your last separation, had been amicably and justly terminated. I lost no time in taking those measures which were most likely to bring them to such a termination, by special missions charged with such powers and instructions as in the event of failure could leave no imputation on either our moderation or forbearance. The delays which have since taken place in our negotiations with the British government appears to have proceeded from causes which do not forbid the expectation that during the course of the session I may be enabled to lay before you their final issue. What will be that of the negotiations for settling our differences with Spain, nothing which had taken place at the date of the last dispatches enables us to pronounce. On the western side of the Mississippi she advanced in considerable force, and took post at the settlement of Bayou Pierre, on the Red River. This village was originally settled by France, was held by her as long as she held Louisiana, and was delivered to Spain only as a part of Louisiana. Being small, insulated, and distant, it was not observed, at the moment of redelivery to France and the United States, that she continued a guard of half a dozen men which had been stationed there. A proposition, however, having been lately made by our commander-in-chief, to assume the Sabine River as a temporary line of separation between the troops of the two nations until the issue of our negotiation shall be known; this has been referred by the

Spanish commandant to his superior, and in the meantime, he has withdrawn his force to the western side of the Sabine River. The correspondence on this subject, now communicated, will exhibit more particularly the present state of things in that quarter.

The nature of that country requires indispensably that an unusual proportion of the force employed there should be cavalry or mounted infantry. In order, therefore, that the commanding officer might be enabled to act with effect, I had authorized him to call on the governors of Orleans and Mississippi for a corps of five hundred volunteer cavalry. The temporary arrangement he has proposed may perhaps render this unnecessary. But I inform you with great pleasure of the promptitude with which the inhabitants of those territories have tendered their services in defense of their country. It has done honor to themselves, entitled them to the confidence of their fellow citizens in every part of the Union, and must strengthen the general determination to protect them efficaciously under all circumstances which may occur.

Having received information that in another part of the United States a great number of private individuals were combining together, arming and organizing themselves contrary to law, to carry on military expeditions against the territories of Spain, I thought it necessary, by proclamations as well as by special orders, to take measures for preventing and suppressing this enterprise, for seizing the vessels, arms, and other means provided for it, and for arresting and bringing to justice its authors and abettors. It was due to that good faith which ought ever to be the rule of action in public as well as in private transactions; it was due to good order and regular government, that while the public force was acting strictly on the defensive and merely to protect our citizens from aggression, the criminal attempts of private individuals to decide for their country the question of peace or war, by commencing active and unauthorized hostilities, should be promptly and efficaciously suppressed.

Whether it will be necessary to enlarge our regular force will depend on the result of our negotiation with Spain; but as it is uncertain when that result will be known, the provisional measures requisite for that, and to meet any pressure intervening in that quarter, will be a subject for your early consideration.

The possession of both banks of the Mississippi reducing to a single point the defense of that river, its waters, and the country adjacent, it becomes highly necessary to provide for that point a more adequate security. Some position above its mouth, commanding the passage of the river, should be rendered sufficiently strong to cover the armed vessels which may be stationed there for defense, and in conjunction with them to present an insuperable obstacle to any force attempting to pass. The approaches to the city of New Orleans, from the eastern quarter also, will require to be examined, and more effectually guarded. For the internal support of the country, the encouragement of a strong settlement on the western side of the Mississippi, within reach of New Orleans, will be worthy the consideration of the legislature.

The gunboats authorized by an act of the last session are so advanced that they will be ready for service in the ensuing spring. Circumstances permitted us to allow the time necessary for their more solid construction. As a much larger number will still be wanting to place our seaport towns and waters in that state of defense to which we are competent and they entitled, a similar appropriation for a further provision for them is recommended for the ensuing year.

A further appropriation will also be necessary for repairing fortifications already established, and the erection of such works as may have real effect in obstructing the approach of an enemy to our seaport towns, or their remaining before them.

In a country whose Constitution is derived from the will of the people, directly expressed by their free suffrages; where the principal executive functionaries, and those of the legislature, are renewed by them at short periods; where under the characters of jurors, they exercise in person the greatest portion of the judiciary powers; where the laws are consequently so formed and administered as to bear with equal weight and favor on all, restraining no man in the pursuits of honest industry, and securing to everyone the property which that acquires, it would not be supposed that any safeguards could be needed against insurrection or enterprise on the public peace or authority. The laws, however, aware that these should not be trusted to moral restraints only, have wisely provided punishments for these crimes when committed. But would it not be salutary to give also the means of preventing their commission? Where an enterprise is meditated by private individuals against a foreign nation in amity with the United States, powers of prevention to a certain extent are given by the laws; would they not be as reasonable and useful were the enterprise preparing against the United States? While adverting to this branch of the law, it is proper to observe that in enterprises meditated against foreign nations, the ordinary process of binding to the observance of the peace and good behavior, could it be extended to acts to be done out of the jurisdiction of the United States, would be effectual in some cases where the offender is able to keep out of sight every indication of his purpose which could draw on him the exercise of the powers now given by law.

The states on the coast of Barbary seem generally disposed at present to respect our peace and friendship; with Tunis alone some uncertainty remains. Persuaded that it is our interest to maintain our peace with them on equal terms, or not at all, I propose to send in due time a reinforcement into the Mediterranean, unless previous information shall show it to be unnecessary.

We continue to receive proofs of the growing attachment of our Indian neighbors, and of their disposition to place all their interests under the patronage of the United States. These dispositions are inspired by their confidence in our justice, and in the sincere concern we feel for their welfare; and as long as we discharge these high and honorable functions with the integrity and good faith which alone can entitle us to their continuance, we may expect to reap the just reward in their peace and friendship.

The expedition of Messrs. Lewis and Clark, for exploring the river Missouri, and the best communication from that to the Pacific Ocean, has had all the success which could have been expected. They have traced the Missouri nearly to its source, descended the Columbia to the Pacific Ocean, ascertained with accuracy the geography of that interesting communication across our continent, learned the character of the country, of its commerce, and inhabitants; and it is but justice to say that Messrs. Lewis and Clark, and their brave companions, have by this arduous service deserved well of their country.

The attempt to explore the Red River, under the direction of Mr. Freeman, though conducted with a zeal and prudence meriting entire approbation, has not been equally successful. After proceeding up it about six hundred miles, nearly as far as the French settlements had extended while the country was in their possession, our geographers were obliged to return without completing their work.

Very useful additions have also been made to our knowledge of the Mississippi by Lieutenant Pike, who has ascended to its source, and whose journal and map, giving the details of the journey, will shortly be ready for communication to both houses of Congress. Those of Messrs. Lewis and Clark, and Freeman, will require further time to be digested and prepared. These important surveys, in addition to those before possessed, furnish materials for commencing an accurate map of the Mississippi and its western waters. Some principal rivers, however, remain still to be explored, toward which the authorization of Congress, by moderate appropriations, will be requisite.

I congratulate you, fellow citizens, on the approach of the period at which you may interpose your authority constitutionally to withdraw the citizens of the United States from all further participation in those violations of human rights which have been so long continued on the unoffending inhabitants of Africa, and which the morality, the reputation, and the best interests of our country have long been eager to proscribe. Although no law you may pass can take prohibitory effect till the first day of the year one thousand eight hundred and eight, yet the intervening period is not too long to prevent, by timely notice, expeditions which cannot be completed before that day.

The receipts at the treasury during the year ending on the 30th of September last have amounted to near fifteen millions of dollars, which have enabled us, after meeting the current demands, to pay two millions seven hundred thousand dollars of the American claims, in parts of the price of Louisiana; to pay of the funded debt upward of three millions of principal, and nearly four of interest; and in addition, to reimburse, in the course of the present month, near two millions of 5½ percent stock. These payments and reimbursements of the funded debt, with those which have been made in four years and a half preceding, will, at the close of the present year, have extinguished upward of twenty-three millions of principal.

The duties composing the Mediterranean fund will cease by law at the end of the present season. Considering, however, that they are levied chiefly on luxuries, and that we have an impost on salt, a necessary of life, the free use of which otherwise is so important, I recommend to your consideration the suppression of the duties on salt, and the continuation of the Mediterranean fund, instead thereof, for a short time, after which that also will become unnecessary for any purpose now within contemplation.

When both of these branches of revenue shall in this way be relinquished, there will still ere long be an accumulation of moneys in the treasury beyond the installments of public debt which we are permitted by contract to pay. They cannot, then, without a modification assented to by the public creditors, be applied to the extinguishment of this debt, and the complete liberation of our revenues—the most desirable of all objects; nor, if our peace continues, will they be wanting for any other existing purpose. The question, therefore, now comes forward: To what other objects shall these surpluses be appropriated, and the whole surplus of impost, after the entire discharge of the public debt, and during those intervals when the purposes of war shall not call for them? Shall we suppress the impost and give that advantage to foreign over domestic manufactures? On a few articles of more general and necessary use, the suppression in due season will doubtless be right, but the great mass of the articles on which impost is paid is foreign luxuries, purchased by those only who are rich enough to afford themselves the use of them. Their patriotism would certainly prefer its continuance and application to the great purposes of the public education, roads, rivers, canals, and such other objects of public improvement as it may be thought proper to add to the constitutional enumeration of federal powers. By these operations new channels of communication will be opened between the states; the lines of separation will disappear, their interests will be identified, and their union cemented by new and indissoluble ties. Education is here placed among the articles of public care, not that it would be proposed to take its ordinary branches out of the hands of private enterprise, which manages so much better all the concerns to which it is equal; but a public institution can alone supply those sciences which, though rarely called for, are yet necessary to complete the circle, all the parts of which contribute to the improvement of the country, and some of them to its preservation. The subject is now proposed for the consideration of Congress, because, if approved by the time the state legislatures shall have deliberated on this extension of the federal trusts, and the laws shall be passed, and other arrangements made for their execution, the necessary funds will be on hand and without employment. I suppose an amendment to the Constitution, by consent of the states, necessary, because the objects now recommended are not among those enumerated in the Constitution, and to which it permits the public moneys to be applied.

The present consideration of a national establishment for education, particularly, is rendered proper by this circumstance also, that if Congress, approving the proposition, shall yet think it more eligible to found it on a donation of lands, they have it now in their power to endow it with those which will be among the earliest to produce the necessary income. This foundation would have the advantage of being independent on war, which may suspend other improvements by requiring for its own purposes the resources destined for them.

This, fellow citizens, is the state of the public interest at the present moment, and according to the information now possessed. But such is the situation of the nations of Europe, and such too the predicament in which we stand with some of them, that we cannot rely with certainty on the present aspect of our affairs that may change from moment to moment, during the course of your session or after you shall have separated. Our duty is, therefore, to act upon things as they are, and to make a reasonable provision for whatever they may be. Were armies to be raised whenever a speck of war is visible in our horizon, we never should have been without them. Our resources would have been exhausted on dangers which have never happened, instead of being reserved for what is really to take place. A steady, perhaps a quickened pace in preparations for the defense of our seaport towns and waters; an early settlement of the most exposed and vulnerable parts of our country; a militia so organized that its effective portions can be called to any point in the Union, or volunteers instead of them to serve a sufficient time, are means which may always be ready yet never preying on our resources until actually called into use. They will maintain the public interests while a more permanent force shall be in course of preparation. But much will depend on the promptitude with which these means can be brought into activity. If war be forced upon us in spite of our long and vain appeals to the justice of nations, rapid and vigorous movements in its outset will go far toward securing us in its course and issue, and toward throwing its burdens on those who render necessary the resort from reason to force.

The result of our negotiations, or such incidents in their course as may enable us to infer their probable issue; such further movements also on our western frontiers as may show whether war is to be pressed there while negotiation is protracted elsewhere shall be communicated to you from time to time as they become known to me, with whatever other information I possess or may receive, which may aid your deliberations on the great national interests committed to your charge.

MESSAGE TO CONGRESS
ON THE
BURR CONSPIRACY

January 22, 1807

To the Senate and House of Representatives of the United States: Agreeably to the request of the House of Representatives, communicated in their resolution of the 16th instant, I proceed to state under the reserve therein expressed, information received touching an illegal combination of private individuals against the peace and safety of the Union, and a military expedition planned by them against the territories of a power in amity with the United States, with the measures I have pursued for suppressing the same.

I had for some time been in the constant expectation of receiving such further information as would have enabled me to lay before the legislature the termination as well as the beginning and progress of this scene of depravity, so far as it has been acted on the Ohio and its waters. From this the state and safety of the lower country might have been estimated on probable grounds, and the delay was indulged the rather because no circumstance had yet made it necessary to call in the aid of the legislative functions. Information now recently communicated has brought us nearly to the period contemplated. The mass of what I have received, in the course of these transactions, is voluminous, but little has been given under the sanction of an oath so as to constitute formal and legal evidence. It is chiefly in the form of letters, often containing such a mixture of rumors, conjectures, and suspicions as render it difficult to sift out the real facts, and unadvisable to hazard more than general outlines, strengthened by concurrent information or the particular credibility of the relater. In this state of the evidence, delivered sometimes too under the restriction of private confidence, neither safety nor justice will permit the exposing names, except that of the principal actor, whose guilt is placed beyond question.

Sometime in the latter part of September, I received intimations that designs were in agitation in the western country, unlawful and unfriendly to the peace of the Union; and that the prime mover in these was Aaron Burr, heretofore distinguished by the favor of his country. The grounds of these intimations being inconclusive, the objects uncertain, and the fidelity of that country known to be firm, the only measure taken was to urge the informants to use their best endeavors to get further insight into the designs and proceedings of the suspected persons, and to communicate them to me.

It was not until the latter part of October that the objects of the conspiracy began to be perceived, but still so blended and involved in mystery that nothing distinct could be singled out for pursuit. In this state of uncertainty as to the crime contemplated, the acts done, and the legal course to be pursued, I thought it best to send to the scene where these things were principally in transaction a person in whose integrity, understanding, and discretion entire confidence could be reposed, with instructions to investigate the plots going on, to enter into conference (for which he had sufficient credentials) with the governors and all other officers, civil and military, and with their aid to do on the spot whatever should be necessary to discover the designs of the conspirators, arrest their means, bring their persons to punishment, and to call out the force of the country to suppress any unlawful enterprise in which it should be found they were engaged. By this time it was known that many boats were under preparation, stores of provisions collecting, and an unusual number of suspicious characters in motion on the Ohio and its waters. Besides dispatching the confidential agent to that quarter, orders were at the same time sent to the governors of the Orleans and Mississippi territories, and to the commanders of the land and naval forces there, to be on their guard against surprise, and in constant readiness to resist any enterprise which might be attempted on the vessels, posts, or other objects under their care; and on the 8th of November, instructions were forwarded to General Wilkinson to hasten an accommodation with the Spanish commander on the Sabine, and as soon as that was effected, to fall back with his principal force to the hither bank of the Mississippi, for the defense of the intersecting points on that river. By a letter received from that officer on the 25th of November, but dated October 21, we learn that a confidential agent of Aaron Burr had been deputed to him, with communications partly written in cipher and partly oral, explaining his designs, exaggerating his resources, and making such offers of emolument and command to engage him and the army in his unlawful enterprise as he had flattered himself would be successful. The general, with the honor of a soldier and fidelity of a good citizen, immediately dispatched a trusty officer to me with information of what had passed, proceeding to establish such an understanding with the Spanish commandant on the Sabine as permitted him to withdraw his force across the Mississippi, and to enter on measures for opposing the projected enterprise.

The general's letter, which came to hand on the 25th of November, as has been mentioned, and some other information received a few days earlier, when brought together, developed Burr's general designs, different parts of which only had been revealed to different informants. It appeared that he contemplated two distinct objects, which might be carried on either jointly or separately, and either the one or the other first, as circumstances should direct. One of these was the severance of the Union of these States by the Allegheny mountains; the other, an attack on Mexico. A third object was provided, merely ostensible, to wit: the settlement of a pretended purchase of a tract of country on the Washita, claimed by a Baron Bastrop. This was to serve as the pretext for all his preparations, an allurement for such followers as really wished to acquire settlements in that country, and a cover under which to retreat in the event of final discomfiture of both branches of his real design.

He found at once that the attachment of the western country to the present Union was not to be shaken; that its dissolution could not be effected with the consent of its inhabitants, and that his resources were inadequate, as yet, to effect it by force. He took his course then at once, determined to seize on New Orleans, plunder the bank there, possess himself of the military and naval stores, and proceed on his expedition to Mexico; and to this object all his means and preparations were now directed. He collected from all the quarters where himself or his agents possessed influence, all the ardent, restless, desperate, and disaffected persons who were ready for any enterprise analogous to their characters. He seduced good and well-meaning citizens, some by assurances that he possessed the confidence of the government and was acting under its secret patronage, a pretense which obtained some credit from the state of our differences with Spain; and others by offers of land in Bastrop's claim on the Washita.

This was the state of my information of his proceedings about the last of November, at which time, therefore, it was first possible to take specific measures to meet them. The proclamation of November 27, two days after the receipt of General Wilkinson's information, was now issued. Orders were dispatched to every intersecting point on the Ohio and Mississippi, from Pittsburgh to New Orleans, for the employment of such force either of the regulars or of the militia, and of such proceedings also of the civil authorities, as might enable them to seize on all the boats and stores provided for the enterprise, to arrest the persons concerned, and to suppress effectually the further progress of the enterprise. A little before the receipt of these orders in the state of Ohio, our confidential agent, who had been diligently employed in investigating the conspiracy, had acquired sufficient information to open himself to the governor of that state and apply for the immediate exertion of the authority and power of the state to crush the combination. Governor

Tiffin and the legislature, with a promptitude, an energy, and patriotic zeal which entitle them to a distinguished place in the affection of their sister states, effected the seizure of all the boats, provisions, and other preparations within their reach, and thus gave a first blow, materially disabling the enterprise in its outset.

In Kentucky, a premature attempt to bring Burr to justice, without sufficient evidence for his conviction, had produced a popular impression in his favor, and a general disbelief of his guilt. This gave him an unfortunate opportunity of hastening his equipments. The arrival of the proclamation and orders, and the application and information of our confidential agent, at length awakened the authorities of that state to the truth, and then produced the same promptitude and energy of which the neighboring state had set the example. Under an act of their legislature of December 23, militia was instantly ordered to different important points, and measures taken for doing whatever could yet be done. Some boats (accounts vary from five to double or treble that number) and persons (differently estimated from one to three hundred) had in the meantime passed the falls of the Ohio, to rendezvous at the mouth of the Cumberland, with others expected down that river.

Not apprised, till very late, that any boats were building on Cumberland, the effect of the proclamation had been trusted to for some time in the state of Tennessee; but on the 19th of December, similar communications and instructions with those of the neighboring states were dispatched by express to the governor, and a general officer of the western division of the state, and on the 23d of December our confidential agent left Frankfort for Nashville, to put into activity the means of that state also. But by information received yesterday, I learn that on the 22d of December, Mr. Burr descended the Cumberland with two boats merely of accommodation, carrying with him from that state no quota toward his unlawful enterprise. Whether after the arrival of the proclamation, of the orders, or of our agent, any exertion which could be made by that state, or the orders of the governor of Kentucky for calling out the militia at the mouth of Cumberland, would be in time to arrest these boats, and those from the falls of the Ohio, is still doubtful.

On the whole, the fugitives from Ohio, with their associates from Cumberland, or any other place in that quarter, cannot threaten serious danger to the city of New Orleans.

By the same express of December 19, orders were sent to the governors of New Orleans and Mississippi, supplementary to those which had been given on the 25th of November, to hold the militia of their territories in readiness to cooperate for their defense, with the regular troops and armed vessels then under command of General Wilkinson. Great alarm, indeed, was excited at New Orleans by the exaggerated accounts of Mr. Burr, disseminated through his emissaries, of the armies and navies he was to assemble there. General Wilkinson had arrived there himself on the 24th of November, and had immediately put into activity the resources of the place for the purpose of its defense; and on the 10th of December he was joined by his troops from the Sabine. Great zeal was shown by the inhabitants generally, the merchants of the place readily agreeing to the most laudable exertions and sacrifices for manning the armed vessels with their seamen, and the other citizens manifesting unequivocal fidelity to the Union, and a spirit of determined resistance to their expected assailants.

Surmises have been hazarded that this enterprise is to receive aid from certain foreign powers. But these surmises are without proof or probability. The wisdom of the measures sanctioned by Congress at its last session had placed us in the paths of peace and justice with the only powers with whom we had any differences, and nothing has happened since which makes it either their interest or ours to pursue another course. No change of measures has taken place on our part; none ought to take place at this time. With the one, friendly arrangement was then proposed, and the law deemed necessary on the failure of that was suspended to give time for a fair trial of the issue. With the same power, negotiation is still preferred, and provisional measures only are necessary to meet the event of rupture. While, therefore, we do not deflect in the slightest degree from the course we then assumed, and are still pursuing, with mutual consent, to restore a good understanding, we are not to impute to them practices as irreconcilable to interest as to good faith, and changing necessarily the relations of peace and justice between us to those of war. These surmises are, therefore, to be imputed to the vauntings of the author of this enterprise, to multiply his partisans by magnifying the belief of his prospects and support.

By letters from General Wilkinson, of the 14th and 18th of September, which came to hand two days after date of the resolution of the House of Representatives, that is to say, on the morning of the 18th instant, I received the important affidavit, a copy of which I now communicate, with extracts of so much of the letters as come within the scope of the resolution. By these it will be seen that of three of the principal emissaries of Mr. Burr, whom the general had caused to be apprehended, one had been liberated by habeas corpus, and the two others, being those particularly employed in the endeavor to corrupt the general and army of the United States, have been embarked by him for our ports in the Atlantic states, probably on the consideration that an impartial trial could not be expected during the present agitations of New Orleans, and that that city was not as yet a safe place of confinement. As soon as these persons shall arrive, they will be delivered to the custody of the law, and left to such course of trial, both as to place and process, as its functionaries may direct. The presence of the highest judicial authorities, to be assembled at this place within a few days, the means of pursuing a sounder course of proceedings here than elsewhere, and the aid of the executive means, should the judges have occasion to use them render it equally desirable for the criminals as for the public that, being already removed from the place where they were first apprehended, the first regular arrest should take place here, and the course of proceedings receive here its proper direction.

ADDRESS TO
THE CHIEFS OF THE
SHAWNEE NATION

February 19, 1807

My Children, Chiefs of the Shawnee Nation: I have listened to the speeches of the Blackhoof, Blackbeard, and the other head chiefs of the Shawnees, and have considered them well. As all these speeches relate to the public affairs of your nation, I will answer them together.

You express a wish to have your lands laid off separately to yourselves, that you may know what is your own, may have a fixed place to live on, of which you may not be deprived after you shall have built on it, and improved it; you would rather that this should be towards Fort Wayne, and to include the three reserves; you ask a strong writing from us, declaring your right, and observe that the writing you had was taken from you by the Delawares.

After the close of our war with the English, we wished to establish peace and friendship with our Indian neighbors also. In order to do this, the first thing necessary was to fix a firm boundary between them and us, that there might be no trespasses across that by either party. Not knowing then what parts on our border belonged to each Indian nation particularly, we thought it safest to get all those in the north to join in one treaty, and to settle a general boundary line between them and us. We did not intermeddle as to the lines dividing them one from another, because this was their concern, not ours. We therefore met the chiefs of the Wyandots, Delawares, Shawnees, Ottaways, Chippeways, Powtewatamies, Miamis, Eel-Rivers, Weaks, Kickapoos, Pianteshaws, and Kaskaskies, at Greeneville, and agreed on a general boundary which was to divide their lands from those of the whites, making only some particular reserves, for the establishment of trade and intercourse with them. This treaty was eleven years ago, as Blackbeard has said. Since that, some of them have thought it for their advantage to sell us portions of their lands, which has changed the boundaries in some parts; but their rights in the residue remain as they were, and must always be settled among themselves. If the Shawnees and Delawares, and their other neighbors, choose to settle the boundaries between their respective tribes, and to have them marked and recorded in our books, we will mark them as they shall agree among themselves, and will give them strong writings declaring the separate right of each. After which, we will protect each tribe in its respective lands, as well as against other tribes who might attempt to take them from them, as against our own people. The writing which you say the Delawares took from you must have been the copy of the Treaty of Greenville. We will give you another copy to be kept by your nation.

With respect to the reserves, you know they were made for the purpose of establishing convenient stations for trade and intercourse with the tribes within whose boundaries they are. And as circumstances shall render it expedient to make these establishments, it is for your interest, as well as ours, that the possession of these stations should enable us to make them.

You complain that Bluejacket, and a part of your people at Greenville, cheat you in the distribution of your annuity, and take more of it than their just share. It will be difficult to remedy this evil while your nation is living in different settlements. We will, however, direct our agent to inquire, and inform us what are your numbers in each of your settlements, and will then divide the annuities between the settlements justly, according to their numbers. And if we can be of any service in bringing you all together into one place, we will willingly assist you for that purpose. Perhaps your visit to the settlement of your people on the Mississippi under the Flute may assist towards gathering them all into one place from which they may never again remove.

You say that you like our mode of living, that you wish to live as we do, to raise a plenty of food for your children, and to bring them up in good principles; that you adopt our mode of living, and ourselves as your brothers. My children, I rejoice to hear this; it is the wisest resolution you have ever formed, to raise corn and domestic animals, by the culture of the earth, and to let your women spin and weave clothes for you all, instead of depending for these on hunting. Be assured that half the labor and hardships you go through to provide your families by hunting, with food and clothing, if employed in a farm would feed and clothe them better. When the white people first came to this land, they were few, and you were many; now we are many, and you few; and why? Because, by cultivating the earth, we produce plenty to raise our children, while yours, during a part of every year, suffer for want of food, are forced to eat unwholesome things, are exposed to the weather in your hunting camps, get diseases and die. Hence it is that your numbers lessen.

You ask for instruction in our manner of living, for carpenters and blacksmiths. My children, you shall have them. We will do everything in our power to teach you to take care of your wives and children, that you may multiply and be strong. We are sincerely your friends and brothers, we are as unwilling to see your blood spilt in war, as our own. Therefore, we encourage you to live in peace with all nations, that your women and children may live without danger, and without fear. The greatest honor of a man is in doing good to his fellow men, not in destroying them. We have placed Mr. Kirk among you, who will have other persons under him to teach you how to manage farms, and to make clothes for yourselves; and we expect you will put some of your young people to work with the carpenters and smiths we place among you, that they may learn the trades. In this way only can you have a number of tradesmen sufficient for all your people.

You wish me to name to you the person authorized to speak

to you in our name, that you may know whom to believe, and not be deceived by impostors. My children, Governor Harrison is the person we authorize to talk to you in our name. You may depend on his advice, and that it comes from us. He stands between you and us, to convey with truth whatever either of us wishes to say to the other.

My children, I wish you a safe return to your friends and families, that you may retain your resolution of learning to live in our way, that it may give health and comfort to your families, and add members to your nation. In me you will always find a sincere and true friend.

LETTER TO COLONEL
ROBERT FULTON

Monticello, August 16, 1807

Sir:

Your letter of July 28 came to hand just as I was about leaving Washington, and it has not been sooner in my power to acknowledge it. I consider your torpedoes as very valuable means of the defense of harbors, and have no doubt that we should adopt them to a considerable degree. Not that I go the whole length (as I believe you do) of considering them as solely to be relied on. Neither a nation nor those entrusted with its affairs could be justifiable, however sanguine its expectations, in trusting solely to an engine not yet sufficiently tried, under all the circumstances which may occur, and against which we know not as yet what means of parrying may be devised. If, indeed, the mode of attaching them to the cable of a ship be the only one proposed, modes of prevention cannot be difficult. But I have ever looked to the submarine boat as most to be depended on for attaching them, and though I see no mention of it in your letter, or your publications, I am in hopes it is not abandoned as impracticable. I should wish to see a corps of young men trained to this service. It would belong to the engineers if at hand, but being nautical, I suppose we must have a corps of naval engineers, to practice and use them. I do not know whether we have authority to put any part of our existing naval establishment in a course of training, but it shall be the subject of a consultation with the secretary of the navy. General Dearborne has informed you of the urgency of our want of you at New Orleans for the locks there.

I salute you with great respect and esteem.

LETTER TO
CHARLES C. PINCKNEY

Washington, March 30, 1808

Dear Sir:

Your letter of the 8th was received on the 25th, and I proceed to state to you my views of the present state and prospect of foreign affairs, under the confidence that you will use them for your own government and opinions only, and by no means let them get out as from me. With France we are in no *immediate* danger of war. Her future views it is impossible to estimate. The immediate danger we are in of a rupture with England is postponed for this year. This is effected by the embargo, as the question was simply between that and war. That may go on a certain time, perhaps through the year, without the loss of their property to our citizens, but only its remaining unemployed on their hands. A time would come, however, when war would be preferable to a continuance of the embargo. Of this Congress may have to decide at their next meeting. In the meantime, we have good information that a negotiation for peace between France and England is commencing through the medium of Austria. The way for it has been smoothed by a determination expressed by France (through the *Moniteur,* which is their government paper) that herself and her allies will demand from Great Britain no renunciation of her maritime principles; nor will they renounce theirs. Nothing shall be said about them in the treaty, and both sides will be left in the next war to act on their own. No doubt the meaning of this is, that all the *Continental* powers of Europe will form themselves into an armed neutrality, to enforce their own principles. Should peace be made, we shall have safely rode out the storm in peace and prosperity. If we have anything to fear, it will be after that.

Nothing should be spared from this moment in putting our militia in the best condition possible, and procuring arms. I hope that this summer we shall get our whole seaports put into that state of defense, which Congress has thought proportioned to our circumstances and situation; that is to say, put *hors d'insulte* from a maritime attack, by a moderate squadron. If armies are combined with their fleets, then no resource can be provided but to meet them in the field. We propose to raise seven regiments only for the present year, depending always on our militia for the operations of the first year of war. On any other plan, we should be obliged always to keep a large standing army. Congress will adjourn in about three weeks. I hope Captain McComb is getting on well with your defensive works. We shall be able by midsummer, to give you a sufficient number of gunboats to protect Charleston from any vessel which can cross the bar; but the militia of the place must be depended on to fill up the complement of men necessary for action in the moment of an attack, as we shall man them, in ordinary, but with their navigating crew of eight or ten good seamen.

I salute you with great esteem and respect.

ADDRESS TO THE DEPUTIES OF THE CHEROKEES OF THE UPPER AND LOWER TOWNS

January 9, 1809

My Children: I understand from the speeches which you have delivered me that there is a difference of disposition among the people of both parts of your nation, some of them desiring to remain on their lands, to betake themselves to agriculture and the industrious occupations of civilized life, while others, retaining their attachment to the hunter life, and having little game on their present lands, are desirous to remove across the Mississippi to some of the vacant lands of the United States, where game is abundant. I am pleased to find so many disposed to ensure, by the cultivation of the earth, a plentiful subsistence for their families, and to improve their minds by education; but I do not blame those who, having been brought up from their infancy to the pursuit of game, desire still to follow it to distant countries. I know how difficult it is for men to change the habits in which they have been raised. The United States, my children, are the friends of both parties, and as far as can reasonably be asked, they will be willing to satisfy the wishes of both. Those who remain may be assured of our patronage, our aid, and good neighborhood; those who wish to remove are permitted to send an exploring party to reconnoiter the country on the waters of the Arkansas and White rivers, and the higher up the better, as they will be the longer unapproached by our settlements, which will begin at the mouths of those rivers. The regular districts of the government of St. Louis are already laid off to the St. Francis. When this party shall have found a tract of country suiting the emigrants, and not claimed by other Indians, we will arrange with them and you the exchange of that for a just portion of the country they leave, and to a part of which proportioned to their numbers they have a right. Every aid towards their removal, and what will be necessary for them there, will then be freely administered to them, and when established in their new settlements, we shall still consider them as our children, give them the benefit of exchanging their peltries for what they want at our factories, and always hold them firmly by the hand.

I will now, my children, proceed to answer your kind address on my retiring from the government. Sensible that I am become too old to watch over the extensive concerns of the seventeen states and their territories, I requested my fellow citizens to permit me to retire, to live with my family, and to choose another president for themselves and father for you. They have done so; and in a short time I shall retire, and resign into his hands the care of your and our concerns. Be assured, my children, that he will have the same friendly dispositions towards you which I have had, and that you will find in him a true and affectionate father. Indeed, this is now the disposition of all our people towards you; they look upon you as brethren, born in the same land, and having the same interests. Tell your people, therefore, to entertain no uneasiness on account of this change, for there will be no change as to them. Deliver to them my adieux, and my prayers to the Great Spirit for their happiness. Tell them that during my administration I have held their hand fast in mine, and that I will put it into the hand of their new father, who will hold it as I have done.

ADDRESS TO
THE INHABITANTS OF
ALBEMARLE COUNTY,
VIRGINIA

April 3, 1809

Returning to the scenes of my birth and early life, to the society of those with whom I was raised, and who have been ever dear to me, I receive, fellow citizens and neighbors, with inexpressible pleasure, the cordial welcome you are so good as to give me. Long absent on duties which the history of a wonderful era made incumbent on those called to them, the pomp, the turmoil, the bustle and splendor of office have drawn but deeper sighs for the tranquil and irresponsible occupations of private life, for the enjoyment of an affectionate intercourse with you, my neighbors and friends, and the endearments of family love, which nature has given us all, as the sweetener of every hour. For these I gladly lay down the distressing burden of power, and seek, with my fellow citizens, repose and safety under the watchful cares, the labors, and perplexities of younger and abler minds. The anxieties you express to administer to my happiness, do, of themselves, confer that happiness; and the measure will be complete if my endeavors to fulfill my duties in the several public stations to which I have been called have obtained for me the approbation of my country. The part which I have acted on the theater of public life has been before them; and to their sentence I submit it; but the testimony of my native county, of the individuals who have known me in private life, to my conduct in its various duties and relations, is the more grateful, as proceeding from eyewitnesses and observers, from triers of the vicinage.

Of you, then, my neighbors, I may ask, in the face of the world, "Whose ox have I taken, or whom have I defrauded? Whom have I oppressed, or of whose hand have I received a bribe to blind mine eyes therewith?" On your verdict I rest with conscious security. Your wishes for my happiness are received with just sensibility, and I offer sincere prayers for your own welfare and prosperity.

LETTER TO GENERAL
THADDEUS KOSCIUSKO

Monticello, February 26, 1810

My dear General and Friend:

I have rarely written to you; never but by safe conveyances; and avoiding everything political, lest coming from one in the station I then held it might be imputed injuriously to our country, or perhaps even excite jealousy of you. Hence my letters were necessarily dry. Retired now from public concerns, totally unconnected with them, and avoiding all curiosity about what is done or intended, what I say is from myself only, the workings of my own mind, imputable to nobody else.

The anxieties which I know you have felt on seeing exposed to the justlings of a warring world a country to which, in early life, you devoted your sword and services when oppressed by foreign dominion, were worthy of your philanthropy and disinterested attachment to the freedom and happiness of man. Although we have not made all the provisions which might be necessary for a war in the field of Europe, yet we have not been inattentive to such as would be necessary here. From the moment that the affair of the Chesapeake rendered the prospect of war imminent, every faculty was exerted to be prepared for it, and I think I may venture to solace you with the assurance that we are, in a good degree, prepared. Military stores for many campaigns are on hand, all the necessary articles (sulphur excepted), and the art of preparing them among ourselves, abundantly; arms in our magazines for more men than will ever be required in the field, and forty thousand new stand yearly added, of our own fabrication, superior to any we have ever seen from Europe; heavy artillery much beyond our need; an increasing stock of field pieces, several founderies casting one every other day each; a military school of about fifty students, which has been in operation a dozen years; and the manufacture of men constantly going on, and adding forty thousand young soldiers to our force every year that the war is deferred. At all our seaport towns of the least consequence we have erected works of defense and assigned them gunboats, carrying one or two heavy pieces, either eighteen, twenty-four, or thirty-two pounders, sufficient in the smaller harbors to repel the predatory attacks of privateers or single armed ships, and proportioned in the larger harbors to such more serious attacks as they may probably be exposed to. All these were nearly completed, and their gunboats in readiness, when I retired from the government. The works of New York and New Orleans alone, being on a much larger scale, are not yet completed. The former will be finished this summer, mounting 438 guns, and, with the aid of from fifty to one hundred gunboats, will be adequate to the resistance of any fleet which will ever be trusted across the Atlantic. The works for New Orleans are less advanced. These are our preparations. They are very different from what you will be told by newspapers, and travelers, even Americans. But it is not to them the government communicates the public condition. Ask one of them if he knows the exact state of any particular harbor, and you will find probably that he does not know even that of the one he comes from. You will ask, perhaps, where are the proof of these preparations for one who cannot go and see them. I answer, in the acts of Congress, authorizing such preparations, and in your knowledge of me, that, if authorized, they would be executed.

Two measures have not been adopted, which I pressed on Congress repeatedly at their meetings. The one, to settle the whole ungranted territory of Orleans, by donations of land to able-bodied young men, to be engaged and carried there at the public expense, who would constitute a force always ready on the spot to defend New Orleans. The other was to class the militia according to the years of their birth, and make all those from twenty to twenty-five liable to be trained and called into service at a moment's warning. This would have given us a force of three hundred thousand young men, prepared by proper training, for service in any part of the United States; while those who had passed through that period would remain at home, liable to be used in their own or adjacent states. These two measures would have completed what I deemed necessary for the entire security of our country. They would have given me, on my retirement from the government of the nation, the consolatory reflection that having found, when I was called to it, not a single seaport town in a condition to repel a levy of contribution by a single privateer or pirate, I had left every harbor so prepared by works and gunboats as to be in a reasonable state of security against any probable attack; the territory of Orleans acquired, and planted with an internal force sufficient for its protection; and the whole territory of the United States organized by such a classification of its male force as would give it the benefit of all its young population for active service, and that of a middle and advanced age for stationary defense. But these measures will, I hope, be completed by my successor, who, to the purest principles of republican patriotism, adds a wisdom and foresight second to no man on earth.

So much as to my country. Now a word as to myself. I am retired to Monticello, where, in the bosom of my family, and surrounded by my books, I enjoy a repose to which I have been long a stranger. My mornings are devoted to correspondence. From breakfast to dinner, I am in my shops, my garden, or on horseback among my farms; from dinner to dark, I give to society and recreation with my neighbors and friends; and from candlelight to early bedtime, I read. My health is perfect; and my strength considerably reinforced by the activity of the course I pursue; perhaps it is as great as usually falls to the lot of near sixty-seven years of age. I talk of ploughs and harrows, of seeding and harvesting, with my neighbors, and of politics too, if they choose, with as little reserve as the rest of my fellow citizens, and feel, at length, the blessing of being free to say and do what I please, without being responsible for it to any mortal.

A part of my occupation, and by no means the least pleasing, is the direction of the studies of such young men as ask it. They place themselves in the neighboring village, and have the use of my library and counsel, and make a part of my society. In advising the course of their reading, I endeavor to keep their attention fixed on the main objects of all science, the freedom and happiness of man; so that coming to bear a share in the councils and government of their country, they will keep ever in view the sole objects of all legitimate government. . . .

Instead of the unalloyed happiness of retiring unembarrassed and independent, to the enjoyment of my estate, which is ample for my limited views, I have to pass such a length of time in a thralldom of mind never before known to me. Except for this, my happiness would have been perfect. That yours may never know disturbance, and that you may enjoy as many years of life as health and ease to yourself shall wish, is the sincere prayer of your constant and affectionate friend.

LETTER TO
DR. BENJAMIN RUSH

Monticello, January 16, 1811
Dear Sir:

I had been considering for some days whether it was not time, by a letter, to bring myself to your recollection, when I received your welcome favor of the 2d instant. I had before heard of the heart-rending calamity you mention, and had sincerely sympathized with your afflictions. But I had not made it the subject of a letter, because I knew that condolences were but renewals of grief. Yet I thought, and still think, this is one of the cases wherein we should "not sorrow, even as others who have no hope." . . .

You ask if I have read Hartley? I have not. My present course of life admits less reading than I wish. From breakfast, or noon at latest, to dinner, I am mostly on horseback, attending to my farm or other concerns, which I find healthful to my body, mind, and affairs; and the few hours I can pass in my cabinet are devoured by correspondences; not those with my intimate friends, with whom I delight to interchange sentiments, but with others, who, writing to me on concerns of their own in which I have had an agency, or from motives of mere respect and approbation, are entitled to be answered with respect and a return of good will. My hope is that this obstacle to the delights of retirement will wear away with the oblivion which follows that, and that I may at length be indulged in those studious pursuits, from which nothing but revolutionary duties would ever have called me.

I shall receive your proposed publication and read it with the pleasure which everything gives me from your pen. Although much of a skeptic in the practice of medicine, I read with pleasure its ingenious theories.

I receive with sensibility your observations on the discontinuance of friendly correspondence between Mr. Adams and myself, and the concern you take in its restoration. This discontinuance has not proceeded from me, nor from the want of sincere desire and of effort on my part, to renew our intercourse. You know the perfect coincidence of principle and of action, in the early part of the Revolution, which produced a high degree of mutual respect and esteem between Mr. Adams and myself. Certainly no man was ever truer than he was, in that day, to those principles of rational republicanism which, after the necessity of throwing off our monarchy, dictated all our efforts in the establishment of a new government. And although he swerved, afterwards, towards the principles of the English constitution, our friendship did not abate on that account. While he was vice president, and I secretary of state, I received a letter from President Washington, then at Mount Vernon, desiring me to call together the heads of departments, and to invite Mr. Adams to join us (which, by-the-bye, was the only instance of that being done) in order to determine on some measure which required dispatch; and he desired me to act on it, as decided, without again recurring to him. I invited them to dine with me, and after dinner, sitting at our wine, having settled our question, other conversation came on, in which a collision of opinion arose between Mr. Adams and Colonel Hamilton on the merits of the British constitution, Mr. Adams giving it as his opinion that, if some of its defects and abuses were corrected, it would be the most perfect constitution of government ever devised by man. Hamilton, on the contrary, asserted that with its existing vices, it was the most perfect model of government that could be formed; and that the correction of its vices would render it an impracticable government. And this you may be assured was the real line of difference between the political principles of these two gentlemen. Another incident took place on the same occasion, which will further delineate Mr. Hamilton's political principles. The room being hung around with a collection of the portraits of remarkable men, among them were those of Bacon, Newton, and Locke, Hamilton asked me who they were. I told him they were my trinity of the three greatest men the world had ever produced, naming them. He paused for some time: "The greatest man," said he, "that ever lived, was Julius Caesar." Mr. Adams was honest as a politician, as well as a man; Hamilton honest as a man, but as a politician believing in the necessity of either force or corruption to govern men.

You remember the machinery which the Federalists played off, about that time, to beat down the friends to the real principles of our Constitution, to silence by terror every expression in their favor, to bring us into war with France and alliance with England, and finally to homologize our Constitution with that of England. Mr. Adams, you know, was overwhelmed with feverish addresses, dictated by the fear, and often by the pen, of the *bloody buoy,* and was seduced by them into some open indications of his new principles of government, and in fact was so elated as to mix with his kindness a little superciliousness towards me. Even Mrs. Adams, with all her good sense and prudence, was sensibly flushed. And you recollect the short suspension of our intercourse, and the circumstance which gave rise to it, which you were so good as to bring to an early explanation, and have set to rights, to the cordial satisfaction of us all. The nation at length passed condemnation on the political principles of the Federalists by refusing to continue Mr. Adams in the presidency. On the day on which we learned in Philadelphia the vote of the city of New York, which it was well known would decide the vote of the state, and that, again, the vote of the Union, I called on Mr. Adams on some official business. He was very sensibly affected, and accosted me with these words: "Well, I understand that you are to beat me in this contest, and I will only say that I will be as faithful a subject as any you will have." "Mr. Adams," said I, "this is no personal contest between you and me. Two systems of principles on the subject of government divide our fellow citizens into two parties. With one of these you concur, and I with the other. As we have been longer on the public stage than most of those now living, our names happen to be more generally known. One of these parties, therefore, has put your name at its head, the other mine. Were we both to die today, tomorrow two other names would be in the place of ours, without any change in the motion of the machinery. Its motion is from its principle, not from you or myself." "I believe you are right," said he, "that we are but passive instruments, and should not suffer this matter to affect our personal dispositions." But he did not long retain this just view of the subject. I have always believed that the thousand calumnies which the Federalists, in bitterness of heart, and mortification at their ejection, daily invented against me, were carried to him by their busy intriguers, and made some impression. When the election between Burr and myself was kept in suspense by the Federalists, and they were meditating to place the president of the Senate at the head of the government, I called on Mr. Adams with a view to have this desperate measure prevented by his negative. He grew warm in an instant, and said with a vehemence he had not used towards me before, "Sir, the event of the election is within your own power. You have only to say you will do justice to the public creditors, maintain the navy, and not disturb those holding offices, and the government will instantly be put into your hands. We know it is the wish of the people it should be so." "Mr. Adams," said I, "I know not what part of my conduct, in either public or private life, can have authorized a doubt of my fidelity to the public engagements. I say, however, I will not come into the government by capitulation. I will not enter on it but in perfect freedom to follow the dictates of my own judgment." I had before given the same answer to the same intimation from Gouverneur Morris. "Then," said he, "things must take their course." I turned the conversation to something else, and soon took my leave. It was the first time in our lives we had ever parted with anything like dissatisfaction. And then followed those scenes of midnight appointment, which have been condemned by all men. The last day of his political power, the last hours, and even beyond the midnight, were employed in filling all offices, and especially permanent ones, with the bitterest Federalists, and providing for me the alternative either to execute the government by my enemies, whose study it would be to thwart and defeat all my measures, or to incur the odium of such numerous removals from office as might bear me down. A little time and reflection effaced in my mind this temporary dissatisfaction with Mr. Adams, and restored me to that just estimate of his virtues and passions, which a long acquaintance had enabled me to fix. And my first wish became that of making his retirement easy by any means in my power; for it was understood he was not rich. I suggested to some Republican members of the delegation from his state the giving him, either directly or indirectly, an office, the most lucrative in that state, and then offered to be resigned, if they thought he would not deem it affrontive. They were of opinion he would take great offense at the offer; and moreover, that the body of republicans would consider such a step in the outset as arguing very ill of the course I meant to pursue. I dropped the idea, therefore, but did not cease to wish for some opportunity of renewing our friendly understanding.

Two or three years after, having had the misfortune to lose a daughter, between whom and Mrs. Adams there had been a considerable attachment, she made it the occasion of writing me a letter, in which, with the tenderest expressions of concern at this event, she carefully avoided a single one of friendship towards myself, and even concluded it with the wishes "of her who *once* took pleasure in subscribing herself your friend, Abigail Adams." Unpromising as was the complexion of this letter, I determined to make an effort towards removing the cloud from between us. This brought on a correspondence which I now enclose for your perusal, after which be so good as to return it to me, as I have never communicated it to any mortal breathing, before. I send it to you, to convince you I have not been wanting either in the desire or the endeavor to remove this misunderstanding. Indeed, I thought it highly disgraceful to us both, as indicating minds not sufficiently elevated to prevent a public competition from affecting our personal friendship. I soon found from the correspondence that conciliation was desperate, and yielding to an intimation in her last letter, I ceased from further explanation. I have the same good opinion of Mr. Adams which I ever had. I know him to be an honest man, an able one with his pen, and he was a powerful advocate on the floor of Congress. He has been alienated from me by belief in the lying suggestions contrived for electioneering purposes, that I perhaps mixed in the activity and intrigues of the occasion. My most intimate friends can testify that I was perfectly passive. They would sometimes, indeed, tell me what was going on; but no man ever heard me take part in such conversations; and none ever misrepresented Mr. Adams in my presence without my asserting his just character. With very confidential persons I have doubtless disapproved of the principles and practices of his administration. This was unavoidable. But never with those with whom it could do him any injury. Decency would have required this conduct from me, if disposition had not; and I am satisfied Mr. Adams's conduct was equally honorable towards me. But I think it part of his character to suspect foul play in those of whom he is jealous, and not easily to relinquish his suspicions.

I have gone, my dear friend, into these details, that you might know everything which had passed between us, might be fully possessed of the state of facts and dispositions, and judge for yourself whether they admit a revival of that friendly intercourse for which you are so kindly solicitous. I shall certainly not be wanting in anything on my part which may second your efforts, which will be the easier with me, inasmuch as I do not entertain a sentiment of Mr. Adams the expression of which could give him reasonable offense. And I submit the whole to yourself, with the assurance that whatever be the issue, my friendship and respect for yourself will remain unaltered and unalterable.

LETTER TO
DR. ROBERT PATTERSON

Monticello, November 10, 1811

Dear Sir:

I write this letter separate, because you may perhaps think something in the other of the same date worth communicating to the committee.

I accept, willingly, Mr. Voigt's offer to make me a timepiece, and with the kind of pendulum he proposes. I wish it to be as good as hands can make it, in everything useful, but no unnecessary labor to be spent on mere ornament. A plain but neat mahogany case will be preferred.

I have a curiosity to try the length of the pendulum vibrating seconds here, and would wish Mr. Voigt to prepare one which could be substituted for that of the clock occasionally, without requiring anything more than unhanging the one and hanging the other in its place. The bob should be spherical, of lead, and its radius, I presume, about one inch. As I should not have the convenience of a room of uniform temperature, the suspending rod should be such as not to be affected by heat or cold, nor yet so heavy as to effect too sensibly the center of oscillation. Would not a rod of wood not larger than a large wire answer this double view? I remember Mr. Rittenhouse told me he had made experiments on some occasion on the expansibility of wood lengthwise by heat, which satisfied him it was as good as the gridiron for a suspender of the bob. By the experiments on the strength of wood and iron in supporting weights appended to them, iron has been found but about six times as strong as wood, while its specific gravity is eight times as great. Consequently, a rod of it of equal strength will weigh but three-fourths of one of iron, and disturb the center of oscillation less in proportion. A rod of wood of white oak, e.g., not larger than a seine twine, would probably support a spherical bob of lead of one inch radius. It might be worked down to that size, I suppose, by the cabinet-makers, who are in the practice of preparing smaller threads of wood for inlaying. The difficulty would be in making it fast to the bob at one end, and scapement at the other, so as to regulate the length with ease and accuracy. This Mr. Voigt's ingenuity can supply, and in all things I would submit the whole matter to your direction to him, and be thankful to you to give it. Yours affectionately.

LETTER TO
DR. BENJAMIN RUSH

Poplar Forest, December 5, 1811

Dear Sir:

While at Monticello I am so much engrossed by business or society that I can only write on matters of strong urgency. Here I have leisure, as I have everywhere the disposition to think of my friends. I recur, therefore, to the subject of your kind letters relating to Mr. Adams and myself, which a late occurrence has again presented to me. I communicated to you the correspondence which had parted Mrs. Adams and myself, in proof that I could not give friendship in exchange for such sentiments as she had recently taken up towards myself, and avowed and maintained in her letters to me. Nothing but a total renunciation of these could admit a reconciliation, and that could be cordial only in proportion as the return to ancient opinions was believed sincere. In these jaundiced sentiments of hers I had associated Mr. Adams, knowing the weight which her opinions had with him, and notwithstanding she declared in her letters that they were not communicated to him. A late incident has satisfied me that I wronged him as well as her, in not yielding entire confidence to this assurance on her part. Two of the Mr. ———, my neighbors and friends, took a tour to the northward during the last summer. In Boston they fell into company with Mr. Adams, and by his invitation passed a day with him at Braintree. He spoke out to them everything which came uppermost, and as it occurred to his mind, without any reserve; and seemed most disposed to dwell on those things which happened during his own administration. He spoke of his *masters,* as he called his heads of departments, as acting above his control, and often against his

287

opinions. Among many other topics, he adverted to the unprincipled licentiousness of the press against myself, adding, "I
always loved Jefferson, and still love him."

This is enough for me. I only needed this knowledge to
revive towards him all the affections of the most cordial moments of our lives. Changing a single word only in Dr. Franklin's character of him, I knew him to be always an honest man,
often a great one, but sometimes incorrect and precipitate in his
judgments; and it is known to those who have ever heard me
speak of Mr. Adams that I have ever done him justice myself,
and defended him when assailed by others, with the single
exception as to political opinions. But with a man possessing so
many other estimable qualities, why should we be dissocialized
by mere differences of opinion in politics, in religion, in philosophy, or anything else. His opinions are as honestly formed as my
own. Our different views of the same subject are the result of a
difference in our organization and experience. I never withdrew
from the society of any man on this account, although many
have done it from me; much less should I do it from one with
whom I had gone through, with hand and heart, so many trying
scenes. I wish, therefore, but for an apposite occasion to express
to Mr. Adams my unchanged affections for him. There is an
awkwardness which hangs over the resuming a correspondence
so long discontinued, unless something could arise which should
call for a letter. Time and chance may perhaps generate such an
occasion, of which I shall not be wanting in promptitude to
avail myself. From this fusion of mutual affections, Mrs. Adams
is of course separated. It will only be necessary that I never name
her. In your letters to Mr. Adams, you can, perhaps, suggest my
continued cordiality towards him, and knowing this, should an
occasion of writing first present itself to him, he will perhaps
avail himself of it, as I certainly will, should it first occur to me.
No ground for jealousy now existing, he will certainly give fair
play to the natural warmth of his heart. Perhaps I may open the
way in some letter to my old friend Gerry, who I know is in
habits of the greatest intimacy with him.

I have thus, my friend, laid open my heart to you, because you were so kind as to take an interest in healing again revolutionary affections, which have ceased in expression only, but not in their existence. God ever bless you, and preserve you in life and health.

LETTER TO
JOHN ADAMS

Monticello, January 21, 1812

Dear Sir:

I thank you beforehand (for they are not yet arrived) for the specimens of homespun you have been so kind as to forward me by post. I doubt not their excellence, knowing how far you are advanced in these things in your quarter. Here we do little in the fine way, but in coarse and middling goods a great deal. Every family in the country is a manufactory within itself, and is very generally able to make within itself all the stouter and middling stuffs for its own clothing and household use. We consider a sheep for every person in the family as sufficient to clothe it, in addition to the cotton, hemp, and flax which we raise ourselves. For fine stuff we shall depend on your northern manufactories. Of these, that is to say, of company establishments, we have none. We use little machinery. The spinning jenny, and loom with the flying shuttle, can be managed in a family; but nothing more complicated. The economy and thriftiness resulting from our household manufactures are such that they will never again be laid aside; and nothing more salutary for us has ever happened than the British obstructions to our demands for their manufactures. Restore free intercourse when they will, their commerce with us will have totally changed its form, and the articles we shall in future want from them will not exceed their own consumption of our produce.

A letter from you calls up recollections very dear to my mind. It carries me back to the times when, beset with difficulties and dangers, we were fellow laborers in the same cause, struggling for what is most valuable to man, his right of self-government. Laboring always at the same oar, with some wave ever ahead, threatening to overwhelm us, and yet passing harmless under our bark, we knew not how we rode through the storm with heart and hand, and made a happy port. Still we did not expect to be without rubs and difficulties; and we have had them. First, the detention of the western posts, then the coalition of Pilnitz, outlawing our commerce with France, and the British enforcement of the outlawry. In your day, French depredations; in mine, English, and the Berlin and Milan decrees; now, the English orders of council, and the piracies they authorize. When these shall be over, it will be the impressment of our seamen or something else; and so we have gone on, and so we shall go on, puzzled and prospering beyond example in the history of man. And I do believe we shall continue to growl, to multiply and prosper until we exhibit an association, powerful, wise, and happy, beyond what has yet been seen by men. As for France and England, with all their preeminence in science, the one is a den of robbers, and the other of pirates. And if science produces no better fruits than tyranny, murder, rapine, and destitution of national morality, I would rather wish our country to be ignorant, honest, and estimable, as our neighboring savages are. But whither is senile garrulity leading me? Into politics, of which I have taken final leave. I think little of them and say less. I have given up newspapers in exchange for Tacitus and Thucydides, for Newton and Euclid, and I find myself much the happier. Sometimes, indeed, I look back to former occurrences, in remembrance of our old friends and fellow laborers, who have fallen before us. Of the signers of the Declaration of Independence, I see now living not more than half a dozen on your side of the Potomac, and on this side, myself alone. You and I have been wonderfully spared, and myself with remarkable health, and a considerable activity of body and mind. I am on horseback three or four hours of every day, visit three or four times a year a possession I have ninety miles distant, performing the winter journey on horseback. I walk little, however, a single mile being too much for me, and I live in the midst of my grandchildren, one of whom has lately promoted me to be a great-grandfather. I have heard with pleasure that you also retain good health, and a greater power of exercise in walking than I do. But I would rather have heard this from yourself, and that, writing a letter like mine, full of egotisms, and of details of your health, your habits, occupations, and enjoyments, I should have the pleasure of knowing that in the race of life, you do not keep, in its physical decline, the same distance ahead of me which you have done in political honors and achievements. No circumstances have lessened the interest I feel in these particulars respecting yourself; none have suspended for one moment my sincere esteem for you, and I now salute you with unchanged affection and respect.

LETTER TO PRESIDENT JAMES MADISON

Monticello, June 29, 1812

Dear Sir:

I duly received your favor of the 22d covering the declaration of war. It is entirely popular here, the only opinion being that it should have been issued the moment the season admitted the militia to enter Canada. . . . To continue the war popular, two things are necessary mainly: (1) to stop Indian barbarities; the conquest of Canada will do this; (2) to furnish markets for our produce, say indeed for our flour, for tobacco is already given up, and seemingly without reluctance. The great profits of the wheat crop have allured everyone to it; and never was such a crop on the ground as that which we generally begin to cut this day. It would be mortifying to the farmer to see such a one rot in his barn. It would soon sicken him to war. Nor can this be a matter of wonder or of blame on him. Ours is the only country on earth where war is an instantaneous and total suspension of all the objects of his industry and support. For carrying our produce to foreign markets our own ships, neutral ships, and even enemy ships under neutral flag, which I would wink at, will probably suffice. But the coasting trade is of double importance, because both seller and buyer are disappointed, and both are our own citizens. You will remember that in this trade our greatest distress in the last war was produced by our own pilot boats taken by the British and kept as tenders to their larger vessels. These being the swiftest vessels on the ocean, they took them and selected the swiftest from the whole mass. Filled with men they scoured everything along shore, and completely cut up that coasting business which might otherwise have been carried on within the range of vessels of force and draught. Why should not we then line our coast with vessels of pilot-boat construction, filled with men, armed with cannonades, and only so much larger as to assure the mastery of the pilot boat? The British cannot counterwork us by building similar ones, because the fact is, however unaccountable, that our builders alone understand that construction. It is on our own pilot boats the British will depend, which our larger vessels may thus retake. These, however, are the ideas of a landsman only; Mr. Hamilton's judgment will test their soundness.

Our militia are much afraid of being called to Norfolk at this season. They all declare a preference of a march to Canada. I trust however that Governor Barbour will attend to circumstances, and so apportion the service among the counties that those acclimated by birth or residence may perform the summer tour, and the winter service be allotted to the upper counties.

I trouble you with a letter for General Kosciusko. It covers a bill of exchange from Mr. Barnes for him, and is therefore of great importance to him. Hoping you will have the goodness so far to befriend the general as to give it your safest conveyance, I commit it to you, with the assurance of my sincere affections.

LETTER TO
DR. WALTER JONES

Monticello, January 2, 1814

Dear Sir:

Your favor of November 25 reached this place December 21, having been near a month on the way. How this could happen I know not, as we have two mails a week both from Fredericksburg and Richmond. It found me just returned from a long journey and absence, during which so much business had accumulated, commanding the first attentions, that another week has been added to the delay.

I deplore, with you, the putrid state into which our newspapers have passed, and the malignity, the vulgarity, and mendacious spirit of those who write for them; and I enclose you a recent sample, the production of a New England judge, as a proof of the abyss of degradation into which we are fallen. These ordures are rapidly depraving the public taste, and lessening its relish for sound food. As vehicles of information, and a curb on our functionaries, they have rendered themselves useless, by forfeiting all title to belief. That this has, in a great degree, been produced by the violence and malignity of party spirit, I agree with you; and I have read with great pleasure the paper you enclosed me on that subject, which I now return. It is at the same time a perfect model of the style of discussion which candor and decency should observe, of the tone which renders difference of opinion even amiable, and a succinct, correct, and dispassionate history of the origin and progress of party among us. It might be incorporated as it stands, and without changing a word, into the history of the present epoch, and would give to posterity a fairer view of the times than they will probably derive from other sources. In reading it with great satisfaction, there was but a single passage where I wished a little more development of a very sound and catholic idea; a single intercalation to rest it solidly on true bottom. It is near the end of the first page, where you make a statement of genuine republican maxims, saying that "the people ought to possess as much political power as can possibly exist with the order and security of society." Instead of this, I would say that "the people, being the only safe depository of power, should exercise in person every function which their qualifications enable them to exercise, consistently with the order and security of society; that we now find them equal to the election of those who shall be invested with their executive and legislative powers, and to act themselves in the judiciary, as judges in questions of fact; that the range of their powers ought to be enlarged," etc. This gives both the reason and exemplication of the maxim you express, that they "ought to possess as much political power," etc. I see nothing to correct either in your facts or principles.

You say that in taking General Washington on your shoulders, to bear him harmless through the federal coalition, you encounter a perilous topic. I do not think so. You have given the genuine history of the course of his mind through the trying scenes in which it was engaged, and of the seductions by which it was deceived, but not depraved. I think I knew General Washington intimately and thoroughly; and were I called on to delineate his character, it should be in terms like these.

His mind was great and powerful, without being of the very first order; his penetration strong, though not so acute as that of a Newton, Bacon, or Locke; and as far as he saw, no judgment was ever sounder. It was slow in operation, being little aided by invention or imagination, but sure in conclusion. Hence the common remark of his officers of the advantage he derived from councils of war, where hearing all suggestions, he selected whatever was best; and certainly no general ever planned his battles more judiciously. But if deranged during the course of the action, if any member of his plan was dislocated by sudden circumstances, he was slow in readjustment. The consequence was that he often failed in the field, and rarely against an enemy in station, as at Boston and York. He was incapable of fear, meeting personal dangers with the calmest unconcern. Perhaps the strongest feature in his character was prudence, never acting until every circumstance, every consideration, was maturely weighed; refraining if he saw a doubt, but, when once decided, going through with his purpose, whatever obstacles opposed. His integrity was most pure, his justice the most inflexible I have ever known, no motives of interest or consanguinity, of friendship or hatred, being able to bias his decision. He was, indeed, in every sense of the words, a wise, a good, and a great man. His temper was naturally irritable and high-toned; but reflection and resolution had obtained a firm and habitual ascendency over it. If ever, however, it broke its bonds, he was most tremendous in his wrath. In his expenses he was honorable, but exact; liberal in contributions to whatever promised utility; but frowning and unyielding on all visionary projects, and all unworthy calls on his charity. His heart was not warm in its affections; but he exactly calculated every man's value, and gave him a solid esteem proportioned to it. His person, you know, was fine, his stature exactly what one would wish, his deportment easy, erect, and noble; the best horseman of his age, and the most graceful figure that could be seen on horseback. Although in the circle of his friends, where he might be unreserved with safety, he took a free share in conversation, his colloquial talents were not above mediocrity, possessing neither copiousness of ideas nor fluency of words. In public, when called on for a sudden opinion, he was unready, short, and embarrassed. Yet he wrote readily, rather diffusely, in an easy and correct style. This he had acquired by conversation with the world, for his education was merely reading, writing, and common arithmetic, to which he added surveying at a later day. His time was employed in action chiefly, reading little, and that only in agriculture and English history. His correspondence became necessarily extensive, and, with journalizing his agricultural proceedings, occupied most of his leisure hours within doors. On the whole, his character was, in its mass, perfect, in nothing bad, in few points indifferent; and it may truly be said that never did nature and fortune combine more perfectly to make a man great, and to place him in the same constellation with whatever worthies have merited from man an everlasting remembrance. For his was the singular destiny and merit of leading the armies of his country successfully through an arduous war, for the establishment of its independence; of conducting its councils through the birth of a government, new in its forms and principles, until it had settled down into a quiet and orderly train; and of scrupulously obeying the laws through the whole of his career, civil and military, of which the history of the world furnishes no other example.

How, then, can it be perilous for you to take such a man on your shoulders? I am satisfied the great body of Republicans think of him as I do. We were, indeed, dissatisfied with him on his ratification of the British treaty. But this was short-lived. We knew his honesty, the wiles with which he was encompassed, and that age had already began to relax the firmness of his purposes; and I am convinced he is more deeply seated in the love and gratitude of the Republicans than in the Pharisaical homage of the federal monarchists. For he was no monarchist from preference of his judgment. The soundness of that gave him correct views of the rights of man, and his severe justice devoted him to them. He has often declared to me that he considered our new Constitution as an experiment on the practicability of republican government, and with what dose of liberty man could be trusted for his own good; that he was determined the experiment should have a fair trial, and would lose the last drop of his blood in support of it. And these declarations he repeated to me the oftener and more pointedly, because he knew my suspicions of Colonel Hamilton's views, and probably had heard from him the same declarations which I had, to wit, that "the British constitution, with its unequal representation, corruption, and other existing abuses, was the most perfect government which had ever been established on earth, and that a reformation of those abuses would make it an impracticable government." I do believe that General Washington had not a firm confidence in the durability of our government. He was naturally distrustful of men, and inclined to gloomy apprehensions; and I was ever persuaded that a belief that we must at length end in something like a British constitution had some weight in his adoption of the ceremonies of levees, birthdays, pompous meetings with Congress, and other forms of the same character, calculated to prepare us gradually for a change which he believed possible, and to let it come on with as little shock as might be to the public mind.

These are my opinions of General Washington, which I would vouch at the judgment seat of God, having been formed on an acquaintance of thirty years. I served with him in the Virginia legislature from 1769 to the Revolutionary War, and again, a short time in Congress, until he left us to take command of the army. During the war and after it we corresponded occasionally, and in the four years of my continuance in the office of Secretary of State, our intercourse was daily, confidential, and cordial. After I retired from that office, great and malignant pains were taken by our federal monarchists, and not entirely without effect, to make him view me as a theorist, holding French principles of government, which would lead infallibly to licentiousness and anarchy. And to this he listened the more easily, from my known disapprobation of the British treaty. I never saw him afterwards, or these malignant insinuations should have been dissipated before his just judgment, as mists before the sun. I felt on his death, with my countrymen, that "verily a great man hath fallen this day in Israel."

More time and recollection would enable me to add many other traits of his character; but why add them to you who knew him well? And I cannot justify to myself a longer detention of your paper.

Vale, proprieque tuum, me esse tibi persuadeas.

LETTER TO
SAMUEL H. SMITH

Monticello, September 21, 1814

Dear Sir:

I learn from the newspapers that the vandalism of our enemy has triumphed at Washington over science as well as the arts, by the destruction of the public library with the noble edifice in which it was deposited. Of this transaction, as of that of Copenhagen, the world will entertain but one sentiment. They will see a nation suddenly withdrawn from a great war, full armed and full handed, taking advantage of another whom they had recently forced into it, unarmed, and unprepared, to indulge themselves in acts of barbarism which do not belong to a civilized age. When Van Ghent destroyed their shipping at Chatham, and De Ruyter rode triumphantly up the Thames, he might in like manner, by the acknowledgment of their own historians, have forced all their ships up to London bridge, and there have burnt them, the tower, and city, had these examples been then set. London, when thus menaced, was near a thousand years old, Washington is but in its teens.

I presume it will be among the early objects of Congress to recommence their collection. This will be difficult while the war continues, and intercourse with Europe is attended with so much risk. You know my collection, its condition and extent. I have been fifty years making it, and have spared no pains, opportunity, or expense to make it what it is. While residing in Paris, I devoted every afternoon I was disengaged, for a summer or two, in examining all the principal bookstores, turning over every book with my own hand, and putting by everything which related to America, and indeed whatever was rare and valuable in every science. Besides this, I had standing orders during the whole time I was in Europe, on its principal book-marts, particularly Amsterdam, Frankfort, Madrid, and London, for such works relating to America as could not be found in Paris. So that in that department particularly, such a collection was made as probably can never again be effected, because it is hardly probably that the same opportunities, the same time, industry, perseverance, and expense, with some knowledge of the bibliography of the subject, would again happen to be in concurrence. During the same period, and after my return to America, I was led to procure, also, whatever related to the duties of those in the high concerns of the nation. So that the collection, which I suppose is of between nine and ten thousand volumes, while it includes what is chiefly valuable in science and literature generally, extends more particularly to whatever belongs to the American statesman. In the diplomatic and parliamentary branches, it is particularly full. It is long since I have been sensible it ought not to continue private property, and had provided that at my death, Congress should have the refusal of it at their own price. But the loss they have now incurred, makes the present the proper moment for their accommodation, without regard to the small remnant of time and the barren use of my enjoying it. I ask of your friendship, therefore, to make for me the tender of it to the library committee of Congress, not knowing myself of whom the committee consists. I enclose you the catalogue, which will enable them to judge of its contents. Nearly the whole are well bound, abundance of them elegantly, and of the choicest editions existing. They may be valued by persons named by themselves, and the payment made convenient to the public. It may be, for instance, in such annual installments as the law of Congress has left at their disposal, or in stock of any of their late loans, or of any loan they may institute at this session, so as to spare the present calls of our country, and await its days of peace and prosperity. They may enter, nevertheless, into immediate use of it, as eighteen or twenty wagons would place it in Washington in a single trip of a fortnight. I should be willing indeed, to retain a few of the books, to amuse the time

I have yet to pass, which might be valued with the rest, but not included in the sum of valuation until they should be restored at my death, which I would carefully provide for, so that the whole library as it stands in the catalogue at this moment should be theirs without any garbling. Those I should like to retain would be chiefly classical and mathematical, some few in other branches, and particularly one of the five encyclopedias in the catalogue. But this, if not acceptable, would not be urged. I must add that I have not revised the library since I came home to live, so that it is probable some of the books may be missing, except in the chapters of law and divinity, which have been revised and stand exactly as in the catalogue. The return of the catalogue will of course be needed, whether the tender be accepted or not. I do not know that it contains any branch of science which Congress would wish to exclude from their collection; there is, in fact, no subject to which a member of Congress may not have occasion to refer. But such a wish would not correspond with my views of preventing its dismemberment. My desire is either to place it in their hands entire, or to preserve it so here. I am engaged in making an alphabetical index of the author's names, to be annexed to the catalogue, which I will forward to you as soon as completed. Any agreement you shall be so good as to take the trouble of entering into with the committee, I hereby confirm. Accept the assurance of my great esteem and respect.

LETTER TO PRESIDENT JAMES MADISON

Monticello, March 23, 1815

Dear Sir:

I duly received your favor of the 12th, and with it the pamphlet on the causes and conduct of the war, which I now return. I have read it with great pleasure, but with irresistible desire that it should be published. The reasons in favor of this are strong, and those against it are so easily gotten over, that there appears to me no balance between them.

1. We need it in Europe. They have totally mistaken our character. Accustomed to rise at a feather themselves, and to be always fighting, they will see in our conduct, fairly stated, that acquiescence under wrong, to a certain degree, is wisdom, and not pusillanimity; and that peace and happiness are preferable to that false honor which, by eternal wars, keeps their people in eternal labor, want, and wretchedness.

2. It is necessary for the people of England, who have been deceived as to the causes and conduct of the war, and do not entertain a doubt that it was entirely wanton and wicked on our part, and under the order of Bonaparte. By rectifying their ideas, it will tend to that conciliation which is absolutely necessary to the peace and prosperity of both nations.

3. It is necessary for our own people—who, although they have known the details as they went along, yet have been so plied with false facts and false views by the Federalists that some impression has been left that all has not been right.

It may be said that it will be thought unfriendly. But truths necessary for our own character must not be supressed out of tenderness to its calumniators. Although written, generally, with great moderation, there may be some things in the pamphlet which may perhaps irritate. The characterizing every act, for example, by its appropriate epithet, is not necessary to show its deformity to an intelligent reader. The naked narrative will present it truly to his mind, and the more strongly, from its moderation, as he will perceive that no exaggeration is aimed at. Rubbing down these roughnesses, and they are neither many nor prominent, and preserving the original date, might, I think, remove all the offensiveness, and give more effect to the publication. Indeed, I think that a soothing postscript, addressed to the interests, the prospects, and the sober reason of both nations, would make it acceptable to both. The trifling expense of reprinting it ought not to be considered a moment. Mr. Gallatin could have it translated into French, and suffer it to get abroad in Europe without either avowal or disavowal. But it would be useful to print some copies of an appendix, containing all the documents referred to, to be preserved in libraries, and to facilitate to the present and future writers of history, the acquisition of the materials which test the truth it contains.

I sincerely congratulate you on the peace, and, more especially on the eclat with which the war was closed. The affair of New Orleans was fraught with useful lessons to ourselves, our enemies, and our friends, and will powerfully influence our future relations with the nations of Europe. It will show them we mean to take no part in their wars, and count no odds when when engaged in our own. I presume that, having spared to the pride of England her formal acknowledgment of the atrocity of impressment in an article of the treaty, she will concur in a convention for relinquishing it. Without this, she must understand that the present is but a truce, determinable on the first act of impressment of an American citizen, committed by any officer of hers. Would it not be better that this convention should be a separate act, unconnected with any treaty of commerce, and made an indispensable preliminary to all other treaty? If blended with a treaty of commerce, she will make it the price of injurious concessions. Indeed, we are infinitely better without such treaties with any nation. We cannot too distinctly detach ourselves from the European system, which is essentially belligerent, nor too sedulously cultivate an American system, essentially pacific. But if we go into commercial treaties at all, they should be with all, at the same time, with whom we have important commercial relations. France, Spain, Portugal, Holland, Denmark, Sweden, Russia all should proceed *pari passu.* Our ministers marching in phalanx on the same line, and intercommunicating freely, each will be supported by the weight of the whole mass, and the facility with which the other nations will agree to equal terms of intercourse will discountenance the selfish higglings of England, or justify our rejection of them. Perhaps, with all of them, it would be best to have but the single article *gentis amicissimae,* leaving everything else to the usages and courtesies of civilized nations. But all these things wil occur to yourself, with their counterconsideration.

Mr. Smith wrote to me on the transportation of the library, and, particularly, that it is submitted to your direction. He mentioned, also, that Dougherty would be engaged to superintend it. No one will more carefully and faithfully execute all those duties which would belong to a wagon-master. But it requires a character acquainted with books to receive the library. I am now employing as many hours of every day as my strength will permit in arranging the books, and putting every one in its place on the shelves, corresponding with its order on the catalogue, and shall have them numbered correspondently. This operation will employ me a considerable time yet. Then I should wish a competent agent to attend, and, with the catalogue in his hand, see that every book is on the shelves, and have their lids nailed on, one by one, as he proceeds. This would take such a person about two days; after which, Dougherty's business would be the mere mechanical removal, at convenience. I enclose you a letter from Mr. Milligan, offering his service, which would not cost more than eight or ten days' reasonable compensation. This is necessary for my safety and your satisfaction, as a just caution for the public. You know that there are persons, both in and out of the public councils, who will seize every occasion of imputation on either of us, the more difficult to be repelled in this case, in which a negative could not be proved. If you approve of it, therefore, as soon as I am through the review, I will give notice to Mr. Milligan, or any other person you will name, to come on immediately. Indeed it would be well worthwhile to add to his duty that of covering the books with a little paper (the good bindings, at least) and filling the vacancies of the presses with paper parings, to be brought from Washington. This would add little more to the time, as he could carry on both operations at once.

Accept the assurance of my constant and affectionate friendship and respect.

LETTER TO
SAMUEL KERCHIVAL

Monticello, July 12, 1816

Sir:

I duly received your favor of June 13, with the copy of the letters on the calling a convention, on which you are pleased to ask my opinion. I have not been in the habit of mysterious reserve on any subject, nor of buttoning up my opinions within my own doublet. On the contrary, while in public service especially, I thought the public entitled to frankness and intimately to know whom they employed. But I am now retired: I resign myself, as a passenger, with confidence to those at present at the helm, and ask but for rest, peace, and good will. The question you propose, on equal representation, has become a party one, in which I wish to take no public share. Yet, if it be asked for your own satisfaction only, and not to be quoted before the public, I have no motive to withhold it, and the less from you, as it coincides with your own. At the birth of our Republic, I committed that opinion to the world, in the draft of a constitution annexed to the *Notes on Virginia,* in which a provision was inserted for a representation permanently equal. The infancy of the subject at that moment, and our inexperience of self-government, occasioned gross departures in that draft from genuine republican canons. In truth, the abuses of monarchy had so much filled all the space of political contemplation that we imagined everything republican which was not monarchy. We had not yet penetrated to the mother principle that "governments are republican only in proportion as they embody the will of their people, and execute it." Hence, our first constitutions had really no leading principles in them. But experience and reflection have but more and more confirmed me in the particular importance of the equal representation then proposed. On that point, then, I am entirely in sentiment with your letters, and only lament that a copyright of your pamphlet prevents their appearance in the newspapers, where alone they would be generally read, and produce general effect. The present vacancy too, of other matter, would give them place in every paper, and bring the question home to every man's conscience.

But inequality of representation in both houses of our legislature is not the only republican heresy in this first essay of our revolutionary patriots at forming a constitution. For let it be agreed that a government is republican in proportion as every member composing it has his equal voice in the direction of its concerns—not indeed in person, which would be impracticable beyond the limits of a city, or small township, but by representatives chosen by himself, and responsible to him at short periods; and let us bring to the test of this canon every branch of our Constitution.

In the legislature, the House of Representatives is chosen by less than half the people, and not at all in proportion to those who do choose. The Senate are still more disproportionate, and for long terms of irresponsibility. In the executive, the governor is entirely independent of the choice of the people, and of their control; his council equally so, and at best but a fifth wheel to a wagon. In the judiciary, the judges of the highest courts are dependent on none but themselves. In England, where judges were named and removable at the will of an hereditary executive, from which branch most misrule was feared, and has flowed, it was a great point gained, by fixing them for life, to make them independent of that executive. But in a government founded on the public will, this principle operates in an opposite direction, and against that will. There, too, they were still removable on a concurrence of the executive and legislative branches. But we have made them independent of the nation itself. They are irremovable, but by their own body, for any depravities of conduct, and even by their own body for the imbecilities of dotage. The justices of the inferior courts are

self-chosen, are for life, and perpetuate their own body in succession forever, so that a faction once possessing themselves of
the bench of a county can never be broken up, but hold their
county in chains, forever indissoluble. Yet these justices are the
real executive as well as judiciary, in all our minor and most
ordinary concerns. They tax us at will; fill the office of sheriff,
the most important of all the executive officers of the county;
name nearly all our military leaders, which leaders, once named,
are removable but by themselves. The juries, our judges of all
fact, and of law when they choose it, are not selected by the
people, nor amenable to them. They are chosen by an officer
named by the court and executive. Chosen, did I say? Picked up
by the sheriff from the loungings of the courtyard, after everything respectable has retired from it. Where then is our republicanism to be found? Not in our Constitution certainly, but
merely in the spirit of our people. That would oblige even a
despot to govern us republicanly. Owing to this spirit, and to
nothing in the form of our Constitution, all things have gone
well. But this fact, so triumphantly misquoted by the enemies
of reformation, is not the fruit of our Constitution, but has
prevailed in spite of it. Our functionaries have done well, because generally honest men. If any were not so, they feared to
show it.

But, it will be said, it is easier to find faults than to amend
them. I do not think their amendment so difficult as is pretended. Only lay down true principles, and adhere to them
inflexibly. Do not be frightened into their surrender by the
alarms of the timid, or the croakings of wealth against the
ascendency of the people. If experience be called for, appeal to
that of our fifteen or twenty governments for forty years, and
show me where the people have done half the mischief in these
forty years that a single despot would have done in a single year;
or show half the riots and rebellions, the crimes and the punishments, which have taken place in any single nation, under kingly
government, during the same period. The true foundation of
republican government is the equal right of every citizen, in his

person and property, and in their management. Try by this, as a tally, every provision of our Constitution, and see if it hangs directly on the will of the people. Reduce your legislature to a convenient number for full but orderly discussion. Let every man who fights or pays exercise his just and equal right in their election. Submit them to approbation or rejection at short intervals. Let the executive be chosen in the same way, and for the same term, by those whose agent he is to be; and leave no screen of a council behind which to skulk from responsibility. It has been thought that the people are not competent electors of judges *learned in the law*. But I do not know that this is true, and, if doubtful, we should follow principle. In this, as in many other elections, they would be guided by reputation, which would not err oftener, perhaps, than the present mode of appointment. In one state of the Union, at least, it has long been tried, and with the most satisfactory success. The judges of Connecticut have been chosen by the people every six months, for nearly two centuries, and I believe there has hardly ever been an instance of change: so powerful is the curb of incessant responsibility. If prejudice, however, derived from a monarchical institution, is still to prevail against the vital elective principle of our own, and if the existing example among ourselves of periodical election of judges by the people be still mistrusted, let us at least not adopt the evil, and reject the good, of the English precedent; let us retain amovability on the concurrence of the executive and legislative branches, and nomination by the executive alone. Nomination to office is an executive function. To give it to the legislature, as we do, is a violation of the principle of the separation of powers. It swerves the members from correctness by temptations to intrigue for office themselves and to a corrupt barter of votes, and destroys responsibility by dividing it among a multitude. By leaving nomination in its proper place, among executive functions, the principle of the distribution of power is preserved, and responsibility weighs with its heaviest force on a single head.

The organization of our county administrations may be

thought more difficult. But follow principle, and the knot unties itself. Divide the counties into wards of such size as that every citizen can attend, when called on, and act in person. Ascribe to them the government of their wards in all things relating to themselves exclusively. A justice, chosen by themselves, in each, a constable, a military company, a patrol, a school, the care of their own poor, their own portion of the public roads, the choice of one or more jurors to serve in some court, and the delivery, within their own wards, of their own votes for all elective officers of higher sphere, will relieve the county administration of nearly all its business, will have it better done, and by making every citizen an acting member of the government, and in the offices nearest and most interesting to him, will attach him by his strongest feelings to the independence of his country, and its republican Constitution. The justices thus chosen by every ward would constitute the county court, would do its judiciary business, direct roads and bridges, levy county and poor rates, and administer all the matters of common interest to the whole country. These wards, called townships in New England, are the vital principle of their governments, and have proved themselves the wisest invention ever devised by the wit of man for the perfect exercise of self-government, and for its preservation. We should thus marshal our government into: (1) the general federal republic, for all concerns foreign and federal; (2) that of the state, for what relates to our own citizens exclusively; (3) the county republics, for the duties and concerns of the county; and (4) the ward republics, for the small and yet numerous and interesting concerns of the neighborhood; and in government, as well as in every other business of life, it is by division and subdivision of duties alone that all matters, great and small, can be managed to perfection. And the whole is cemented by giving to every citizen, personally, a part in the administration of the public affairs.

The sum of these amendments is: (1) general suffrage; (2) equal representation in the legislature; (3) an executive chosen by the people; (4) judges elective or amovable; (5) justices, jurors, and sheriffs elective; (6) ward divisions; and (7) periodical amendments of the Constitution.

I have thrown out these as loose heads of amendment for consideration and correction; and their object is to secure self-government by the republicanism of our Constitution, as well as by the spirit of the people; and to nourish and perpetuate that spirit. I am not among those who fear the people. They, and not the rich, are our dependence for continued freedom. And to preserve their independence, we must not let our rulers load us with perpetual debt. We must make our election between *economy and liberty,* or *profusion and servitude.* If we run into such debts as that we must be taxed in our meat and in our drink, in our necessaries and our comforts, in our labors and our amusements, for our callings and our creeds, as the people of England are, our people, like them, must come to labor sixteen hours in the twenty-four, give the earnings of fifteen of these to the government for their debts and daily expenses; and the sixteenth being insufficient to afford us bread, we must live, as they now do, on oatmeal and potatoes; have no time to think, no means of calling the mismanagers to account; but be glad to obtain subsistence by hiring ourselves to rivet their chains on the necks of our fellow sufferers. Our land-holders, too, like theirs, retaining indeed the title and stewardship of estates called theirs, but held really in trust for the treasury, must wander, like theirs, in foreign countries, and be contented with penury, obscurity, exile, and the glory of the nation. This example reads to us the salutary lesson that private fortunes are destroyed by public as well as by private extravagance. And this is the tendency of all human governments. A departure from principle in one instance becomes a precedent for a second; that second for a third; and so on, till the bulk of the society is reduced to be mere automatons of misery, to have no sensibilities left but for sinning and suffering. Then begins, indeed, the *bellum omnium in omnia,* which some philosophers observing to be so general in this world, have mistaken it for the natural, instead of the abusive, state of man. And the fore-horse of this frightful team is public debt. Taxation follows that, and in its train wretchedness and oppression.

Some men look at constitutions with sanctimonious reverence, and deem them like the ark of the covenant, too sacred to be touched. They ascribe to the men of the preceding age a wisdom more than human, and suppose what they did to be beyond amendment. I knew that age well; I belonged to it, and labored with it. It deserved well of its country. It was very like the present, but without the experience of the present; and forty years of experience in government is worth a century of book-reading; and this they would say themselves, were they to rise from the dead. I am certainly not an advocate for frequent and untried changes in laws and constitutions. I think moderate imperfections had better be borne with; because, when once known, we accommodate ourselves to them, and find practical means of correcting their ill effects. But I know also that laws and institutions must go hand in hand with the progress of the human mind. As that becomes more developed, more enlightened, as new discoveries are made, new truths disclosed, and manners and opinions change with the change of circumstances, institutions must advance also, and keep pace with the times. We might as well require a man to wear still the coat which fitted him when a boy, as civilized society to remain ever under the regimen of their barbarous ancestors. It is this preposterous idea which has lately deluged Europe in blood. Their monarchs, instead of wisely yielding to the gradual change of circumstances, of favoring progressive accommodation to progressive improvement, have clung to old abuses, entrenched themselves behind steady habits, and obliged their subjects to seek through blood and violence rash and ruinous innovations, which, had they been referred to the peaceful deliberations and collected wisdom of the nation, would have been put into acceptable and salutary forms. Let us follow no such examples, nor weakly believe that one generation is not as capable as another of taking care of itself, and of ordering its own affairs. Let us, as our sister states have done, avail ourselves of our reason and experience, to correct the crude essays of our first and unexperienced, although wise, virtuous, and well-meaning councils. And lastly, let us provide in our Constitution for its revision at stated periods. What these periods should be, nature herself indicates. By the European tables of mortality, of the adults living at any one moment of time, a majority will be dead in about nineteen years. At the end of that period then, a new majority is come into place; or, in other words, a new generation. Each generation is as independent of the one preceding as that was of all which had gone before. It has then, like them, a right to choose for itself the form of government it believes most promotive of its own happiness; consequently, to accommodate to the circumstances in which it finds itself, that received from its predecessors; and it is for the peace and good of mankind, that a solemn opportunity of doing this every nineteen or twenty years should be provided by the Constitution; so that it may be handed on, with periodical repairs, from generation to generation, to the end of time, if anything human can so long endure. It is now forty years since the constitution of Virginia was formed. The same tables inform us, that, within that period, two-thirds of the adults then living are now dead. Have then the remaining third, even if they had the wish, the right to hold in obedience to their will, and to laws heretofore made by them, the other two-thirds, who, with themselves, compose the present mass of adults? If they have not, who has? The dead? But the dead have no rights. They are nothing; and nothing cannot own something. Where there is no substance, there can be no accident. This corporeal globe, and everything upon it, belong to its present corporeal inhabitants, during their generation. They alone have a right to direct what is the concern of themselves alone, and to declare the law of that direction; and this declaration can only be made by their majority. That majority, then, has a right to depute representatives to a convention, and to make the constitution what they think will be the best for themselves. But how collect their voice? This is the real difficulty. If invited by private authority, or county or district meetings, these divisions are so large that few will attend; and their voice will be imperfectly or falsely pronounce. Here, then, would be one of the advantages of the ward divisions I have proposed. The mayor of every ward, on a question like the present, would call his ward together, take the simple yea or nay of its members, convey these to the county court, who would hand on those of all its wards to the proper general authority; and the voice of the whole people would be thus fairly, fully, and peaceably expressed, discussed, and decided by the common reason of the society. If this avenue be shut to the call of sufferance, it will make itself heard through that of force, and we shall go on, as other nations are doing, in the endless circle of oppression, rebellion, reformation, again; and so on forever.

These, sir, are my opinions of the governments we see among men, and of the principles by which alone we may prevent our own from falling into the same dreadful track. I have given them at greater length than your letter called for. But I cannot say things by halves; and I confide them to your honor, so to use them as to preserve me from the gridiron of the public papers. If you shall approve and enforce them, as you have done that of equal representation, they may do some good. If not, keep them to yourself as the effusions of withered age and useless time. I shall, with not the less truth, assure you of my great respect and consideration.

DRAFT OF AN ACT
FOR ESTABLISHING
ELEMENTARY SCHOOLS

1817

I. Be it enacted by the General Assembly of Virginia, That at the first session of the superior court in every county within this commonwealth, next ensuing the passage of this act, the judge thereof shall appoint three discreet and well-informed persons, residents of the county, and not being ministers of the gospel* of any denomination, to serve as visitors of the elementary schools in the said county; of which appointment the sheriff shall, within fifteen days thereafter deliver a certificate, under the hand of the clerk of the said court, to each of the persons so appointed.

II. The said visitors shall meet at the courthouse of their county on the first county court day after they shall have received notice of their appointment, and afterwards at such times and places as they, or any two of them, with reasonable notice to the third, shall have agreed; and shall proceed to divide their county into wards,† by metes and bounds so designated as to

---

*Ministers of the gospel are excluded to avoid jealousy from the other sects, were the public education committed to the ministers of a particular one—and with more reason than in the case of their exclusion from the legislative and executive functions.

†This designation of the size of a ward is founded on these considerations: (1) that the population which furnishes a company of militia will generally about furnish children enough for a school; (2) that in most instances, at present, the militia captaincies being laid off compactly by known and convenient metes and bounds, many will be adopted without change, and others will furnish a canvas to work on and to reform; (3) that these wards, once established, will be found convenient and salutary aids in the administration of government, of which they will constitute the organic elements, and the first integral members in the composition of the military.

comprehend each, about the number of militia sufficient for a company, and so also as not to divide, and throw into different wards* the lands of any one person held in one body; which division into wards shall, within six months from the date of their appointment, be completely designated, published, and reported, by their metes and bounds, to the office of the clerk of the Superior Court, there to be recorded, subject, however, to such alterations, from time to time afterwards, as changes of circumstances shall, in the opinion of the said visitors or their successors, with the approbation of the said court, render expedient.

III. The original division into wards being made, the visitors shall appoint days for the first meeting of every ward, at such place as they shall name within the same, of which appointment notice shall be given at least two weeks before the day of meeting, by advertisement at some public place within the ward, requiring every free, white male citizen, of full age, resident within the ward, to meet at the place, and by the hour of twelve of the day so appointed, at which meeting some one of the visitors shall also attend, and a majority of the said warders being in attendance, the visitor present shall propose to them to decide by a majority of their votes—(1) the location of a schoolhouse for the ward, and a dwelling-house for the teacher (the owner of the ground consenting thereto); (2) the size and structure of the said houses; and (3) whether the same shall be built by the joint labor of the warders, or by their pecuniary contributions; and also (4) to elect by a plurality of their votes a warden, resident, who shall direct and superintend the said buildings, and be charged with their future care.

---

*The prohibition to place among different wards the lands of a single individual, held in a body is: (1) to save the proprietor from the perplexity of multiplied responsibilities; and (2) to prevent arbitrary and inconsistent apportionments, by different wardens, of the comparative values of the different portions of his lands in their respective wards.

IV. And if they decide that the said buildings* shall be erected by the joint labor of the warders, then all persons within the said ward liable to work in the highways shall attend at the order of the warden, and, under his direction, shall labor thereon until completed, under the same penalties as provided by law to enforce labor on the highways. And if they decide on erection by pecuniary contributions, the residents and owners of property within the ward shall contribute toward the cost, each in proportion to the taxes they last paid to the state for their persons and for the same property: of which the sheriff or commissioners shall furnish a statement to the warden, who, according to the ratio of that statement, shall apportion and assess the quota of contribution for each, and be authorized to demand, receive, and apply the same to the purposes of the contribution, and to render account thereof, as in all other his pecuniary transactions for the school, to the visitors; and on failure of payment by any contributor, the sheriff, on the order of the warden, shall collect and render the same under like powers and regulations as provided for the collection of the public taxes. And in every case it shall be the duty of the warden to have the buildings completed within six months from the date of his election.

V. It shall be the duty of the said visitors to seek and to employ for every ward,† whenever the number and ages of its

*It is presumed that the wards will generally build such log-houses for the school and teacher as they now do, and will join force and build them themselves, experience proving them to be as comfortable as they are cheap. Nor would it be advisable to build expensive houses in the country wards, which, from changes in their population, will be liable to changes of their boundaries and consequent displacements of their center, drawing with it a removal of their schoolhouse. In towns, better houses may be more safely built, or rented for both purposes.

†Estimating eight hundred militia to a county, there will be twelve captaincies or wards in a county on an average. Suppose each of these, three years in every six, to have children enough for a school, who have not yet had three years' schooling; such a county will employ six teachers, each serving two wards by alternate terms. These teachers will be taken from the laboring classes, as they are now, to wit: from that which furnishes mechanics, overseers, and tillers of the earth; and they will chiefly be the cripples, the weakly, and the old of that class, who will have been qualified for these functions by

children require it, a person of good moral character, qualified to teach reading, writing, numeral arithmetic, and geography, whose subsistence shall be furnished by the residents and proprietors of the ward, either in money or in kind, at the choice of each contributor, and in the ratio of their public taxes, to be apportioned and levied as on the failures before provided for. The teacher shall also have the use of the house and accommodations provided for him, and shall moreover receive annually such standing wages as the visitors shall have determined to be proportioned on the residents and proprietors of the ward, and

---

the ward schools themselves. If put on a footing then, for wages and subsistence, with the young and the able of their class, they will be liberally compensated: say with $150 wages and the usual allowance of meat and bread. The subsistence will probably be contributed in kind by the warders, out of their family stock. The wages alone will be a pecuniary tax of about $900. To a county, this addition would be of about one-fifth of the taxes we now pay to the state, or about one-fifth of 1 percent on every man's taxable property—if tax can be called that which we give to our children in the most valuable of all forms, that of instruction. Were those schools to be established on the public funds, and to be managed by the governor and council, or the commissioners of the literary fund, brick houses to be built for the schools and teachers, high wages and subsistence given them, they would be badly managed, depraved by abuses, and would exhaust the whole literary fund. While under the eye and animadversion of the wards, and the control of the wardens and visitors, economy, diligence, and correctness of conduct will be enforced, the whole literary fund will be spared to complete the general system of education, by colleges in every district for instruction in the languages and a university for the whole of the higher sciences; and this, by an addition to our contributions almost insensible, and which, in fact, will not be felt as a burden, because applied immediately and visibly to the good of our children.

A question of some doubt might be raised on the latter part of this section, as to the rights and duties of society towards its members, infant and adult. Is it a right or a duty in society to take care of their infant members in opposition to the will of the parent? How far does this right and duty extend? To guard the life of the infant, his property, his instruction, his morals? The Roman father was supreme in all these; we draw a line, but where? Public sentiment does not seem to have traced it precisely. Nor is it necessary in the present case. It is better to tolerate the rare instance of a parent refusing to let his child be educated than to shock the common feelings and ideas by the forcible asportation and education of the infant against the will of the father. What is proposed here is to remove the objection of expense by offering education gratis, and to strengthen parental excitement by the disfranchisement of his child while uneducated. Society has certainly a right to disavow him whom they offer, and are not permitted to qualify for the duties of a citizen. If we do not force instruction, let us at least strengthen the motives to receive it when offered.

to be paid, levied, and applied as before provided in other cases of pecuniary contribution. At this school shall be received and instructed gratis every infant of competent age who has not already had three years schooling. And it is declared and enacted, that no person unborn or under the age of twelve years at the passing of this act, and who is *compos mentis,* shall, after the age of fifteen years, be a citizen of this commonwealth until he or she can read readily in some tongue, native or acquired.

VI. To keep up a constant succession of visitors, the judge of the Superior Court of every county shall at his first session in every bisextile year, appoint visitors as before characterized, either the same or others, at his discretion. And in case of the death or resignation of any visitor during the term of his appointment, or of his removal by the said judge for good cause, moral or physical, he shall appoint another to serve until the next bisextile appointment. Which visitors shall have their first meeting at their courthouse on the county court day next ensuing their appointment, and afterwards at such times and places as themselves or any two of them with reasonable notice to the third shall agree. But the election of wardens shall be annually, at the first meeting of the ward after the month of March, until which election the warden last elected shall continue in office.

VII. All ward meetings shall be at their schoolhouse, and on a failure of the meeting of a majority of the wardens on the call of a visitor, or of their warden, such visitor or warden may call another meeting.

VIII. At all times when repairs or alterations of the buildings before provided for shall be wanting, it shall be the duty of the warden or of a visitor to call a ward meeting and to take the same measures towards such repairs or alterations as are herein before authorized for the original buildings.

IX. When, on the application of any warden, authorized thereto by the vote of his ward, the judge of the Superior Court shall be of opinion that the contributors of any particular ward are disproportionably and oppressively overburdened with an unusual number of children of noncontributors of their ward, he may direct an order to the county court to assess in their next county levy the whole or such part of the extra burden as he shall think excessive and unreasonable, to be paid to the warden for its proper use, to which order the said county court is required to conform.

X. The said teachers shall, in all things relating to the education and government of their pupils, be under the direction and control of the visitors; but no religious reading, instruction, or exercise shall be prescribed or practiced inconsistent with the tenets of any religious sect or denomination.

XI. Some one of the visitors, once in every year at least, shall visit the several schools: shall inquire into the proceedings and practices thereat: shall examine the progress of the pupils, and give to those who excel in reading, in writing, in arithmetic, or in geography such honorary marks and testimonies of approbation as may encourage and excite to industry and emulation.

XII. All decisions and proceedings of the visitors relative to the original designation of wards at any time before the buildings are begun, or changes of wards at any time after, to the quantum of subsistence, or wages allowed to the teacher, and to the rules prescribed to him for the education and government of his pupils, shall be subject to be controlled and corrected by the judge of the superior court of the county, on the complaint of any individual aggrieved or interested.

LETTER TO
DR. VINE UTLEY

Monticello, March 21, 1819

Sir:

Your letter of February 18 came to hand on the 1st instant; and the request of the history of my physical habits would have puzzled me not a little, had it not been for the model with which you accompanied it, of Dr. Rush's answer to a similar inquiry. I live so much like other people that I might refer to ordinary life as the history of my own. Like my friend the doctor, I have lived temperately, eating little animal food, and that not as an aliment so much as a condiment for the vegetables, which constitute my principal diet. I double, however, the doctor's glass and a half of wine, and even treble it with a friend; but halve its effects by drinking the weak wines only. The ardent wines I cannot drink, nor do I use ardent spirits in any form. Malt liquors and cider are my table drinks, and my breakfast, like that also of my friend, is of tea and coffee. I have been blest with organs of digestion which accept and concoct, without ever murmuring, whatever the palate chooses to consign to them, and I have not yet lost a tooth by age. I was a hard student until I entered on the business of life, the duties of which leave no idle time to those disposed to fulfill them; and now, retired, and at the age of seventy-six, I am again a hard student. Indeed, my fondness for reading and study revolts me from the drudgery of letter writing. And a stiff wrist, the consequence of an early dislocation, makes writing both slow and painful. I am not so regular in my sleep as the doctor says he was, devoting to it from five to eight hours, according as my company or the book I am reading interests me; and I never go to bed without an hour or half hour's previous reading of something moral, whereon to ruminate in the intervals of sleep. But whether I retire to bed early or late, I rise with the sun. I use spectacles at night, but not necessarily in the day, unless in reading small print. My hearing is distinct in particular conversation, but confused when several voices cross each other, which unfits me for the society of the table. I have been more fortunate than my friend in the article of health. So free from catarrhs that I have not had one (in the breast, I mean) on an average of eight or ten years through life. I ascribe this exemption partly to the habit of bathing my feet in cold water every morning, for sixty years past. A fever of more than twenty-four hours I have not had above two or three times in my life. A periodical headache has afflicted me occasionally, once, perhaps, in six or eight years, for two or three weeks at a time, which seems now to have left me; and except on a late occasion of indisposition, I enjoy good health; too feeble, indeed, to walk much, but riding without fatigue six or eight miles a day, and sometimes thirty or forty. I may end these egotisms, therefore, as I began, by saying that my life has been so much like that of other people, that I might say with Horace, to everyone *"nomine mutato, narratur fabula de te."* I must not end, however, without due thanks for the kind sentiments of regard you are so good as to express towards myself; and with my acknowledgments for these, be pleased to accept the assurances of my respect and esteem.

LETTER TO GENERAL
JAMES BRECKINRIDGE

Monticello, April 9, 1822

Dear General:

Your favor of March 28 was received on the 7th instant. We failed in having a quorum on the 1st. Mr. Johnson and General Taylor were laboring for Lithgow in Richmond, and Mr. Madison was unwell. On the score of business it was immaterial, as there was not a single measure to be proposed. The loss was of the gratification of meeting in society with those whom we esteem. This is the valuable effect of our semiannual meetings, jubilees, in fact, for feasting the mind and fostering the best affections of the heart towards those who merit them.

The four rows of buildings of accommodation are so nearly completed that they are certain of being entirely so in the course of the summer; and our funds, as you have seen stated in our last report, are sufficient to meet the expense, except that the delays in collecting the arrears of subscriptions oblige us to borrow temporarily from this year's annuity, which, according to that report, had another destination. These buildings done, we are to rest on our oars, and passively await the will of the legislature. Our future course is a plain one. We have proceeded from the beginning on the sound determination to finish the buildings before opening the institution; because, once opened, all its funds will be absorbed by professors' salaries, etc., and nothing remain ever to finish the buildings. And we have thought it better to begin two or three years later, in the full extent proposed, than to open, and go on forever, with a halfway establishment. Of the wisdom of this proceeding, and of its greater good to the public finally, I cannot a moment doubt. Our part then is to pursue with steadiness what is right, turning neither to right nor left for the intrigues or popular delusions of the day, assured that the public approbation will in the end be with us. The councils of the legislature, at their late session, were poisoned unfortunately by the question of the seat of government, and the consequent jealousies of our views in erecting the large building still wanting. This lost us some friends who feel a sincere interest in favor of the university, but a stronger one in the question respecting the seat of government. They seem not to have considered that the seat of the government, and that of the university, are incompatible with one another; that if the former were to come here, the latter must be removed. Even Oxford and Cambridge placed in the middle of London, they would be deserted as seats of learning, and as proper places for training youth. These groundless jealousies, it is to be hoped, will be dissipated by sober reflection, during the separation of the members; and they will perceive, before their next meeting, that the large building, without which the institution cannot proceed, has nothing to do with the question of the seat of government. If, however, the ensuing session should still refuse their patronage, a second or a third will think better, and result finally in fulfilling the object of our aim, the securing to our country a full and perpetual institution for all the useful sciences—one which will restore us to our former station in the confederacy. It may be a year or two later indeed; but it will replace us in full grade, and not leave us among the mere subalterns of the league. Patience and steady perseverance on our part will secure the blessed end. If we shrink, it is gone forever. Our autumnal meeting will be interesting. The question will be whether we shall relinquish the scale of a real university, the rallying center of the South and the West, or let it sink to that of a common academy. I hope you will be with us, and give us the benefit of your firm and enlarged views. I am not at all disheartened with what has passed, nor disposed to give up the ship. We have only to lie still, to do and say nothing, and firmly avoid opening. The public opinion is advancing. It is coming to our aid and will force the institution on to consummation. The numbers are great, and many from great distances, who visit it daily as an object of curiosity. They become strengthened if friends, converted if enemies, and all loud and zealous advocates, and will shortly give full tone to the public voice. Our motto should be: "Be not wearied with well-doing." Accept the assurance of my affectionate friendship and respect.

LETTER TO PRESIDENT
JAMES MONROE

Monticello, October 24, 1823

Dear Sir:

The question presented by the letters you have sent me is the most momentous which has ever been offered to my contemplation since that of Independence. That made us a nation, this sets our compass and points the course which we are to steer through the ocean of time opening on us. And never could we embark on it under circumstances more auspicious. Our first and fundamental maxim should be never to entangle ourselves in the broils of Europe. Our second, never to suffer Europe to intermeddle with cisatlantic affairs. America, North and South, has a set of interests distinct from those of Europe, and peculiarly her own. She should therefore have a system of her own, separate and apart from that of Europe. While the last is laboring to become the domicile of despotism, our endeavor should surely be to make our hemisphere that of freedom. One nation, most of all, could disturb us in this pursuit; she now offers to lead, aid, and accompany us in it. By acceding to her proposition, we detach her from the bands, bring her mighty weight into the scale of free government, and emancipate a continent at one stroke, which might otherwise linger long in doubt and difficulty. Great Britain is the nation which can do us the most harm of any one, or all, on earth; and with her on our side we need not fear the whole world. With her then, we should most sedulously cherish a cordial friendship; and nothing would tend more to knit our affections than to be fighting once more, side by side, in the same cause. Not that I would purchase even her amity at the price of taking part in her wars. But the war in which the present proposition might engage us, should that be its consequence, is not her war, but ours. Its object is to introduce and establish the American system, of keeping out of our land all foreign powers, of never permitting those of Europe to intermeddle with the affairs of our nations. It is to maintain our own principle, not to depart from it. And if, to facilitate this, we can effect a division in the body of the European powers, and draw over to our side its most powerful member, surely we should do it. But I am clearly of Mr. Canning's opinion that it will prevent instead of provoking war. With Great Britain withdrawn from their scale and shifted into that of our two continents, all Europe combined would not undertake such a war. For how would they propose to get at either enemy without superior fleets? Nor is the occasion to be slighted, which this proposition offers, of declaring our protest against the atrocious violations of the rights of nations, by the interference of anyone in the internal affairs of another, so flagitiously begun by Bonaparte, and now continued by the equally lawless Alliance, calling itself Holy.

But we have first to ask ourselves a question. Do we wish to acquire to our own confederacy any one or more of the Spanish provinces? I candidly confess that I have ever looked on Cuba as the most interesting addition which could ever be made to our system of states. The control which, with Florida Point, this island would give us over the Gulf of Mexico, and the countries and isthmus bordering on it, as well as all those whose waters flow into it, would fill up the measure of our political well-being. Yet, as I am sensible that this can never be obtained, even with her own consent, but by war; and its independence, which is our second interest (and especially its independence of England), can be secured without it, I have no hesitation in abandoning my first wish to future chances, and accepting its independence, with peace and the friendship of England, rather than its association, at the expense of war and her enmity.

I could honestly, therefore, join in the declaration proposed, that we aim not at the acquisition of any of those possessions; that we will not stand in the way of any amicable arrangement between them and the mother country; but that we will oppose, with all our means, the forcible interposition of any other power, as auxiliary, stipendiary, or under any other form or pretext, and most especially, their transfer to any power by conquest, cession, or acquisition in any other way. I should think it, therefore, advisable, that the executive should encourage the British government to a continuance in the dispositions expressed in these letters, by an assurance of his concurrence with them as far as his authority goes; and that as it may lead to war, the declaration of which requires an act of Congress, the case shall be laid before them for consideration at their first meeting, and under the reasonable aspect in which it is seen by himself.

I have been so long weaned from political subjects, and have so long ceased to take any interest in them, that I am sensible I am not qualified to offer opinions on them worthy of any attention. But the question now proposed involves consequences so lasting, and effects so decisive of our future destinies, as to rekindle all the interest I have heretofore felt on such occasions, and to induce me to the hazard of opinions, which will prove only my wish to contribute still my mite towards anything which may be useful to our country. And praying you to accept it at only what it is worth, I add the assurance of my constant and affectionate friendship and respect.

LETTER TO
RICHARD RUSH

Dear Sir:

I have heretofore informed you that our legislature had undertaken the establishment of a University in Virginia; that it was placed in my neighborhood, and under the direction of a board of seven visitors, of whom I am one, Mr. Madison another, and others equally worthy of confidence. We have been four or five years engaged in erecting our buildings, all of which are now ready to receive their tenants, one excepted, which the present season will put into a state for use. The last session of our legislature had by new donations liberated the revenue of fifteen M. D. a year, with which they had before endowed the institution, and we propose to open it the beginning of the next year. We require the intervening time for seeking out and engaging professors. As to these we have determined to receive no one who is not of the first order of science in his line; and as such in every branch cannot be obtained with us, we propose to seek some of them at least in the countries ahead of us in science, and preferably in Great Britain, the land of our own language, habits, and manners. But how to find out those who are of the first grade of science, of sober correct habits and morals, harmonizing tempers, talents for communication, is the difficulty. Our first step is to send a special agent to the universities of Oxford, Cambridge, and Edinburgh to make the selection for us; and the person appointed for this office is the gentleman who will hand you this letter—Mr. Francis Walker Gilmer—the best-educated subject we have raised since the Revolution, highly qualified in all the important branches of science, professing particularly that of the law, which he has practiced some years at our

Supreme Court with good success and flattering prospects. His morals, his amiable temper and discretion will do justice to any confidence you may be willing to place in him, for I commit him to you as his mentor and guide in the business he goes on. We do not certainly expect to obtain such known characters as were the Cullens, the Robertsons, and Porsons of Great Britain, men of the first eminence established there in reputation and office, and with emoluments not to be bettered anywhere. But we know that there is another race treading on their heels, preparing to take their places, and as well and sometimes better qualified to fill them. These while unsettled, surrounded by a crowd of competitors, of equal claims and perhaps superior credit and interest, may prefer a comfortable certainty here for an uncertain hope there, and a lingering delay even of that. From this description we expect we may draw professors equal to those of the highest name. The difficulty is to distinguish them; for we are told that so overcharged are all branches of business in that country, and such the difficulty of getting the means of living, that it is deemed allowable in ethics for even the most honorable minds to give highly exaggerated recommendations and certificates to enable a friend or protegé to get into a livelihood; and that the moment our agent should be known to be on such a mission, he would be overwhelmed by applications from numerous pretenders, all of whom, worthy or unworthy, would be supported by such recommendations and such names as would confound all discrimination. On this head our trust and hope is in you. Your knowledge of the state of things, your means of finding out a character or two at each place, truly trustworthy, and into whose hands you can commit our agent with entire safety, for information, caution, and cooperation, induces me to request your patronage and aid in our endeavors to obtain such men, and such only as will fulfill our views. An unlucky selection in the outset would forever blast our prospects. From our information of the character of the different universities, we expect we should go to Oxford for our classical professor, to Cambridge for those of mathematics, natural philosophy, and natural history, and to Edinburgh for a professor of anatomy, and the elements or outlines only of medicine. We have still our eye on Mr. Blaetterman for the professorship of modern languages, and Mr. Gilmer is instructed to engage him, if no very material objection to him may have arisen unknown to us. We can place in Mr. Gilmer's hands but a moderate sum at present for merely textbooks to begin with, and for indispensable articles of apparatus, mathematical, astronomical, physical, chemical, and anatomical. We are in the hope of a sum of fifty thousand dollars, as soon as we can get a settlement passed through the public offices. My experience in dealing with the bookseller Lackington, on your recommendation, has induced me to recommend him to Mr. Gilmer, and if we can engage his fidelity, we may put into his hands the larger supply of books when we are ready to call for it, and particularly what we shall propose to seek in England.

Although I have troubled you with many particulars, I yet leave abundance for verbal explanation with Mr. Gilmer, who possesses a full knowledge of everything, and our full confidence in everything. He takes with him plans of our establishment, which we think it may be encouraging to show to the persons to whom he will make propositions, as well to let them see the comforts provided for themselves, as to show by the extensiveness and expense of the scale, that it is no ephemeral thing to which they are invited.

With my earnest solicitations that you will give us all your aid in an undertaking on which we rest the hopes and happiness of our country, accept the assurances of my sincere friendship, attachment, and respect.

LETTER TO
ROGER C. WEIGHTMAN

Monticello, June 24, 1826

Respected Sir:

The kind invitation I receive from you, on the part of the citizens of the city of Washington, to be present with them at their celebration on the fiftieth anniversary of American Independence, as one of the surviving signers of an instrument pregnant with our own, and the fate of the world, is most flattering to myself, and heightened by the honorable accompaniment proposed for the comfort of such a journey. It adds sensibly to the sufferings of sickness to be deprived by it of a personal participation in the rejoicings of that day. But acquiescence is a duty, under circumstances not placed among those we are permitted to control. I should, indeed, with peculiar delight, have met and exchanged there congratulations personally with the small band, the remnant of that host of worthies, who joined with us on that day, in the bold and doubtful election we were to make for our country, between submission or the sword; and to have enjoyed with them the consolatory fact that our fellow citizens, after half a century of experience and prosperity, continue to approve the choice we made. May it be to the world, what I believe it will be (to some parts sooner, to others later, but finally to all)—the signal of arousing men to burst the chains under which monkish ignorance and superstition had persuaded them to bind themselves, and to assume the blessings and security of self-government. That form which we have substituted restores the free right to the unbounded exercise of reason and freedom of opinion. All eyes are opened, or opening, to the rights of man. The general spread of the light of science has already laid open to every view the palpable truth that the mass of mankind has not been born with saddles on their backs, nor a favored few booted and spurred, ready to ride them legitimately, by the grace of God. These are grounds of hope for others. For ourselves, let the annual return of this day forever refresh our recollections of these rights, and an undiminished devotion to them.

I will ask permission here to express the pleasure with which I should have met my ancient neighbors of the city of Washington and its vicinities, with whom I passed so many years of a pleasing social intercourse; an intercourse which so much relieved the anxieties of the public cares, and left impressions so deeply engraved in my affections, as never to be forgotten. With my regret that ill health forbids me the gratification of an acceptance, be pleased to receive for yourself, and those for whom you write, the assurance of my highest respect and friendly attachments.